From Thought to Action

From Thought to Action

DEVELOPING A SOCIAL JUSTICE ORIENTATION

Amy Aldridge Sanford

Texas A&M University-Corpus Christi

cognella®

SAN DIEGO

Bassim Hamadeh, CEO and Publisher
Todd R. Armstrong, Publisher
Tony Paese, Project Editor
Jess Estrella, Senior Graphic Designer
Trey Soto, Licensing Associate
Natalie Piccotti, Director of Marketing
Kassie Graves, Vice President of Editorial
Jamie Giganti, Director of Academic Publishing

Cover image copyright © 2014 iStockphoto LP/omergenc.
copyright © 2015 Depositphotos/Slanapotam.
copyright © 2019 iStockphoto LP/Egor Shabanov.

Printed in the United States of America.

cognella® | ACADEMIC PUBLISHING

3970 Sorrento Valley Blvd., Ste. 500, San Diego, CA 92121

Dedication

For the people who give me life—
Mom, Dad, Walker family, Aunt Vickie, Dana, Gene, Rusty, and my
forever students.

The traditional college student is an activist in transition—most students
are not yet regular adults with major responsibilities, but neither are they
kids to be ignored. It's the perfect place to hone one's righteousness before
heading out to the big bad real world.
—Baumgardner & Richards, *Grassroots,* 2005, p. 89

Brief Contents

Detailed Contents

Foreword

José Angel Gutierréz, PhD, JD, Emeritus

L IKE THE ENERGY-INFUSED drinks too many millennials chug today along with the hits of strong coffee, this book is a kick-starter for those at the starting blocks of the race to do something in life. Dr. Amy Aldridge Sanford has made a new contribution to the limited material in the literature on moving from the status quo to direct action—not an easy jump-start to make for most people, especially students overdosed on parental and societal dos and don'ts. I was one of those once.

I recall the rage I felt when, in my first social studies class in junior high (which was still segregated), our Anglo teacher showed us slides from archeological sites in Maya land in Mexico and present-day Guatemala. She had taken them while on vacation and wanted to show them to us as she began her lesson plan on the Spanish conquest of Mexico. My parents had instilled in me instructions to respect my teachers and never talk back to an older person. So I kept my mouth shut. Mouth agape, I looked at the magnificent structures and their size. Once home, I did ask my mother why the teacher knew about those things, could go there and take pictures, and we didn't. My mother confessed she did not know anything about that either but, while she only went to the eighth grade, still had not been taught anything about pre-Columbian peoples and their history by her Anglo teachers. My father was more dismissive of my questions and cold in his response. He simply said in Spanish, *"Los indios perdieron; los que pierden no escriben la historia."* Translation: "The Indians lost; those that lose do not write the history." I did not understand his analysis but, again, kept my mouth shut.

Such items of information and knowledge missing in my brain began to bother me over the years into high school and college. Like a 3-year-old fascinated with newfound word power, I never stopped asking "Why?" More often than not, the responses to my "Why?"s were dismissive and cold like that of my father. I began to learn about power relations while in this formative stage. I did not know what that was, but I did know, see, feel, and learn that others, usually Anglos, could do things I could not, and the "Why?" was usually answered by my Chicano peers with "Because we are Mexicans." Fortunately, my education into the world of power relations started early in 1956–1962. First, my father died in 1956 when I was 12 years of age. My mother and I had to become migrant workers to make ends meet. Second, my student body changed in composition from majority Anglo to Chicano between the 1959 and 1960 school years. We could organize and win, for the first time, elective offices such as club, class, and student body president. Third, in my hometown of Crystal City, Texas, in 1961, Chicano workers at the Del Monte plant and others who were members of the *Sociedad de Miguel Hidalgo*, a mutual benefit society, started organizing an electoral campaign to win control of the city council. This was an era of no Voting Rights Act, the poll tax, and the pathological and criminal Texas Rangers (not the baseball team!) keeping the Mexicans in line. The five Chicano candidates did win that election in April 1963, only to be ousted in the subsequent election in 1965 by a coalition of Anglos and middle-class Mexican Americans. Being a middle-class Mexican American simply meant you did not have to head north into the Midwest annually in search of seasonal agricultural work because you worked for and depended on Anglos for a livelihood. But the victory by *Los Cinco Candidatos*, as they were called in Spanish, left me with a strong conviction that Chicanos could not only take political control of our city government but also that we should. My turn to do that began in 1967, when five of us created the Mexican American Youth Organization (MAYO) and began organizing school walkouts of classes to protest poor educational opportunity. I did about 30 plus of them; others across the nation did another 300 plus. The most notorious and publicized were the Chicano student walkouts by students in five high schools in Los Angeles, California, in March 1968. The HBO movie *Walkout* has memorialized that civil rights history. The one in my hometown in 1969 is documented in several documentaries and most recently when I received the 2019 National Hispanic Hero Award (see https://youtu.be/rx_soif-Blk).

By the late '60s, I was in graduate school and having to write long research papers in every class. The biggest obstacle was the references my professors insisted I have to document my research. After completing my master's at St. Mary's University, I became the only Chicano in the entire University of Texas system enrolled in a PhD program in Austin in 1968. There were but a handful of books on the Chicano experience then. My only recourse was to rely on participant observation as my primary research tool. I wrote a chapter for my dissertation on power relations that I witnessed, which I called "Gringo Tricks." Later, I published that chapter and elaborated on power relations in *A Gringo Manual on How to Handle Mexicans* (2nd ed.) and its sequel, *A Chicano Manual on How to Handle Gringos*, both published by the University of Houston's Arte Publico Press, in 2001 and 2003, respectively. In the first book, I elaborate on the process of power relations (pp. 3–11), and in the sequel, I reduce the process to three quick questions on page xiii and provide some analysis in the next two pages.

The three questions I posed, and that Dr. Aldridge Sanford discusses at length in 10 very readable chapters that follow, are:

1. How does the world work?
2. How do I make the world work for me?
3. How do I make the world?

Those who seek social justice did not make the world or, to be clearer, the status quo. The world as it is, the status quo, is contextual—what you know, where you live, and life from day to day—your neighborhood, city, school, county, region, state, and nation. Those who maintain that status quo are the architects, owners, supporters, and those not engaged. They benefit and profit immensely from this system. Those not engaged get the crumbs of the benefits and profits; nevertheless, they get something and remain passive, quiet, and not engaged in direct action. The world as it is works for them. In the United States, all states, and most counties, it is the Anglo community that benefits and profits from this economic elites system. As we push forward demographically into 2030, 2040, 2050, and beyond, the critical mass of people will not be Anglos or white, if we want to use racial classifications; instead, those who will replace them will be minorities—racial, ethnic, and gendered. These replacements, however, will not all be in accord with making a different world. Many will just want to change the color of faces, the personnel now in charge of how the world works. Others, like myself and believers in the pursuit of social justice, will want to make a world to our liking. Herein lies the political struggle between those two broad camps into the future.

Readers of this text will learn how others have fared and how they moved from inaction or status quo to action in many arenas. You will learn, if you want to make the world, to channel your anger and rage into strategic direct action. You will learn that some people, many of whom you care deeply about, do not agree with your views, much less your actions. You must learn to compartmentalize your feelings and not let those personal relations stop or freeze your imperative to make the world. You must remake the world so others can enjoy life under better-quality conditions than before. Is that not the goal of humankind—our goal right now?

Preface

F ROM THOUGHT TO *Action: Developing a Social Justice Orientation* is the book I wanted to give my students for more than a decade. My university teaching career is dedicated to preparing and teaching social justice–oriented courses in conservative regions of the United States, and as a result, I have watched students struggle as they try to find their way to a "woke" status regarding the marginalized and disenfranchised. Additionally, many of my professor friends have emailed and private messaged me on Facebook to share similar stories about  their students. (They also wanted book recommendations). As students' social justice consciousness is raised, so are their levels of anger, frustration, and hopelessness. The students are angry at their parents for their homophobia, racism, etc.; at their high school teachers for not giving them more information sooner; and at their professor(s) for teaching them things they cannot unknow. It was common for students to complain to me that television watching was ruined for them as a result of something they learned in class and that they could no longer communicate with less woke family members without becoming very frustrated.

I was also very frustrated with my students, but for a different reason. They rarely moved beyond talk. It was uncommon for them to take action on things that bothered them the most—like Chick-fil-A. I heard students complain about the "homophobic" chicken many times over the years, but I never saw them devise a campaign to draw business away from the Chick-fil-A on campus. I knew they needed more instruction regarding activism. Again, I needed a book to help guide them on their journeys, which can often take years, but again, I had nothing comprehensive to recommend. Instead, I would give them (and my professor friends) a list of several books (many of them are referenced in the following pages) in the hopes they could piece something together.

Reading *From Thought to Action: Developing a Social Justice Orientation* will help students manage the discomfort that accompanies a newly raised social justice consciousness. The purpose of the book is to help students (a) focus on common humanity, (b) feel less isolated during their social justice journeys, and (c) figure out how to move from thought to action. In the social and behavioral sciences, especially in conservative spaces in the United States, the majority of student majors struggle with information they have never really considered before—information about the marginalized, disenfranchised, underserved, and invisible. A student needs the opportunity to process and figure out what to do with their raised consciousness *before* they go out to face the world on their own—where they can position themselves to never hear about these problems again.

From Thought to Action: Developing a Social Justice Orientation gives teachers and learners the opportunity to process together while reading the book and considering the discussion starters at the end of each chapter. These questions can be used for face-to-face discussion, online message boards, and as prompts for reflective essays. Additionally, each chapter includes a list of books, video clips, movies, etc. that relate to or inspired information in the chapter. Readers can reference items on this list to expand their understanding of what may be new information for them.

Who Should Read This Book?

Stage models help us understand what is required of a person who is on a journey toward activism. One such example is the five-stage feminist identification model (FIM). Stage 1 is the *status quo*; no consciousness-raising has occurred. To reach Stage 2, a person must recognize that there is oppression in society. Some people will never have that epiphany and will remain in Stage 1 throughout their entire lives. We all know people like this. They are either very naïve or benefit greatly from an oppressive system. People in this latter group use the term "bootstraps"—as in a person needs to pull themselves up by the bootstraps. This book will probably *not* be very helpful to people who would use that phrase with a straight face. They will likely need a little more convincing before reading this text.

In Stage 3, people become angry about the oppression—angry at themselves, angry at their parents, angry at the oppressive system, angry at people who never pointed out this oppression before. This stage of anger could last months, years, or even a lifetime. During this stage, a person will seek the company of like-minded individuals with whom they can talk, share books, attend events, etc. It is during the fourth stage that a person identifies completely with a group and can label oneself as feminist, Chican@,[1] an LGBTQ+ ally, etc. When and if a person can work through the anger, they can move to the fifth and final stage of effective activism.

Feminist Identification Model	
Downing & Roush (1985)	
Stage 1: Passive Acceptance	Acceptance of traditional patriarchal sex roles
Stage 2: Revelation	Awareness of marginalization and oppression
Stage 3: Embeddedness-Emanation	Seeking relationships with like-minded people
Stage 4: Synthesis	Integration of new social justice identity
Stage 5: Active Commitment	Doing the social justice work

This book is for anyone who has made it past the first stage and is living with a newfound social justice consciousness. There are chapters in this book that will help a person in Stage 2 understand their anger, and there are chapters that will help someone in Stage 5 who is ready to do something about the oppression. This book is also for the mentors and teachers who often get sought out for advice by the newly liberated. We would love to see the people we mentor move to activism. This book provides space for that conversation.

A Guide to the Chapters

This text includes 10 chapters that do not have to be read in order. Readers will come to this book at different places in their journeys and may desire to start with the information that most resonates with them. In the first chapter, readers

---

1   The @ symbol is used in Chican@ to allow for the word to be gender-neutral.

will become familiar with the concept of a social justice consciousness or orientation and will learn about my journey. As a white poor kid raised on the Holy Bible and government cheese in rural Oklahoma, I certainly made some mistakes along the way to a social justice consciousness. My hope is that both students and my colleagues can use my (flawed) journey to discuss their own—mistakes and all. In Chapters 2–4, readers will be given some common terminology and recent histories of both well-known social movements (women's suffrage and the labor movement) and lesser-known social movements (Chican@ civil rights and the American Indian Movement) within the United States. Be prepared. This information is typically what makes students unhappy with their history teachers.

In Chapter 5, turning points for some well-known and lesser-known activists are presented. The chapter includes stories from the lives of Clara Luper, a high school teacher in Oklahoma who led some of the earliest sit-ins of the U.S. Black civil rights movement; Judy Shepard, a gay rights activist whose son Matthew Shepard was beaten and left for dead in rural Wyoming; Mitch Landrieu, the former mayor of New Orleans who ordered the removal of Confederate statues in the city; and Malala Yousafzai, a recipient of the Nobel Peace Prize at the age of 17 because of her advocacy for educating girls in her home country of Pakistan. Their turning points and dozens of others will help students pinpoint important moments in their own journeys. In Chapter 6, there is a long list of potential activist causes for the readers, including immigration, ageism, sexual orientation, and disability. Readers will consider which of these causes to adopt and how to best take action. Among other actions, an activist can write a letter, start an online petition, or organize a boycott. All will be explored in the chapter.

One of the toughest tasks of activism is convincing others to care and take action. In Chapter 7, readers will look at different approaches to dialogue, conversational partners, and how to handle the naysayers (including family and friends) who may have a hard time understanding a person's newfound social justice orientation. Activism requires effective leadership and grouping. In Chapter 8, readers will learn about leadership styles, common leadership mistakes, and examples from some of the most effective movement leaders in history, including Bayard Rustin, Bella Abzug, and Wilma Mankiller. Chapter 9 includes information about groups, coalitions, and common challenges in organizing. In Chapter 10, risks and rewards of social activism will be presented. Risks include defamation of one's character, loss of employment, arrest, trauma, and even death. Many people have made great sacrifices for the progress of equality. The book will end on a high note with a discussion about the rewards of social justice activism.

Acknowledgments

My sincerest gratitude to the following individuals who read drafts of chapters, discussed ideas with me, and/or otherwise inspired me during the long journey of writing this book.

Pat Arneson (Duquesne University, Department of Communication & Rhetorical Studies)

Bilaye Benibo (Texas A&M University-Corpus Christi, Department of Psychology & Sociology)

David Blanke (Texas A&M University-Corpus Christi, Department of Humanities)

Laura D. Boren (Georgia Southwestern State University, Division of Student Engagement and Success)

Ryan G. Cannonie (Oklahoma's District 27, Assistant District Attorney)

Kristopher D. Copeland (Tulsa Community College, Division of Academic Affairs)

Deborah Cunningham Breede (Coastal Carolina University, Department of Communication, Media, & Culture)

Lahoma Davidson (Flint Rock Development, Owner and Lead Consultant)

Jason Del Gandio (Temple University, Department of Communication and Social Influence)

Jennifer C. Dunn (Dominican University, Department of Communication Arts and Sciences)

Amber M. Fite-Morgan (University of North Alabama, Office of General Counsel)

Lawrence R. Frey (University of Colorado Boulder, Department of Communication)

William Gardner (University of Washington, Department of Health Metric Sciences)

Alberto González (Bowling Green State University, School of Media & Communication)

Tabitha Hart (San José State University, Department of Communication Studies)

Sarah Janda (Cameron University, Department of Social Sciences)

Malynnda A. Johnson (Indiana State University, Department of Communication)

Sarah Johnson (Medical University of South Carolina, Education, Student Life, & Engagement)

David H. Kahl, Jr. (Penn State Behrend, School of Humanities & Social Sciences)

John C. B. LaRue (Texas A&M University-Corpus Christi, Office of Compliance)

Tiburcio Lince (Tarleton State University, Office of Diversity & Inclusion)

Casandra Lorentson (KCS Public Relations, Communications Manager)

Jennifer Martin Emami (Texas Woman's University, Department of Multicultural Women's and Gender Studies)

Eddah Mbula Mutua (St. Cloud State University, Department of Communication Studies)

Heather Nesemeier (Minnesota State University Moorhead, Office of Online Learning)

Sandra Pensoneau-Conway (Southern Illinois University Carbondale, Department of Communication Studies)

Steve Poulter (Newman University, English Department)

Anthony Quiroz (Texas A&M University-Corpus Christi, Department of Humanities)

Rishi Raj (Texas A&M University-Corpus Christi, Department of Educational Leadership)

Jessica Reemer (WMC-TV Nashville, Digital Content Manager)

Ariana Rodriguez (Texas A&M University-Corpus Christi, Islander Feminists)

Bradlee Ross (Connors State College, Division of Communications & Fine Arts)

Elaina M. Ross (Northeastern State University, Department of Communication and Media Studies)

C. Kyle Rudick (University of Northern Iowa, Department of Communication Studies)

Amy Sanders McCarter (Cherokee Nation Businesses, Community Relations Coordinator)

Robin VanMeter (Direct Energy, Diversity and Inclusion Manager of North America)

Wendy Walker (Texas A&M University-Corpus Christi, Department of English)

Justin D. Walton (Cameron University, Department of Communication Studies)

Frank Wiley (WEWS Cleveland, Anchor)

Kimberly M. Weismann (Williston State College, Arts and Human Sciences Department)

Further Reading

Cross, W. E. (1971). Negro-to-Black conversion experience: Toward a psychology of Black liberation. *Black World*, *20*(9), 13–27.

Downing, N. E., & Roush, K. L. (1985). From passive acceptance to active commitment: A model of feminist identity development for women. *The Counseling Psychologist*, *13*(4), 695–709.

FIGURE CREDITS

Protesters are seen in June 2011 in support of the Tucson Unified School District's Mexican American Studies program.

CHAPTER 1

Raised by Racists and Murphy Brown

Racist.   *Un-American.*

                 Radical ideas.

      Victim rhetoric.   *Subversive thinking.*

T HESE WERE THE words and phrases used by Arizona lawmakers to describe the Mexican American Studies program in the state's public schools. In Tucson, the courses had been successfully taught since the mid-1990s, when they were first introduced as part of the district's desegregation plan. The topics were popular in the school district, which included a 60% Latinx[1] population, and the courses were often counted for graduation credits in history and literature. This pleased many Latinx students and their families who felt their histories and experiences were inadequately reflected in the majority of the district's existing courses. During the time period that the Mexican American curriculum was taught, dropout rates for Latinx students decreased in Tucson. The students reported that they felt empowered and less isolated from the school's curriculum. In a city that had a long history of racial segregation, brown-skinned students held their heads high and took pride in their heritage. They could name oppression and seek change. Their **social justice consciousness** had been raised, and they wanted to raise the consciousness of others around them.

It was in this climate that in 2006, national lawmakers began to discuss a bill that would classify all people without documentation as felons. The Tucson students responded with walkouts across the city that lasted for days.

---

1   The term Latinx (pronounced La-teen-ex) is used where appropriate as a gender-neutral alternative to Latino. There is a growing concern that using multiple labels (e.g., Latina, Hispanic, Latino, Brown) for similar people can hinder a group's ability to experience cohesion and solidarity.

The student protesters felt that illegal immigrants from Mexico were unfairly targeted in the legislation and that furthermore, all immigrants should be allowed to remain in the United States and better their lives. In one day, more than 1,300 students walked out of their Tucson schools. School administrators said they had concerns about the students' safety and disruptions to the school day. The administrators turned to Dolores Huerta, the iconic labor leader and civil rights activist (read more about her in Chapter 2) and asked her to speak to the students at an all-school assembly. Her job, as described to her by the school administrators, was to encourage the students to stop the walkouts and find other outlets for their activism. At the assembly, Huerta suggested that the students start a postcard campaign to the Republican National Convention asking why Arizona's Republican lawmakers hated people who were Latinx. As soon as she uttered, "Republicans hate Latinos" the students loudly applauded.

Figure 1.1 Dolores Huerta speaking at a campaign rally in 2016.

That response proved to be too much for the state's politicians, who debated banning Mexican American Studies courses within the state's public schools. During these debates, there were accusations that the Tucson students and their teachers hated America and wanted the region returned to Mexico. By 2012, all Mexican American courses for K–12 students were outlawed in Arizona. House Bill

2281 stated classes could no longer be "designed primarily for pupils of a particular ethnic group," nor could they "promote the overthrow of the United States government." A group of students responded by filing a federal lawsuit against the state superintendent, and in August 2017, U.S. District Court Judge A. Wallace Tashima ruled that the law was unconstitutional and discriminatory.

Developing a Social Justice Orientation

British philosopher John Locke made the term "consciousness" popular with his 17th-century book *An Essay Concerning Human Understanding*. Today, "consciousness" is typically discussed as a heightened sense of awareness about oneself in relation to personal surroundings. In other words, until a person becomes conscious of something (e.g., a person, an event, an idea, or an injustice), they[2] will be oblivious to it. During the 1960s and 1970s, women's rights advocates held consciousness-raising groups (often in people's homes) to raise awareness about issues regarding women (more about these groups in Chapter 3). Discussions might include topics like equal pay for equal work, sexual harassment, and women's health. It was thought that once a woman's consciousness was raised, she would be more likely to take action on issues that concerned her. Indeed, during the time of women's liberation in the 1960s and 1970s, women did often take to the streets to fight for justice as they saw it.

"Social justice" is a term embraced by people who work to promote a society in which diversity and difference are celebrated and not ignored or belittled. In other words, social justice is their goal. An "orientation" is a person's beliefs or attitudes toward a subject. Once a person's social justice consciousness is heightened, it is likely that their **social justice orientation** (SJO) will increase as well. Attaining a heightened SJO involves three components: (a) embracing personal history; (b) sympathizing with other people's histories; and (c) a desire to end oppression of the marginalized.

Taking an inventory of one's own personal history can be painful and time-consuming, but it is only through peeling back these storied layers that each of us understands why we believe what we do. There are happy moments (e.g., recognizing that a TV show helped your 8-year-old self frame feminism positively), but there are also those difficult moments (e.g., the memory of making fun of that kid who wore the same clothes every day in your sixth-grade homeroom). In the latter example, you were the oppressor, and as painful as it may be, you must own that

---

2   In the spirit of inclusivity of all genders and biological sexes, the pronouns they, them, and their are used as singular pronouns when the preferred pronoun of a person is unknown.

ugly truth to gain a healthy SJO. Embracing a personal history involves embracing the good and the bad and recognizing what caused the behaviors. It means coming to terms with intersections of oppression and privilege and the simultaneous experience of being both the oppressed and the oppressor.

It is only through recognizing and sympathizing with each other's histories or lived experiences that we appreciate other people's modern-day **truths** and **implicit biases**. Modern-day truths are a set of personal rules each of us lives by. You learned your rules (or truths) early in your life from members of your family, neighborhood and school friends, clergy, and teachers. You also learned from popular culture, including television, radio, magazines, and, in the last 20 years, from the Internet. These truths affect your implicit biases (which reside deep in your subconscious), including both favorable and unfavorable assessments based on people's appearance. Let's take a look at Emily and DeAndre and each of their truths and implicit biases.

> To test your implicit biases, visit Project Implicit at harvard.edu.

Emily, a white[3] woman, always went to schools where she was in the racial majority. In fact, one of the only Black classmates she ever had was in third grade, and from what Emily remembers, he was always in trouble with the teacher for sleeping in class. Obviously, she decided, he never took his schoolwork seriously enough. As Emily grew older, the evening news taught her that Black men were dangerous, and her uncle, also white, regularly used racial slurs when talking about Black people. Today, Emily crosses the street when a Black man approaches from the other direction. In her mind, it is just a precaution.

From an early age, DeAndre saw men who looked like him with their mug shots on the evening news. He heard the white news anchors discuss Black men's alleged crimes with disgust. It felt like they spat the words out. He has seen white women (like Emily) clutch their purses tighter when he passed them on the street. White plainclothes loss prevention officers have followed DeAndre in department stores. He has heard the stories of Terence Crutcher, Philando Castile, Alton Sterling, and Eric Garner. DeAndre's dad taught him how to be overly polite when questioned by police and to always keep his hands visible during a traffic stop. DeAndre learned not to trust white people. In his mind, it is just a protective measure.

Both Emily and DeAndre have historical reasons to think and behave the way they do. The media, school systems, family, and law enforcement have victimized

---

3   The term "white," when used to describe a person's racial makeup, will not be capitalized in this book. Black is capitalized as a subversive response to the historical erasure of Black people's experiences.

both of them. A person with a social justice orientation recognizes *and* sympathizes with the lived experiences of not only Emily and DeAndre but also the news producers and anchors, teachers, Emily's uncle, DeAndre's dad, and law enforcement as well as other people in their stories.

Finally, a person with a healthy SJO can spot oppression of the marginalized and have a strong desire to call it out and end it. This is why the young Mexican American scholars in Tucson enthusiastically applauded Dolores Huerta in 2006. The students felt that Republican lawmakers were marginalizing immigrants from south of the U.S. border, and they wanted to stop the oppression. They were excited to find out that a very important person like Huerta recognized the oppression as well.

The end goal for anyone with an SJO should be **equality** and **equity** for all, no matter their race, ethnicity, physical or mental abilities, class, gender identity, sexual orientation, religion, country of origin, or age. People with an SJO want to improve the quality of life for those who have been marginalized and desire for everyone to live free of oppression. Both the marginalized and the privileged can work for this goal by standing side-by-side to amplify the voices and narratives of the unheard and dialoguing with others in the hopes of raising other people's social justice consciousness. That is activism. Chances are you picked up this book because you want to turn your newfound SJO into action.

My Journey to a Social Justice Orientation

I was born in the mid-1970s. I would like to say that my parents were old hippies who raised me with a strong liberal bias, but that was not the reality. In fact, my white parents, one raised by a middle-class couple in a suburb of Wichita, Kansas, and the other by his grandparents in rural, impoverished southeast Oklahoma, were racists. They moved me 30 miles south from the city of my birth (a racially diverse city of 40,000 in Northeast Oklahoma) to a homogeneous town of 1,200 to ensure that I did not attend middle school with nonwhites. As a preteen and teen, I continuously corrected my parents' racist speech and fought for the right to date outside of my race. "But your children would suffer," they would say—making the assumption that all couples want to have children. My mom thought Elvis Presley's birthday should be a federal holiday if my all-white high school canceled classes for Martin Luther King Day in January (which they never did).

My ethnocentric parents did raise me to speak my mind, though. When I argued with them, I felt heard and respected. This resulted in a strong sense of self—no small feat for a girl child in the buckle of the Bible Belt in the late 20th century.

My financially strapped parents allowed me to pursue everything that interested me: ballet, soccer, bowling, roller skating, Girl Scouts, church youth group, class president, the student newspaper, and competitive speaking. It was through these activities that I honed my personal leadership, but more importantly, it was through these activities that I met and read about people who were different from me. My ideas about disability and ability were framed in the third grade at a Girl Scout jamboree when I heard about the personal triumphs of Helen Keller. At 14 years old, my first time in an airplane took me to Washington, DC, to compete in a national speech contest, where I saw same-sex couples holding hands in the subway and had to make sense of a romantic coupling that I had never seen before. After that trip, my Southern Baptist preacher could no longer tell me how same-sex couples looked and acted; I had witnessed examples with my own eyes. Although I did not have the language to explain it then, same-sex couples were no longer the unknown **"Other"** to me.

The impact of 1980s popular culture cannot be undervalued when it comes to my formative years. The 13-inch black-and-white television in my bedroom provided me with an escape when I sought solitude from my homogenous surroundings. News broadcaster Murphy Brown never made apologies for her demands, business owner Julia Sugarbaker from *Designing Women* could only be pushed so far before she would deliver one of her infamous feminist diatribes, and Janet Jackson was a performer who was in *Control* when MTV still played music videos. These pop icons modeled strength and dignity for me; I knew no other women like them in my day-to-day life. They gave me alternatives to the female submissiveness I witnessed within my community. The strongest women I knew were my teachers, and they always had to answer to the male principal or the male superintendent or the all-male school board.

My undergraduate college experience was financed by Pell Grants and scholarship money. My small regional university had been founded as a female seminary by Cherokee Indians 150 years earlier and was just 60 miles from where I had attended high school. Within a few weeks, it felt like thousands of miles from my hometown. One of my earliest memories of college was the white, male, middle-aged English composition professor who called out a younger white male for his privilege. We had read a biographical sketch of an author who was a member of the National Association of Black Journalists. The student, who thought himself clever and amongst friends, asked the teacher if there was a National Association of *White* Journalists. The professor, without missing a beat, answered, "I imagine it's just called the National Association of Journalists." I laughed. I was the only one. The professor looked at me and nodded. He knew his words were not wasted.

Additionally, I traveled with the speech and debate team two weekends a month, when I heard college students in their mid-20s, who were more liberal and well-read than just about anybody I had ever known, discuss current events for hours in the van crossing highways in middle America. Bill Clinton's Welfare to Work was hotly contested at the time. Until those van rides, I had never heard anyone sympathize with people on welfare. My friends and family told me that welfare recipients were simply Black female drug addicts with too many children who drove Cadillacs while scamming the system because they did not want to work. I learned from the debaters that the majority of people on welfare were white and that many people on welfare would like to work but had a hard time finding affordable, safe childcare within their neighborhoods.

My undergraduate major was secondary education, and when it came time to complete my full internship, I opted to teach speech and theater at the middle school my parents had not wanted me to attend as a student nearly a decade earlier. (It was defiant, but it felt like Julia Sugarbaker would approve). This school was a place where the majority of the students could not participate in extracurricular activities because they had no way home after the school buses ran. The parents were often at work or just did not have reliable transportation or childcare for the other children in their families. To have enough talent (and warm bodies) to put on a school play, I would drive many students home after rehearsals. My favorite passengers were a small group of sharp, energetic, funny 12- and 13-year-old boys. I had a close bond with one of the boys because his older brother and I had attended grade school together and our families had been neighbors back then. By the time I became a teacher, the older brother was in prison, and his mom wanted me to spend as much time as possible with her younger son Latrell. She hoped he would really like school. I would usually take Latrell and his friends home last and would allow them to tag along on my personal errands. It was during such an errand that I began to understand **marginalization** through **profiling**.

It was the end of the school year, and I needed some graduation gifts and decided to check out a jewelry counter at a major department store in the local mall. The three boys waited patiently within my sight while I looked at the merchandise. I made my selections and waited for a salesperson to ring me up, but the workers appeared distracted by something behind me. As they shared knowing glances, I turned to see Latrell and his friends laughing about obnoxiously large purses and playfully punching each other. I quietly told the salesperson closest to me that the boys were with me. She looked relieved but continued to keep an eye on them. It was then I realized that those boys would become Black men, and chances were they would always be profiled and viewed suspiciously in this store and others like it.

After completing the teaching internship, I started graduate school and taught college classes at a women's minimum-security prison once a week to supplement my meager graduate assistant income. Oklahoma had the highest rate of female incarceration in the country, and I quickly learned that many of the women's "crimes" were attached to feeding or protecting their children. One of the students had stabbed an abusive husband, and another had written bogus checks to pay her family's bills. Other women were in for minor drug charges. Some of the women kept in touch with me after their releases. They had one thing in common—they could not find jobs. Even fast-food managers did not want to hire people who checked the felony box on the employment application. I didn't know how these women could ever get back on their feet without a job, and in fact, many of them did not. They ended up making money any way they knew how, from selling dope to stealing to writing bad checks to finding romantic partners who were also committing crimes.

At the age of 24, for the first time, I moved outside the state of my birth—600 miles away—to pursue a PhD at the University of Iowa. It was during this time that I felt I finally achieved full social justice consciousness. It took losing my best friend. Rusty and I met in college during my sophomore year and became so close within a couple of years that we shared an apartment. We did everything together— ate meals, shopped for clothes, studied, laughed until we were on our hands and knees, spent holidays with each other's families, and cared for each other when we were sick. We loved each other and had a closeness that other people envied. I felt very lucky to have him in my life.

Not long after I left Oklahoma for graduate school in Iowa, Rusty reluctantly told me that he was gay. It took 600 miles of distance for him to tell me something he had known for years. He knew what was coming; we had both grown up with the same **Truth**. Our upbringing in the Southern Baptist tradition had prepared me for this moment. Instead of accepting Rusty's sexuality, I told him that it was a sin against God and quoted scripture at him. I told him that he should make a choice to never date a man and that we must pray. Little did I know that Rusty had been "praying the gay away" for years and had even participated in faith-based conversion therapy. By the time he came out to me, he was ready to be out to everybody; it did not take him long to grow tired of my judgment. We soon lost contact. Judging Rusty is the biggest regret of my life. Today, after many apologies and much guilt on my part, we are slowly building a relationship, but I missed out on 13 years of his life—including the death of his grandmother and his wedding ceremony.

I had to reevaluate everything I believed after losing Rusty. The University of Iowa was a good place to do that. The university and the town had a long history of encouraging and embracing diversity. In 1970, UI was the first university in the United States to recognize an LGBTQ+ student group. Twenty years later, it was the first university in the country to extend same-sex partner benefits to university employees and their families. The graduate students voted to unionize in the 1990s. I took graduate classes with a person who was female-to-male trans and unapologetically corrected me when I used the wrong pronoun. I read ethnographic books and academic journal articles that made the "Other" familiar. I began to empathize with people's oppression and committed to never hurt anyone again like I had hurt Rusty. The 3 years I spent in Iowa were a turning point for my social justice consciousness/orientation.

In 2004, I moved back to Oklahoma when I was hired as an instructor by my university *alma mater*. I was determined to challenge the students' paradigms, just like the English composition teacher had done for me a decade earlier. In my free time, I educated myself about American histories and minority experiences. During my 9 years on the faculty, I created and taught many consciousness-raising (and eyebrow-raising) courses, including Women in Leadership, Privilege and Marginalization, and Rhetoric of U.S. Women's Movements. Additionally, I partnered with faculty and staff to create a minor in women's and gender studies, a multidisciplinary program that encouraged professors throughout the campus to offer courses centered on gender identity, sexual orientation, class, ability, race, and ethnicity. I like to think that my undergraduate self would have taken those classes and reached full social justice consciousness before graduate school.

During my time as a faculty member at my *alma mater*, I witnessed students, faculty, staff, administration, and members of the community experience raised social justice consciousness, but I also witnessed a lot of frustration. Initially, people's frustrations tended to center on challenges from friends and family who believed in a Truth to which the students no longer subscribed. They needed something to do with their new knowledge. They needed to take action. A book like this one could have helped guide them through that process.

SJO Is a Journey

Achieving an SJO does not happen overnight. If you have experienced some level of social justice consciousness and are on the journey to an SJO, this book will help you. As witnessed by my story, coming to an SJO is a gradual, ongoing process of learning, experiencing, and evolving. I was well into by 30s before I called myself a feminist or an activist, and in the process of writing this book, I had many consciousness-raising moments as I read feedback from thoughtful reviewers. Achieving full social justice consciousness is a journey on which you may take one step back for every two steps forward. It is often very uncomfortable as you learn people's histories and recognize your role in the oppression of people on the margins.

People who have not yet achieved an SJO often have two characteristics in common: (a) a lack of recognition of systematic oppression and its harms and (b) a belief in ultimate or absolute Truth. They are not necessarily bad people, but they usually benefit from the **status quo** and are resistant to change. They tend to subscribe to **postracist** and **postfeminist** beliefs and will say that they are "color-blind" and "tolerate" people who are different. This language is problematic, because people of color are not ashamed of their race or ethnicity. They want to be seen for who they are, which includes the color of their skin. They just do not want to be discriminated against or simply "tolerated" as a result of their race. They want to be embraced, accepted, and appreciated.

People who lack an SJO also often believe that everyone has equal opportunity, since they believe there is no oppression. We saw this with Tom Horne, Arizona's state superintendent of public instruction and author of HB 2281, which banned ethnic studies in Arizona. In an interview with PBS, Horne admonished the Tucson teachers in the Mexican American studies programs for making race a part of their identities. Horne, a middle-aged white man, said, "I believe that what's important about us [U.S. Americans] is that we're individuals. And what matters is what we know and what we can do and what is our character and not what race we happen to been [sic] born into." Notice Horne's emphasis on the individual and each person's responsibility. In contrast, people with a raised social justice consciousness tend to focus on the collective and how problems can be solved together. Horne, in his privilege, cannot recognize that a person's race may cause discrimination when it comes to their education, potential for employment, shopping at the mall, etc.

A person with absolutely no level of social justice consciousness may lack compassion for others because they truly believe everyone has the very same opportunities for success because America operates as a **meritocracy**, where hard work and a good attitude always pay off. Born into poverty to a single teen who was kicked out of her parents' house? Grow up in foster care where you never completed an entire school year in one place? Go to a high school where there was gang activity and you had to go through a metal detector every day? Does not matter. A person who lacks compassion will believe that you can (and should be) just as successful as the planned child born to two financially secure parents in the suburbs who went to private school. People with little to no social justice consciousness may believe there is no need for affirmative action because everybody has equal opportunity. They might complain that Miss Black America is an example of reverse racism; there is no recognition that beauty standards are based on the dominant culture in the United States.

People living without any social justice consciousness are often guided by a Truth derived from a set of "rules" that, in their minds, are not debatable. Guides come from religious texts, family rituals, personal values and experiences, friend networks, organizations, media personalities, literature, educators, and/or the law. These guides often tell those who subscribe to them what to think about races, sexual orientations, sex roles, etc. For example, some Protestants will point to scripture in the Christian Bible to make the point that homosexuality is a crime against God and nature. Therefore, when people seek marriage equality for everybody, many Bible subscribers feel very strongly that this is wrong. Education provides another example regarding Truth. If a person receives an education where they rarely hear or read about women or people of color in the discussion of United States history and that dialogue is further reinforced at home, that person will subscribe to the Truth (with a capital T) that women and people of color played insignificant roles in the development of the country. The textbook, the teacher, and the family will be the holders of Truth unless someone teaches the child to think critically. A Truth is very hard to change because a person has a lot to lose, including eternal salvation, family relationships, and/or the GPA needed to get into top-ranked colleges. People who live by Truth believe it is *the* correct way to live and will often encourage others to adopt their beliefs.

A Word About White Privilege and White Guilt

I recognize that although I was raised in poverty and am female, I still speak from a place of privilege as a result of my whiteness. For most of my life, I have lived surrounded by people who look like me at home, at school, at work, at church, in popular culture, and in my community. In 2013, I moved to South Texas, where 60% of my city's population is Hispanic. However, at work, the majority of my colleagues and supervisors are white. There is no doubt that my life has been easier because of my race. In most situations, it gives me automatic credibility. Retail employees do not follow me around stores or count the clothing items before I go into a dressing room; there is no assumption that I will steal. No guest has ever mistaken me for a housekeeper at a hotel; after all, I am white, like most of the guests.

As a result of this automatic credibility, I have an overabundance of confidence *and privilege*. On those rare occasions when I am in the racial minority, I know it is only a matter of time or distance until I can be back amongst the ruling majority. It has always been my choice to be a racial minority.

It is my sincerest hope that I do not come to this book as a result of White Guilt or from a desire to be the White Savior. I do not speak for the oppressed; my desire is to raise people's consciousness with stories and experiences from the margins. I do not wish to co-opt anyone's narrative or act as anyone's savior. I write this book because I know there are a lot of people like me who were raised being taught to oppress and have now experienced an awakening. We want to stop the cycle of oppression and be a part of the solution. I hope this book helps you make sense of a new social justice consciousness/orientation and that the tips and stories provided in these pages inspire you.

Review

This book is for readers who have experienced some level of awareness, or consciousness, regarding social justice and desire to continue progress toward equality for all oppressed people. This progress requires personal reflection and sympathy for all people's lived experiences, either of which can be quite uncomfortable. People who have not achieved social justice consciousness tend to like things the way they have always been, whereas people with a social justice orientation want to challenge and change the status quo, which they view as flawed because it is racist, heteronormative, sexist, ableist, etc. People without social justice consciousness believe each individual has the same opportunities for success and should "pull themselves up by their bootstraps" to achieve their potential. People with social justice consciousness believe circumstances and systemic oppression make it very hard for some people to achieve their dreams. They believe in social programs because we are collectively each other's responsibility.

Discussion Starters

1. The high school students in Tucson walked out of their schools to show their disapproval of national lawmakers. Do you believe that was an effective strategy? Why or why not?

2. How can a person achieve a raised social justice consciousness (heightened sense of awareness) but not change their social justice orientation (beliefs and attitudes)?

3. From where do you get your truths or Truth? Give some examples.

4. The author shared her journey to social justice orientation. In what areas do you struggle with your journey? Have you reached social justice consciousness?

5. The author gives an example of experiencing racial privilege and witnessing racial discrimination in a major department store. Give examples of when you have experienced or witnessed privilege or discrimination.

Further Reading/Viewing

Banned in Arizona [Video file]. (2013, February 15). *Need to Know*. PBS. Retrieved from http://video.pbs.org/video/2335625906/

Conley, G. (2016). *Boy erased: A memoir of identity, faith, and family*. New York, NY: Riverhead Books.

Herraras, M. (2013, November 1). Dolores Huerta: There's more to the story than Republican mythology. *Tucson Weekly*. Retrieved from http://www.tucsonweekly.com/TheRange/archives/2013/11/01/dolores-huerta-theres-more-to-the-story-than-republican-mythology

Jones, V. (2017). *Beyond the messy truth: How we came apart, how we come together*. New York, NY: Ballantine Books.

Levin, J. (2019). *The queen*. New York, NY: Little, Brown and Company.

OBear, K. (2017). *... But I'm not racist: Tools for well-meaning whites*. New York, NY: Midpoint Trade Books Inc.

FIGURE CREDITS

Carrie Nation, a member of the Woman's Christian Temperance Union, is pictured in 1910 with the hatchet she used to destroy saloons.

CHAPTER 2

Social Justice During the 19th Century in the United States

The further we seem to move from a given event or way of life, the easier it is for us to believe that the distance from histori-cally damaging events is progress.

—DeRay Mckesson (2018)

F OR PEOPLE WITH a **social justice orientation**, the United States of America has a troubling history. (And no matter what you have been told, it is not unpatriotic to hold that belief). In the early 17th century, European settlers walked off their boats in what would become the United States and began taking possession of the land from **indigenous peoples**[1] who had farmed it and hunted on it for centuries. The new settlers (i.e., occupiers, colonizers) felt empowered to take the land because of the Discovery Doctrine, a statement from Pope Alexander VI in 1493 claiming that Christians had the right to settle land held by people who were not Christians. Indigenous peoples did not believe land should be fenced off and individually owned but should be a shared resource. This was a major philosophical difference between the new settlers and American Indians. Before long, the settlers turned to their lawmakers to settle the differences, completely ignoring the **sovereignty** of American Indians. In 1823, the Supreme Court of the United States made the Discovery Doctrine federal law.

One of the most devastating legislative moves was the Indian Removal Act of 1830,[2] which resulted in tens of thousands of American Indians being forcefully displaced from their homelands in the Southeast and moved

---

1   Both "indigenous" and "American Indian" will be used interchangeably throughout the book when referring to the original occupants (and their descendants) of what is now the United States.

2   In 1862, the Homestead Act opened up settlement in the western United States, further displacing American Indians and people of Spanish and Mexican descent.

further west so non-Indian occupiers could take official possession of the land. The journeys for American Indians were long and grueling and were accomplished mostly by walking hundreds of miles through treacherous weather and terrain. Thousands of American Indians died along the way from exhaustion, disease, and starvation on what is often referred to as "The Trail of Tears." Today, members of the Cherokee Nation annually commemorate the removal with a 950-mile bike ride along the trail from New Echota, Georgia, to Tahlequah, Oklahoma.

In 1775, the descendants of the aforementioned European settlers challenged British rule of their "American" colonies and fought in the Revolutionary War in hopes of declaring their independence. As you know from textbooks, the European settlers were victorious after 8 years of battle and eventually became the ruling class that made and enforced the laws, including the Constitution. In 1791, just 2 years after the U.S. Constitution was made law, 10 amendments (referred to as The Bill of Rights) were ratified. The First Amendment, which calls for freedom of religion, assembly, speech, and the press, has protected **activists** for hundreds of years.

One of the very best attributes of the United States of America is that citizens are allowed (and sometimes encouraged) to critique and protest its power structures, and those power structures have been protested for centuries by both people with privilege and those with none, including women, immigrants, children, indigenous peoples, the poor, people of color, and members of LGBTQ+ communities. They have fought for the democratic ideas upon which the United States was founded. In this chapter, we will broadly focus on four social justice movements that occurred when the United States was very young. In Chapter 3, more contemporary movements will be discussed.

The activists in the following pages were committed to social justice and fought for what they believed was right, even when it cost them their lives, their families, and/or their livelihoods. During their lives, they often seemed radical (and even mentally ill) to their contemporaries, but with the benefit of time, we can learn from their tactics, beliefs, dedication, and ambition. It is the activists before us who envisioned what the United States could be—a country committed to social justice for all. Below are reviews of the major actors and actions in each social movement. For more in-depth discussions, see the sources recommended at the end of the chapter.

Prohibition of Alcohol (1814–1920)

One of the earliest social movements in the United States centered on the consumption of alcohol. Both **Protestants** and people who were for women's rights (sometimes they were one and the same) fought against the making and distribution of alcohol. This stance caused a major rift between Protestants (who had been in the country for a couple of generations and considered themselves "real Americans") and new immigrants. The Protestants banned alcohol as a result of their religious beliefs, whereas the immigrants, who were often Jewish and Catholic, did not see anything wrong with consuming a few drinks. The Protestants complained that the foreign, drunkard husbands would spend all their money at the saloons and have nothing to pay their family's bills. There were also concerns that the same men would abuse their wives and children. Unfortunately, this was an era when there was no escape or police protection from domestic abuse. People in the suffrage movement (i.e., the women's rights movement) felt like they had to get involved because it involved the protection of women and children. During this time, leagues and unions were a great way for people to organize. The two most successful were the Woman's Christian Temperance Union, founded in 1879, and the Anti-Saloon League, founded in 1895. There were two organizations that preceded them: the American Temperance Society (1826) and the Women's Temperance League (1870).

In 1814, Protestant clergyman Lyman Beecher published a series of sermons about intemperance (i.e., drunkenness). The writings got a lot of attention, and in 1826, Beecher co-founded the American Temperance Society (ATS) in Boston. The group had 1.5 million members (the U.S. population in 1830 was 12.8 million) within 10 years and was able to get the sale of alcohol forbidden in Maine in 1851. Other states soon followed. Unfortunately for Beecher and his parishioners, the laws were ineffective and were wiped off the books by 1860. In 1870, the Women's Temperance League was formed. On Christmas Eve in 1873, the members prayed in front of a saloon in Hillsboro, Ohio, blocking the entrance. The news of their civil disobedience spread, and other women across the nation prayed in front of saloons. In the bigger cities, the activists were often sprayed with hoses, doused in beer, and had stones thrown at them. They did close down some saloons, but with time, the saloons all reopened.

In 1879, Frances Willard was the founding president of the Woman's Christian Temperance Union (WCTU). She traveled across the country and gave speeches in favor of temperance and developed temperance curriculum for public schools. She also partnered with people from the suffrage movement in the hopes of strengthening the cause. (This decision was controversial for the suffrage movement because its members feared gaining new enemies). The Anti-Saloon League (ASL) and Wayne B. Wheeler joined the fight in 1895. It is believed that they did the job Willard and the WCTU could not. Wheeler, an experienced lawyer, told politicians they would lose voter support if he did not like what they did regarding temperance. The ASL, which had its own printing press, distributed anti-saloon propaganda. The ASL focused solely on prohibition of alcohol, while WCTU focused on other women's issues as well.

Between 1900 and 1910, Carrie Nation, who was a member of a local WCTU branch, felt she was called by God to go into saloons and physically destroy them, often with a hatchet. Nation started the crusade in her home state of Kansas, where saloons, while not legal, were plentiful. By 1913, nine states had passed laws to restrict the sale of alcohol. The 16th Amendment was also passed, allowing the federal government to collect income tax. As a result of the amendment, the government no longer needed the taxes from the sale of alcohol as a means of financial security. The ASL had supported the 16th amendment.

In 1913, members of the ASL and WCTU marched together in Washington, D.C., to demand prohibition at the federal level. The groups sent out speakers and signed petitions. In 1917, the Great War (later known as World War I) began, and the ASL used the hatred for Germans in the United States to encourage prohibition, since many of the major brewers were German or had German ancestry. In 1920, the 18th Amendment, prohibiting the production, sale, and transport of "intoxicating liquors," went into effect. The Volstead Act, which provided for the enforcement of the 18th Amendment, defined "intoxicating liquors" and provided penalties for breaking the law. The enforcement of the Volstead Act became almost impossible for the government. Throughout the 1920s, the Dries (supporters of the law) were asked to reconsider the enforcement of the Volstead Act, but they would not budge. Their extremism cost them moderate support, and by 1933, the 21st Amendment, which repealed Prohibition, was ratified.

Abolition of Slavery (1830–1865)

The outcome of the Revolutionary War guaranteed freedom for the European settlers of the United States but not for their African slaves, whose ancestors were forced to migrate and be auctioned off as domestic labor in the British colonies starting in 1619. Families were torn apart on the auction block, and slaves were regularly beaten and killed by their masters. William Lloyd Garrison, who eventually became an influential abolitionist,[3] got involved in the anti-slavery movement around 1830 in Boston. Many Black abolitionists (e.g., Mum Bett, Reverend Richard Allen) had been involved before 1830, but unfortunately, the movement did not get much attention until Garrison, a white man with a newspaper, started to use his ink. In 1833, the New England Anti-Slavery Society was formed; Garrison wrote the charter that 63 people signed at a national gathering in Philadelphia. By 1835, there were 300 chapters of the anti-slavery society and tens of thousands of members. The members hoped to appeal to people's moral compasses to stop the spread of slavery and made pamphlets to send to ministers, politicians, and slave owners. They also had bandanas, songs, chocolate wrappers, and readers they sent out in the hopes of keeping slavery confined to the South.

The anti-slavery propaganda resulted in a backlash from slave owners, who burned the pamphlets, bandanas, etc. and threatened the lives of abolitionists and anti-slavery supporters. By 1840, many white people had left Garrison's anti-slavery society after he told his followers not to vote because he was afraid voting would show support for the government. People believed Garrison had become too radical. Garrison was also pro-women's rights, which upset many activists in the anti-slavery movement. As support was dwindling, Garrison had the good fortune of meeting Frederick Douglass, an escaped slave. They began giving speeches across the North. In 1843, they collected 65,000 signatures on a petition that pressured the Massachusetts legislature to pass the Personal Liberty Act, making it illegal for the state to serve any role in recapturing a slave. Several Northern states followed suit.

In 1845, Garrison published parts of Douglass's autobiography, *Narrative of the Life of Frederick Douglass, an American Slave,* in his newspaper. As a result of the publication, Douglass felt he had to flee to Great Britain because he feared for his life. While there, British citizens bought Douglass's freedom from his former master in the United States. In 1847, much to Garrison's dismay, Douglass moved to New York and started a competing anti-slavery newspaper, *The North Star*. Within 5 years, Douglass and Garrison split over their different approaches to abolition (Garrison believed in nonviolence; Douglass disagreed with Garrison) and ended up attacking each other in their respective newspapers.

Around this time, the United States acquired a great amount of land in the Southwest as a result of the Mexican-American War and the **Treaty of Guadalupe Hidalgo**. California was part of that acquisition and was admitted as a free

---

3   There is a distinction between abolitionists and people who were anti-slavery. Abolitionists fought for the immediate end to slavery; people who were anti-slavery did not want the practice to expand beyond the existing slave states.

state. To appease Southerners who did not want California to be a free state, the **Great Compromise of 1850** was authored. As part of the Compromise, the Fugitive Slave Law was put on the books. The law required that all captured slaves be returned to their masters. Soon, bounty hunters were actively looking for runaway slaves. This felt like a major defeat to abolitionists. Beginning in 1850, Harriet Tubman, a former slave who had escaped her master just a year earlier, started running the **Underground Railroad** operation, which lasted 8 years and freed hundreds of people.

In 1852, in response to the Fugitive Slave Law, an unknown author named Harriet Beecher Stowe (daughter of the aforementioned Pastor Lyman Beecher) published *Uncle Tom's Cabin*, a heart-wrenching book that took aim at the Fugitive Slave Law. It told the personal stories of slaves and their families and the unfair treatment they suffered at the hands of their masters. The mostly female audience fell in love with Beecher Stowe's characters. The book was the best-selling novel during the Victorian era, followed by *Ten Nights in a Bar-Room and What I Saw There (Arthur, 1854)*, a book about prohibition. *Uncle Tom's Cabin* was converted into a play that toured across the country and changed many white people's opinions about slavery.

Seven years after the Fugitive Slave Law, abolitionists suffered another blow when the Dred Scott decision was handed down by the Supreme Court in 1857. Among other comments, the Justices' decision said slaves could not be American citizens and therefore had no standing in court. John Brown, an abolitionist who was tired of nonviolent methods, decided to take the law into his own hands, killing slaveholders. He was quickly linked to Douglass, whom he had met 10 years earlier in New York. Douglass, who had nothing to do with the killings, once again fled the country, this time to Canada. He returned only after authorities of the U.S. government promised not to arrest him.

In 1860, Douglass endorsed Abraham Lincoln—an anti-slavery candidate—for president. When Lincoln won, Southern states responded by seceding from the Union. In response, the U.S. House of Representatives passed an amendment to protect slavery. Douglass had enough. He planned to leave the United States for good in 1861. The Civil War started before his ship sailed for Haiti, so Douglass decided to wait it out in the United States. On New Year's Day 1863, the Emancipation Proclamation was signed by President Lincoln. It declared that if the Union won the Civil War, then all slaves would be free. The Confederacy surrendered in 1864. By the end of 1865, the 13th Amendment was added to the Constitution, banning slavery. (Although, as you will read in the next chapter, Black folks were treated suspiciously and did not gain full citizenship in the United States for another 100 years). Frederick Douglass decided to stay in the United States and died in 1895 as an employee of the federal government in Washington, D.C. His home in the nation's capital is a National Historic Site maintained by the National Parks Service.

Women's Suffrage (1848–1920)

Many of the early leaders of women's suffrage were involved in and inspired by the abolition and temperance movements. In fact, Elizabeth Cady Stanton and Lucretia Mott first met at an anti-slavery convention in England, where they became fast friends. Eight years later, they planned and executed the first women's rights convention (called the Seneca Falls Convention) in Seneca Falls, New York. In the summer of 1848, 300 men and women attended the 2-day convention, advertised in a local newspaper. During the convention, Stanton and friends put forth the Declaration of Sentiments (modeled after the Declaration of Independence), which included resolutions demanding legal rights for women when it came to property, divorce, and child-rearing. Stanton was inspired and influenced by the people of the **Haudenosaunee Confederacy** (Iroquois), whom she lived near in Upstate New York; they were models of democracy, nonviolence, and gender equality. The most contested resolution was women's right to vote. Convention attendees thought the demand was just too radical, but Stanton, the author of the resolution, stood her ground. Frederick Douglass, who also attended the convention, sided with Stanton and spoke eloquently in favor of women's suffrage. He said women need the right to vote to have influence over the laws that govern them. Many historians believe the resolution passed as a result of Douglass's speech.

For the next few years, women met in small **suffrage** societies and attended annual women's rights conventions. Sojourner Truth, who was born into slavery, gave her famous *Ain't I a Woman* speech at a convention in Akron, Ohio, in 1851. In 1854, the national convention was held in Albany, the state capital of New York. The suffragists[4] had gathered thousands of petitions to overhaul the state's laws regarding women. Susan B. Anthony, a feminist orator who had met Stanton a few years earlier, gave the keynote address at the convention. A transcript of Anthony's speech was put on the desk of every state legislator. As a result, statutes regarding women's earnings and custody of children were changed to benefit women. Suffrage societies continued to petition state legislatures across the country, and Anthony and others traveled the country giving speeches about women's rights.

---

4   The term "suffragists" rather than "suffragettes" is used in the text, as the moniker "suffragettes" demeans the work of the movement.

Sojourner Truth (1797–1883): *Ain't I A Woman?*

Delivered 1851

Women's Convention, Akron, Ohio

Well, children, where there is so much racket there must be something out of kilter. I think that 'twixt the negroes of the South and the women at the North, all talking about rights, the white men will be in a fix pretty soon. But what's all this here talking about?

That man over there says that women need to be helped into carriages, and lifted over ditches, and to have the best place everywhere. Nobody ever helps me into carriages, or over mud-puddles, or gives me any best place! And ain't I a woman? Look at me! Look at my arm! I have ploughed and planted, and gathered into barns, and no man could head me! And ain't I a woman? I could work as much and eat as much as a man—when I could get it—and bear the lash as well! And ain't I a woman? I have borne thirteen children, and seen most all sold off to slavery, and when I cried out with my mother's grief, none but Jesus heard me! And ain't I a woman?

Then they talk about this thing in the head; what's this they call it? [Member of audience whispers, "Intellect."] That's it, honey. What's that got to do with women's rights or negroes' rights? If my cup won't hold but a pint, and yours holds a quart, wouldn't you be mean not to let me have my little half measure full?

Then that little man in black there, he says women can't have as much rights as men, 'cause Christ wasn't a woman! Where did your Christ come from? Where did your Christ come from? From God and a woman! Man had nothing to do with Him.

If the first woman God ever made was strong enough to turn the world upside down all alone, these women together ought to be able to turn it back and get it right side up again! And now they is asking to do it, the men better let them.

Obliged to you for hearing me, and now old Sojourner ain't got nothing more to say.

In 1860, the Married Woman's Property Act in New York was passed. It gave women the right to own property, to keep their earnings, to sue, and to share custody of their own children. Women in other states pressured their state legislatures to do the same. Little by little, suffragists were seeing the resolutions from the Declaration of Women's Rights come into existence.

Suffragists gathered 400,000 signatures in support of the 13th Amendment to end slavery but were alarmed by the 14th Amendment in 1865. Although the 14th Amendment stated that no *person* should be denied equal protection under the law, it was interpreted to mean solely *men*, and it gave only Black men (and no women) the right to vote. The suffragists wanted universal suffrage—not

Sojourner Truth, "Ain't I A Woman?" 1851.

just suffrage for men. Many of the suffragists were disappointed when the 14th Amendment passed in 1868. They regrouped and asked for biological sex to be added to the 15th Amendment, which prohibited the federal and state governments from denying a citizen the right to vote based on that citizen's "race, color, or previous condition of servitude." It did not happen. The debates regarding the 14th and 15th amendments drove a wedge between abolitionists and suffragists. New associations were founded, and men were no longer allowed to be officers in the organization founded by Anthony and Stanton.

In 1872, Anthony tried to register to vote. She hoped to be denied so she could be arrested and challenge the 14th Amendment in court. To Anthony's surprise, the men at the ballot box allowed her to register and vote. However, she was arrested 3 weeks later for casting a ballot. She used the trial and her guilty sentence to gain media attention. Coincidentally, 2 years later, the Supreme Court did hear a case from a woman who, unlike Anthony, had been turned away at the ballot box. The justices unanimously decided that the 14th Amendment did not give women the right to vote, and furthermore, each state was told to decide who got to vote within its borders. As a result, Southern states passed laws to disenfranchise Black male voters. These "**Jim Crow**" laws included literacy tests and property requirements for voters.

Shortly after the 1874 Supreme Court loss, suffragists gave up on the judicial branch and focused all their energies on the legislative branch. They wanted a constitutional amendment giving women the right to vote. In 1878, the amendment was proposed in Congress but did not make it out of committee. It was reintroduced in every session of Congress for the next 45 years. By 1892, only four states had given women the right to vote. Stanton and Anthony realized that the fight might have to continue after their deaths. They focused on training the next generation of suffragists. Stanton passed away in 1902, and Anthony followed 4 years later.

The younger generation of suffragists, led by Alice Paul and Lucy Burns, preferred parades over conventions and organized a very famous march in 1913 in Washington, D.C., on the eve of Woodrow Wilson's presidential inauguration. To this day, suffragists have often been critiqued for being racist. In fact, Stanton often worried that the movement was too white-centric. This elitism came to light during that parade in 1913. Ida B. Wells-Barnett, a well-known journalist and suffragist who happened to be Black, expected to march with the women from her Illinois state delegation during the Inauguration Eve parade. Parade organizers told Wells-Barnett that she would have to march in the back with the other Black suffragists, but she refused. Once the parade started, she joined the white women from Illinois. A photographer captured the moment she joined the white delegation.

The new generation of suffragists would picket outside the White House during the Wilson presidency, often embarrassing him when foreign dignitaries came to visit. The president had the women jailed, and Alice Paul went on a hunger strike in prison until she was force-fed. Finally, in 1918, President Wilson, who claimed to be appalled by the force feedings, endorsed women's suffrage before Congress. In 1919, the amendment proposed by Stanton and Anthony in 1878 finally passed Congress. In 1920, it received the proper ratification by the states. It had been 72 years since the Seneca Falls Convention and the Declaration of Sentiments.

Labor Movements (1877–1938?)

The first documented national labor strike occurred in 1877 when railroad employees protested wage cuts in Martinsburg, West Virginia. It lasted 45 days and resulted in a pension plan for the workers. In the next decade, more workers asserted themselves against labor bosses during the Industrial Revolution. Between 1880 and 1900, the number of gainfully employed people in the United States increased by 12 million. People went from autonomously working on their farms to being told what to do in a faster-paced industrial environment where they worked long hours 6 or 7 days a week for low wages. From the beginning, there were tensions between management and subordinates. Additionally, there were culture clashes, as ethnocentric foremen expected the growing immigrant worker populations from European countries to "Americanize" and assimilate.

In May 1886, Chicago became the site of one of the earliest rebellions of factory workers. The city had many immigrant workers who had joined together to fight for better working conditions, including a reduced 8-hour workday. They regularly brought attention to their cause with parades, rallies, and strikes. On May 4, workers rallied in Haymarket Square. This evening was particularly important because the attendees were protesting the deaths of strikers killed by police the night before at the McCormick Harvesting Machine Company plant. The event at Haymarket Square started after dark with just a few hundred attendees listening to speakers but grew to thousands and then dwindled back to hundreds by 10 p.m.

Police officers observed the entire event but moved in at about 10:30 p.m. to forcibly disperse the crowd. As a result of police advancement, a bomb was thrown by a never-identified person. Gunfire followed. At least 11 people were killed, including seven police officers, and nearly 70 people were wounded. In the months that followed, the Chicago police raided 10 labor meeting halls, 17 saloons, and several newspaper offices and houses looking to prove that the bombing was part of a conspiracy led by the rally's organizers. They arrested 200 people. Eight men, six of whom where foreign born, were put on trial. They were referred to as "ignorant foreigners" by the Knights of Labor, the first major labor organization in the United States. All of the men, many of whom had not even been present when the bomb was thrown, were found guilty, and most of them were sentenced to death by hanging.

Many scholars believed what came to be known as the "Haymarket affair" was the most important event in the country's labor movement because it angered people and caused **labor unions** to grow larger and stronger. May Day is linked to this event, and union activists Mary Harris "Mother" Jones, middle-aged at the time, and Emma Goldman, a teenager, were both greatly inspired by Haymarket. Jones would go on to fight for miners and children. Goldman participated in labor strikes as well but was also involved with Margaret Sanger to give women access to birth control and was an advocate for LGBTQ+ rights.

Six years after Haymarket, in 1892, workers at the Carnegie Steel Company's steel mill in Homestead, Pennsylvania, went on strike. Like the grievance of the railroad workers in 1877, the complaint was mostly about unfair wages. Unlike the strike by the railroad workers in West Virginia, this strike did not have a happy conclusion. When managers of the plant tried to bring in replacement workers (often referred to as "scabs" by union members) during the strike, a gun battle ensued between the workers and the agents guarding the replacement workers. Eventually, the governor got involved and sent in troops to take over the mill and allow replacement workers. The labor union fell apart, and many were hired back by the company on the original wage terms.

Two years later, in 1894, workers went on strike against the Pullman Palace Car Company, which had recently slashed their wages as a result of the Depression of 1893. Workers were required to live in Pullman, Illinois, and shop at Pullman-owned stores. While the wages were slashed, the cost of living in the city of Pullman did not decrease. Federal troops were put in place during the strike, which actually resulted in an increase in vandalism and violence. The entirety of the strike took place in the summer of 1894. In the end, the labor union was not successful, and, just like after the Homestead strike, the union dissolved. On a positive note, Labor Day legislation was passed 6 days after the end of this strike, and Pullman, Illinois was found to be "un-American" and was annexed to the city of Chicago. Years later, in 1925, A. Philip Randolph founded the Brotherhood of Sleeping Car Porters, made up of mostly Black employees at Pullman. The organization suc-ceeded in persuading President Franklin D. Roosevelt to sign a 1941 executive order forbidding discrimination in defense industry hiring. Randolph would go on to become an elder statesman in the U.S. Black civil rights movement and is given credit for originating the idea for the historic 1963 **March on Washington for Jobs and Freedom** (often referred to simply as the March on Washington), a march that originally was pitched as a Black employment march but evolved to encompass the broader category of civil rights.

Adult labor was not the only labor concern at the turn of the century. In 1900, about 20 percent of children under the age of 16 were working in mines, mills, and factories for wages. Immigrants and America's poor often prioritized work over school because they needed children to contribute to the household income. The National Child Labor Committee (NCLC) was organized in 1904. Four years later, they hired photographer Lewis Hine to take photos of children at work to use in their publications. Hine would often pose as a fire inspector or a Christian Bible salesman to get access to the places where the children worked. Hine's photos were stunning. Small children, often with no shoes and rags for clothes, were seen operating heavy machines. Much like *Uncle Tom's Cabin* humanized the victims of slavery, Hine's photos humanized the victims of child labor. The members and supporters of the NCLC made it their mission to get children in every state out of factories and into schools. The last state to pass a law requiring school attendance was Mississippi in 1917. In 1906, Upton Sinclair published *The Jungle*, a novel about working conditions in the meatpacking industry in Chicago. It sold 150,000 copies and resulted in the passing of the Meat Inspection Act in 1907.

Probably one of the most well-known and tragic examples of a lack of workplace safety occurred in 1911 in New York City's Garment District. Garment workers had walked off their jobs for years: they demanded better pay, fewer hours, and safer working conditions. The workers, mostly immigrant women, did not make much progress with their demands, and shirtmakers at the Triangle Shirtwaist Factory paid the price. The 10-story building caught fire on March 25th, but employees had been locked into their workspace and could not escape. The workers ended up burning alive or jumping multiple floors to their deaths as people on the street watched helplessly. In the end, 146 people died. It was the deadliest workplace disaster in New York City until September 2001, when terrorists hijacked two planes and flew into the World Trade Center, killing 2,606 people.

It was only after the Triangle tragedy that the state of New York and the nation finally reacted to the needs of labor. New York immediately formed a commission and enacted multiple labor codes. In 1912, the neighboring state of Massachusetts set minimum wage requirements for women and children. The fire also affected national laws. Frances Perkins witnessed the fire, and 27 years later, she was the

Figure 2.1 Photo of young children at work taken by famed photographer Lewis Hine and commissioned by the National Child Labor Committee at the beginning of the 20th Century in the United States.

U.S. Secretary of Labor when Congress passed the Fair Labor Standards Act, which established the 40-hour work week, the minimum wage, and overtime pay and put an end to oppressive child labor. The labor movement unofficially ended in 1938 with the passage of the Fair Labor Standards Act, but that act did not protect Mexican Americans in the Southwest, an area of the country that was hit particularly hard by the Great Depression.

Mexican American labor rights activist Emma Tenayuca was struck by the starvation and poverty of those around her. Tenayuca's first arrest came during a protest for fair wages at a cigar factory in San Antonio, Texas, in 1933. She was 16 years old. As a member of the National Workers Alliance (NWA), she helped lead a strike against the Texan pecan industry in 1938. They were protesting the poor working conditions (which were thought to contribute to tuberculosis) and the pay, which had just been decreased. After weeks of workers' protesting and being gassed, the owners agreed to meet with the workers. The talks resulted in a pay increase for the workers.

More than 20 years later, the immigrants in the fields bordering Mexico organized. It was an age-old labor battle: poor working conditions, bad wages, and child labor. Immigrant children, mostly from Mexico, did not go to school because they were needed in the fields. This caused a cycle of illiteracy and poverty for immigrants and a situation in which they could never get ahead. Dolores Huerta, a schoolteacher whose students were affected, and César Chávez, another community organizer, recognized the problems and co-founded the National Farm Workers Association (NFWA) in 1962. It was later called the United Farm Workers (UFW).

In 1965, farm workers walked off the grape fields in Delano, California, and refused to pick anymore, citing inhumane treatment and low wages. This was the beginning of one of the largest food boycotts in history. Field workers picketed outside grocery stores and encouraged shoppers not to buy grapes. Robert Kennedy, then a senator on a subcommittee regarding migratory labor, made a televised trip to Delano, where he called the sheriff out and gave the strike a national stage. While the nation watched on television and read about it in the newspapers, Chávez led people on a 340-mile pilgrimage through the San Joaquin Valley. This got the attention of mayors and governors and grocery store chains. People in countries outside the United States refused to unload California grapes. Like Alice Paul before him, Chávez went on a fast. His lasted for 25 days. It took 5 years of striking, but chain stores finally decided to stop selling grapes, and the growers came to a collective bargaining agreement with Huerta, Chávez, and other members of the NFWA. Both Chávez (posthumously in 1994) and Huerta (in 2012) were awarded the **Presidential Medal of Freedom**.

Review

Four movements (prohibition, abolition, suffrage, and labor) were particularly important during the early history of the United States of America. Activists preached sermons, participated in public protests, wrote books, went to court, lobbied legislatures, marched, marketed their causes on knickknacks, served time in prison, and gave their lives for their causes. People of color were often devalued by white activists, former friends became foes, and some saw death before their dreams became reality. In Chapter 3, we will examine more modern U.S. social movements, in which ethnic minorities fight back, women resurface, and gay men and lesbian women demand that their voices be heard.

Discussion Starters

1. Many suffragists saw temperance as a women's rights concern. Do you agree? Should suffragists have gotten involved with temperance?

2. Prohibition lasted for a little over a decade. Do you consider that a successful movement? What makes a successful movement?

3. Frederick Douglass and William Lloyd Garrison started as friends in the abolitionist movement but parted ways and began to attack each other in print regarding their differences. How do actions like that affect a movement? How can these situations be avoided?

4. Both Carrie Nation (Prohibition) and John Brown (Abolition) grew tired of nonviolence in their movements. Nation took to destroying property, and Brown killed slaveholders. What do you think of their tactics?

5. It took 72 years and a very concentrated effort for women to gain the right to vote in the United States. What do you believe kept the activists motivated? Are there ways they could have accelerated the process?

6. With the exception of Abolition, people of color were often ignored or pushed to the sidelines when it came to 19th-century movements. What is the best way to acknowledge this in the retelling of history?

Further Reading/Viewing

Arthur, T. S. (1854). *Ten nights in a bar-room and what I saw there*. Brooklyn, NY: A. L. Burt Company.

Blight, D. W. (2018). *Frederick Douglass: Prophet of freedom*. New York, NY: Simon & Schuster.

Bratt, P., & Benson, B. (Producers). Bratt, P. (Director). (2017). *Dolores* [Motion picture]. West Hollywood, CA: 5 Stick Films.

Burns, K., & Barnes, P. (Producers). Burns, K. (Director). (2005). *Not for ourselves alone* [Motion picture]. Walpole, NH: Florentine Films.

Gates, H. L. (2019). *Stony the road: Reconstruction, white supremacy, and the rise of Jim Crow*. New York, NY: Penguin Press.

Gutiérrez, J. A. (2019). *The eagle has eyes: The FBI surveillance of César Estrada Chávez of the United Farm Workers Union of America, 1965–1975*. East Lansing, MI: Michigan State University Press.

Pastorello, K. (2014). *The Progressives: Activism and reform in American society, 1893–1917*. Malden, MA: Wiley Blackwell.

Stevens, D. (1995/1920). *Jailed for freedom: American women win the vote*. Troutdale, OR: NewSage Press.

Sinclair, U. (1906). *The Jungle*. New York, NY: Doubleday, Jabber & Company.

Stowe, H. B. (1852). *Uncle Tom's cabin*. Hertfordshire, United Kingdom: Wordsworth.

von Garnier, K. (Director). Heil, R. (2004). *Iron jawed angels* [Motion picture]. New York City, NY: HBO Films.

Wagner, S. R. (2001). *Sisters in spirit: Iroquois influence on early feminists*. Summertown, TN: Native Voices.

Appendix: Timeline

1493—Issued by Pope Alexander VI, the Doctrine of Discovery stated that land not inhabited by Christians could be discovered and claimed by Christians.

1607—The first colony is founded by European settlers in Jamestown, Virginia.

1775—Revolutionary War begins between Great Britain and the U.S. colonies.

1783—Revolutionary War ends with British surrender.

1789—U.S. Constitution is made law.

1791—Ten amendments (referred to as the Bill of Rights) to the U.S. Constitution are ratified.

1823—The Supreme Court, in a unanimous decision, upheld the Doctrine of Discovery, claiming that it gave European settlers the right to land in the New World (what would become the United States of America).

1826—American Temperance Society is founded.

1830—Indian Removal Act is signed, and the forced removal of American Indians from the Southeast further west begins. Thousands of American Indians die along the way from exhaustion, disease, and starvation.

1830—William Lloyd Garrison becomes involved in the anti-slavery movement in Boston.

1833—The New England Anti-Slavery Society is founded.

1840—Suffragists Elizabeth Cady Stanton and Lucretia Mott meet at an anti-slavery convention in England.

1845—*Narrative of the Life of Frederick Douglass, an American Slave* is published.

1846—Mexican-American War begins.

1847—Douglass begins publishing the anti-slavery newsletter *The North Star.*

1848—Mexican-American War ends.

1848—Seneca Falls Convention (women's rights convention) convenes in Seneca Falls, New York.

1850—Harriet Tubman begins the Underground Railroad.

1850—The Fugitive Slave Law requires that all captured slaves be returned to their masters.

1851—Sojourner Truth delivers *Ain't I a Woman* speech in Akron, Ohio, at the Ohio Women's Rights Convention.

1852—*Uncle Tom's Cabin* is published.

1857—The Dred Scott decision, stating slaves are not American citizens and therefore have no standing in court, is handed down by the Supreme Court.

1860—Frederick Douglass endorses Abraham Lincoln for President.

1861—Civil War begins.

1862—Homestead Act allows "any American" to claim 160 acres of land to build a home and farm on it. In the end, 10% of the area of the United States (mostly west of the Mississippi River) was given to homesteaders.

1863—Emancipation Proclamation is signed.

1865—Civil War ends.

1865—The 13th Amendment is added to the Constitution, banning slavery.

1868—The 14th Amendment is added to the Constitution, giving Black men the right to vote.

1870—Women's Temperance League is founded.

1872—Susan B. Anthony is arrested for voting.

1874—The Supreme Court gives permission to the states to decide who can vote within their borders. Southern states immediately pass laws to disenfranchise Black voters.

1877—In the first documented national labor strike, employees protest wage cuts in Martinsburg, West Virginia.

1878—An amendment is proposed in Congress to give women the right to vote but does not get out of committee. It is reintroduced in every session of Congress for the next 45 years.

1879—Woman's Christian Temperance Union is founded.

1886—Workers rally in Haymarket Square in Chicago. At least 11 people are killed, including seven police officers, and nearly 70 people are wounded.

1892—Workers at steel mill in Homestead, Pennsylvania, go on strike.

1894—Workers at Pullman Palace Car in Illinois go on strike.

1894—Labor Day legislation is passed.

1895—Frederick Douglass dies.

1895—Anti-Saloon League is founded.

1902—Elizabeth Cady Stanton dies.

1904—The National Child Labor Committee is organized.

1906—Susan B. Anthony dies.

1906—Upton Sinclair publishes *The Jungle*.

1911—Triangle Shirtwaist Factory fire occurs.

1913—Members of the WCTU and ASL march together in Washington, D.C., to demand prohibition at the federal level.

1913—The 16th Amendment is added to the Constitution, allowing the federal government to collect income tax. As a result of the amendment, the government no longer needed the taxes from the sale of alcohol as a means of financial security.

1913—March on Washington, D.C., occurs in support of women's suffrage.

1917—World War I begins. The Anti-Saloon League uses the hatred for Germans to encourage prohibition.

1919—The amendment giving women the right to vote (originally proposed by Stanton and Anthony in 1878) passes Congress.

1920—The 18th Amendment is added to the Constitution, prohibiting the production, sale, and transport of "intoxicating liquors."

1920—The 19th Amendment is added to the Constitution, giving women the right to vote.

1933—The 18th Amendment is repealed with the passing of the 21st Amendment.

1933—Emma Tenayuca is arrested at the age of 16 for protesting for fair wages at a cigar factory in San Antonio, Texas.

1938—The Fair Labor Standards Act is passed.

1962—The National Farm Workers Association is founded.

1965—Farm workers walk off the grape fields in Delano, California, protesting inhumane treatment and low wages.

FIGURE CREDITS

Soldiers from the 101st Airborne Division escort the Little Rock Nine students into the all-white Central High School in Little Rock, Arkansas.

CHAPTER 3

Social Justice During the 20th Century in the United States

The false distance of history aims to deceive us into believing that the trauma of racism and injustice is in the past. It plays on our desire for a memory of the past that makes sense and feels good.

—DeRay Mckesson (2018)

C HAPTER 2 PRESENTED the early history of social movements in the United States. We will now move into more modern times and look at social movements that have occurred in the past 100 years, including civil rights for ethnic minorities, women's liberation, and gay and lesbian rights (with little thought given to the other communities that now make up the moniker **LGBTQ+**). It was a time when people engaged in identity politics, coming together based upon shared ethnic, gender, and sexual identities. Unfortunately, the aforementioned movements as well as others (e.g., disability, Japanese American, fat acceptance, animal rights, Cuban American, human trafficking, gun control, transgender communities, Puerto Rican, environmental, immigration, prochoice, anti-war) are often left out or inadequately addressed in the history books we read as requirements of formal education. There are a number of reasons for this void.

Some people believe it is unpatriotic and irresponsible to critique the policies or the people of the dominant culture. Furthermore, they believe America is exceptional and superior to other nations. These are the people who want to see cultural studies banned, such as what happened with Mexican American studies in Arizona in 2012. When cultural studies are banned or limited, then history is predominantly told from the side of the victor. This is referred to as revisionist history—telling the story however the winners would like it told. In these narratives, social movements are seen as public nuisances and not as inspirational tales. There are other people who are embarrassed by the past and want to ignore it and pretend it did not happen.

Those of us who want to learn about social justice and activism in the United States have to look beyond the standard textbooks. We need to ensure that marginalized people's experiences are shared with a larger audience. This chapter tells a few of their stories.

Civil Rights Movements

During the 19th century, new immigrants to the United States fought for their rights, especially when it came to Prohibition and labor. During the 20th century, other ethnic minorities began to take a stand, but most of them were not immigrants. They were natives of the land or were forced to migrate. The ancestors of Mexican Americans, Chican@s,[1] and American Indians were encroached upon, and Black Americans, most of their ancestors from Africa, were forced into the United States as slave labor. The new settlers from Europe made laws and cultural decisions that too often negatively affected others.

Mexican American Civil Rights Movement (1921–1960)

Following the Mexican-American War in 1848, all or part of 10 states—including California, Utah, Arizona, New Mexico, and Texas—were relinquished to the United States as a result of the **Treaty of Guadalupe Hidalgo** (discussed in Chapter 2). The racism directed toward the nation's 77,000 newest citizens was immediate. Lynching of Mexican Americans happened frequently. Signs declaring "No Mexicans Allowed" were commonplace, and Mexican Americans organized to defend their civil rights.

The most well-known organizations at the beginning of the 20th century included the Order of Sons of America (*Orden Hijos de America*), founded in 1921 in San Antonio; the Knights of America (*Los Caballeros de America*), founded in 1927 in San Antonio; and the League of Latin American Citizens, founded in 1927 in Harlingen, Texas. Ben Garza, a leader in the Order of Sons of America, believed it would be to everyone's benefit for the organizations to combine their efforts and to come together under one name, one mission, and one constitution. In 1929, they did just that when 150 people met in Corpus Christi, Texas, to become the League of United Latin American Citizens (LULAC). LULAC members, males only at the time, often had to meet in secret under the dark of night to protect their jobs and their

---

1   The @ symbol is used in Chican@ to allow for the word to be gender-neutral.

lives. The initial FBI surveillance of this group happened in the late 1930s. LULAC wanted people who were Latinx to embrace American citizenship, encouraging Mexican Americans[2] to learn the English language, vote, serve on juries, contribute to their communities, and get educations.

It was within the spirit of this ideology that hundreds of thousands of Mexican Americans volunteered to fight for the United States during World War II (1939–1945). In the end, nearly 9,000 Mexican Americans were killed in action, and 17 soldiers were honored with the Medal of Valor, the nation's highest military honor. During their service, Mexican American soldiers were categorized as "white" and, unlike Black soldiers, fought side by side with **Anglos**. As a result of this equality, the soldiers who were Mexican American felt they had earned the right to equality when they returned home, but that is not what they found. Back home in the United States, they were still refused service in restaurants and faced roadblocks when they tried to claim their GI benefits. Existing veterans' associations (e.g., Veterans of Foreign Wars, American Legion) were all white and lacked awareness and concern when it came to the plight of soldiers of color.

Some of the bad feelings toward Mexican Americans postwar may be attributed to the Zoot Suit Riots that took place between Anglo servicemen stationed in Los Angeles and young Mexican Americans who lived in Los Angeles during the war. Zoot suits were the style at the time, but Anglo servicemen thought the style, along with the attitudes of young Mexican Americans, was arrogant. Both groups often socialized in the same nightspots, and sometimes things turned tense. One night in 1943, a fight started when a serviceman claimed a man who was Mexican American made a move to hit him. That fight turned into a riot that lasted for 10 days. Zoot suits were stripped off Mexican Americans, and the men were left in the streets. In the end, the mayor blamed it on the Mexican American youth, who were citizens of his town, while visiting Anglo servicemen were seen as helpless victims.

Dr. Hector P. Garcia, a veteran of WWII, returned from war to begin a private medical practice in South Texas. He formed the American GI Forum in 1948 to address the concerns of veterans, many of whom were his patients. The next year, in 1949, the widow of Felix Longoria, a man who had died in battle in 1945, contacted Dr. Garcia. Longoria's body had recently been returned to his family in Three Rivers, Texas. Beatrice, his widow, wanted to have a wake for her husband at the local funeral home, but the director would not allow it, remarking in front of witnesses that "the whites would not like it." Dr. Garcia and members of the GI

---

2   Latinx and Mexican American are used interchangeably throughout the text.

Forum got involved and contacted a number of state and national figures hoping to draw attention to the topic. Lyndon B. Johnson, a junior U.S. senator from Texas, answered their call. He interceded, drawing national attention. He invited the Longorias to bury Felix in **Arlington National Cemetery** with full military honors. They took him up on the offer, and the American GI Forum raised the money necessary for the family to travel to Virginia for the burial. Many people consider this the earliest unifying event of the Mexican American civil rights movement.

Two important court decisions affecting Mexican American communities were decided in the mid-20th century. The first came in 1947 when the Ninth Circuit Court of Appeals handed down its decision regarding *Mendez et al. v. Westminster School District of Orange County*. The plaintiffs argued segregating children of Mexican and Latin descent into their own schools was unconstitutional. Students in "Mexican" schools were being subjected to flea and lice inspections, books were older than at the white schools, and the students were solely trained for vocational careers. The lawyers for Mendez et al. argued that students of Latin descent were white. The appeals court agreed. This laid the groundwork for future court cases that would challenge segregated schools.

Then, in 1954, just 2 weeks before the historic **Brown v. Board of Education of Topeka** decision (discussed in more detail below), the U.S. Supreme Court unanimously declared that Mexican Americans were entitled to equal protection under the 14th Amendment in *Hernandez v. Texas*. In this case, Pedro "Pete" Hernandez was found guilty of murder in Edna, Texas, but there were no people of color on his jury. In fact, there had not been any Mexican Americans on juries in that county for more than 25 years. The lawyers argued that Mexican Americans, including Hernandez, were deprived of due process and equal protection under the law. The court ruled that the 14th Amendment allowed for protection for racial minorities beyond Black Americans. Hernandez's legal team was funded by both LULAC and the American GI Forum.

....

14th Amendment

No state shall make or enforce any law which shall abridge the privileges or immunities of citizens of the United States; nor shall any state deprive any person of life, liberty, or property, without due process of law; nor deny to any person within its jurisdiction the equal protection of the laws.

....

John F. Kennedy desperately needed the Latinx vote to win the 1960 presidential election. His wife, Jacqueline Kennedy, spoke Spanish in a televised campaign advertisement, and his campaign encouraged the formation of **Viva Kennedy Clubs** throughout the United States. In return, Kennedy's camp promised political appointments and government positions for people who were Latinx, particularly Mexican Americans. Kennedy was elected by slim margins in the Southwest, and many insiders give Latinx voters the credit for getting him elected, although they were sorely disappointed by the lack of Mexican Americans appointments during Kennedy's administration.

Black Civil Rights Movement (1954–1965)

Although most people point to the *Brown v. Board* decision or the **Montgomery Bus Boycott** of the mid-1950s as the beginning of the Black civil rights movement, it is important to understand the history that led to those life-altering moments. Both *Brown* and Montgomery can be traced back to the 14th Amendment (discussed in the previous chapter), which was ratified in 1868 shortly after the Civil War and promised "equal protection of the laws" for all American citizens. People in the Southern states did not like the amendment but recognized that counting a person who is Black as a whole person instead of three-fifths of a person would allow the South to have more seats in Congress.

As a backlash to the rights provided by the 14th Amendment, states in the South passed **Jim Crow** laws. Among other things, Jim Crow laws required Black people to take literacy tests to vote, to step off sidewalks for white people, to give up bus seats to white passengers, and to not look directly into the eyes of white people. Lynching was often used to enforce Jim Crow laws. In 1890, the state of Louisiana passed a law it called the Separate Car Act, which required anyone with any "Black blood" to sit in a separate railroad car from people who were white. The state believed it was following the 14th Amendment as long as both races were accommodated. In 1892, Homer Plessy, a man of mix raced, agreed to test this **"separate but equal" doctrine** and purposely got himself arrested for sitting in the car reserved for white passengers. Then he challenged the state law throughout the court system. Ultimately, he lost when the case went to the Supreme Court in 1896. As a result of *Plessy v. Ferguson*, "separate but equal" became the law of the land for the next 60 years—until *Brown v. Board of Education of Topeka*.

The **National Association for the Advancement of Colored People (NAACP)** was a civil rights organization founded in 1909—a little more than a decade after the Plessy decision. They quickly established a legal defense fund so people could have their days in court. From the time of the establishment of the NAACP until the Brown case was tried, many Black people migrated from the rural South to larger industrial cities to find work and escape prejudice. Movement to cities allowed for more ideal conditions for activism: people had more money, distance from their oppressors, cultural support, and opportunities to meet in groups. It was in this climate that NAACP lawyer Charles Hamilton Houston and his student Thurgood Marshall built cases against Jim Crow laws. In 1954, NAACP lawyers argued before the Supreme Court that "separate but equal" resulted in inferior accommodations for Black folks in *Brown v. Board of Education of Topeka*. In a 9–0 decision, "separate but equal" was struck down by the U.S. Supreme Court. Schools across the country were told to desegregate. In 1957, nine Black students—forever dubbed the Little Rock Nine—entered the all-white Central High School in Little Rock, Arkansas, and in 1960, Ruby Bridges, a kindergartener, helped to desegregate the elementary schools of New Orleans.

The year after the Brown decision, in December 1955, Rosa Parks, an NAACP member, refused to give up her seat to a white man on a bus in Montgomery, Alabama. Emmett Till, a 14-year-old boy who had been brutally lynched for talking to a white woman in Mississippi 5 months earlier, was her inspiration. Reverend Dr. Martin Luther King, Jr., 26 years old, helped organize a year-long boycott of the Montgomery buses that ultimately resulted in desegregation of the buses. The boycott nearly put the city bus system out of business. Both of these events were victories for the Black civil rights movement and major defeats for the Jim Crow South.

Besides the NAACP, other important organizations during the Black civil rights movement included the Southern Christian Leadership Conference (SCLC) and the Student Nonviolent Coordinating Committee (SNCC). The first president of the SCLC, founded in 1957 in Atlanta, was Dr. King. SNCC was founded in Raleigh, North Carolina, in 1960 by college students and Ella Baker, a middle-aged staff member for the NAACP who often criticized charismatic leadership like that of King. The generational differences between these two particularly civil rights organizations caused turmoil. For examples, members of SCLC did not approve of the lunch counter sit-ins organized by SNCC members in the late 1950s and early 1960s. Members of SNCC, typically organized by Diane Nash and **John Lewis**, would enter restaurants that were segregated and demand to be served in the white spaces. Not surprisingly, they were refused service, food was dumped on their heads, hateful things were said to them, and they were violently pulled from their seats. Members of the SCLC believed the sit-ins were too violent and risky.

The year 1963 was a pivotal one for the movement. In the spring, King and the SCLC went to Birmingham to help local people fight to desegregate a shopping center. King was put in jail on Good Friday and wrote his famous *Letter from Birmingham Jail* in response to a statement of public concern and caution released by a group of Southern white religious leaders. In the letter, he calls out Birmingham leaders for their bigotry and criticizes them for taking too long to act against unjust laws. King's incarceration, along with ongoing protests and the brutality of law enforcement, received national attention as a result of the media. People all over the country were becoming sympathetic to the Black civil rights movement. In June, tragedy struck when Medgar Evers (learn more about him in Chapter 9), the first field secretary for Mississippi's NAACP, was shot in front of his family home in Jackson, Mississippi. In late summer, the historic March on Washington for Jobs and Freedom took place, and King made the famous *I Have a Dream* speech from the steps of the Lincoln Memorial to 250,000 marchers and many other people who watched on television. The movement would not be ignored.

> *Freedom is never voluntarily given by the oppressor; it must be demanded by the oppressed.*
>
> —*Rev. Dr. Martin Luther King, Jr., Letter from Birmingham Jail (April 16, 1963)*

In 1964, the Civil Rights Act, which outlawed discrimination based on race, color, religion, sex, or national origin, was passed. It was a victory, but civil rights activists would not rest until Black people could freely exercise the right to vote. Selma, Alabama, was a place where Black potential voters were disenfranchised by unfair polling taxes and literacy tests. SNCC got involved in early 1963 and worked with local citizens to register them to vote. Government officials were not cooperative, and 2 years later, in 1965, a march was organized from Selma to the state capital of Montgomery. The catalyst for the march was the murder by law enforcement of a 26-year-old activist, Jimmie Lee Jackson. A local organizer quipped that he wanted to bring Jackson's lifeless body to the governor so that "he can see what he's done." They did not take the body, but the march occurred. The first attempt to march became known as Bloody Sunday, as the marchers were beaten and teargassed by law enforcement. The brutality was televised, and by the second failed attempt 2 days later, more sympathizers joined the march. It took three attempts before they made it to Montgomery, where King gave a speech, and the publicity resulted in the **Voting Rights Act of 1965**. John Lewis marked this action as the end of the Black civil rights movement.

Subsequently, **Malcolm X**, a Black civil rights leader many people viewed as the antithesis of MLK for his views on violence in activism, was assassinated in 1965. He was born in 1925 as Malcolm Little, and his father died early in his life. His mom's mental state went downhill quickly, leaving Malcolm to live with relatives. In his early 20s, he was picked up for burglary and sentenced to prison. While serving his time, he studied the teachings of the **Nation of Islam** (NOI) and discussed the group with his brother, who had already become a member. After serving 6 and a half years in prison, Malcolm left with a new name (replacing his "slave" name of Little with an X) and a new mission. By 1953, he had joined the ministry of the NOI and was put in charge of his own congregation in New York City the following year. He quickly became known as someone who would stand up to the police. He would often refer to the sit-ins of the U.S. Black civil rights movement as "beg-ins" and encouraged his followers to intimidate and become physical when necessary to attain Black supremacy. In the couple of years before Malcolm's death, he experienced a split with the leadership of the NOI, made a pilgrimage to **Mecca**, replaced the X with Shabazz, and started to promote integration instead of supremacy.

Chican@ Civil Rights Movement (1968–1974)

Chican@s, a younger generation of Mexican Americans than the ones who elected Kennedy, critiqued LULAC and the GI Forum for being social clubs and assimilationists. They wanted to take their fight to the streets. In the mid-1960s, during the farmworker strikes in Delano mentioned in Chapter 2, Sal Castro was a high school teacher in East Los Angeles (140 miles south of Delano). Castro was concerned because Mexican American students were not welcome in student councils, sports, etc. He witnessed the students being placed into vocational tracks and not in college tracks. About half of the Mexican American students dropped out of LA schools every year. Castro talked to his students about their concerns, and they came up with a list of demands, including courses in Mexican American studies and more teachers who looked like them. The students took the list to the school board, but the board members refused to make any changes. In March 1968, Castro and his students organized the first major Mexican American student walkout when 10,000 students walked out of four high schools in East Los Angeles. They continued to walk out day after day for 2 weeks until their demands were met. Thirteen people (including Castro) were arrested after the walkouts and were charged with conspiracy. There was a 7-day sit-in at the building, where the school board met in the hopes of getting Castro reinstated.

Other student walkouts happened in the following years, including a large one in Crystal City, Texas, from December 9, 1969, until January 5, 1970. The first day of protests included 500 students, parents, and community members and grew to include nearly 2,000 people after a few days. Student organizers held a press conference in San Antonio, visited decision makers in Washington, D.C., and locally registered voters during the walkouts. José Ángel Gutiérrez, a 1962 graduate of Crystal City High School, helped organize the walkouts with his wife, Luz Gutiérrez. He co-founded the Mexican American Youth Organization (MAYO) in the mid-1960s and helped form a new political party, **La Raza Unida** (RUP) in 1968. RUP spread to 17 states and Washington, D.C., and the members shared a goal to get Mexican American candidates elected to political offices. There was a generational divide amongst Mexican American voters. Older voters wanted to work inside the Democratic Party, but Gutiérrez and his supporters did not believe that was possible. In 1972, RUP held a national convention in El Paso, Texas. They were under surveillance by the FBI and CIA, who feared a separatist movement. The organization eventually disbanded as a result of disagreements within the leadership and legislation used to decrease RUP's influence.

As mentioned earlier, there was a great respect for the military in Mexican American communities, but it felt like Mexican American soldiers were dying in disproportional amounts during the **Vietnam War**. The Brown Berets, a pro-Chican@ organization, helped to organize national marches in 1970. It is estimated that 20,000 to 30,000 people participated in one march alone in Los Angeles. Chican@s questioned why Mexican Americans had to die to be accepted by their country. There were horrible police reactions at the protests and rallies. Three people were killed at the Los Angeles march, including two Brown Berets and journalist Ruben Salazar.

Red Power/American Indian Movement (1964–1978)

There are more than 550 American Indian nations or tribes within the United States, each with its own unique history and traditions. The communities do share some similar challenges, though. A great number of American Indians were removed from their homelands as a result of the Indian Removal Act of 1830 (discussed in Chapter 2); the **boarding school movement** of the late 19th century and early 20th century, which was used to assimilate children into the dominant white society; and the Indian Relocation Act of 1956, where American Indians were paid to move to urban areas far away from their ancestral homes. The Relocation Act came with the promise of great jobs and nice housing; these promises did not pan out. All three of these government programs caused families to be separated, which resulted in generations of American Indians who lost touch with the traditions of their ancestors. Both the Red Power movement and American Indian Movement (AIM) saw the uprising of proud American Indians in the 1960s and 1970s who wanted to reclaim the traditions and **sovereignty** of their nations/tribes. They also wanted the U.S. government to make good on their treaty agreements.

Clyde Warrior (Ponca), raised in northern Oklahoma by his grandparents, coined the term "Red Power" in 1966. While in college, he was a leader in many student organizations for American Indian students. Through conference attendance and as a respected powwow dancer, he became well known on a national level and co-founded the National Indian Youth Council (NIYC) with Melvin Thom (Paiute) in 1961. In March 1964, members of NIYC as well as actor Marlon Brando became involved in a civil rights protest when they staged a fish-in on the Puyallup River in Washington to protest a treaty agreement that was not being honored by the U.S government. Warrior referred to this protest as a new era in the history of American Indians and used the term "Red Power" to describe the right of American Indians to be culturally different. The term was not accepted by all American Indian activists. Vine Deloria, Jr., executive director of the National Congress of American Indians (NCAI), thought "Red Power" was brash and abrasive. Over the next few years, Warrior and the NIYC got involved in a protest with Cherokees in Northeast Oklahoma who were unhappy with the opening of a Cherokee village and heritage center in Park Hill, Oklahoma. They believed the "living history" misrepresented their culture. Warrior joined the picket line and also dropped fliers from an airplane during the opening weekend for the center. Warrior's life was cut short, and he died in July 1968 at the age of 28.

Around the time of Warrior's death, AIM was founded by George Mitchell (Ojibwa) and Dennis Banks (Ojibwa) in Minneapolis[3] to fight police brutality. Two hundred people showed up at the first meeting in a church basement. They had AIM patrols who would listen to police scanners and try to break up fights before the police would arrive. They also photographed arrests. When the patrols started, American Indians made up 90% of the population in Minneapolis jails; the number was down to 10% within 6 months. The leaders of AIM consulted with NYIC leaders during the early years. AIM and NYIC formed the American Indian Task Force but parted ways when members of NYIC did not show up at the **Wounded Knee Incident of 1973**.

The occupation of Alcatraz Island by young American Indian activists in late 1969 got America's attention. The occupants wanted to see the **Fort Laramie Treaty of 1868** enforced by the U.S. government. The treaty stated that all land abandoned by the U.S. government would be given to the American Indian people

---

3   Most of Warrior's work had taken place in Washington, Oklahoma, New Mexico, and Colorado. Warrior hardly crossed paths with the men who started AIM.

from whom it was obtained. Alcatraz Island had been abandoned as a federal prison 6 years earlier. The protestors planned to repurpose the old prison and surrounding land into a cultural center. The group was led by Richard Oakes (Mohawk) and the Indians of All Tribes (IOAT). Wilma Mankiller (Cherokee), who would later go on to become the the chief of the Cherokee Nation (read more about her in Chapter 8), was there, and John Trudell (Santee Dakota) acted as a spokesperson for IOAT. Members of AIM, including Banks and Russell Means (Oglala/Lakota), also took part in the occupation. Banks wrote in his autobiography that his time at Alcatraz was a turning point in his activism. He realized that the reclaiming of tribal lands needed to be a focus for AIM. Means said the occupation was a time when young American Indian activists begin to realize that they could call on each other for help. Ultimately, the Alcatraz occupants were removed by the U.S. federal government on June 11, 1971. Oakes died the next year, when he was murdered at the age of 30.

The year 1970 was a busy one for AIM members. They had grown to more than 5,000 nationwide. Cleveland AIM (CLAIM) was chartered by Means and sued the Cleveland Indians baseball team over its mascot.[4] In late August, AIM members joined three Lakota women to occupy Mount Rushmore—a land that was sacred to both the Lakota and Cheyenne. They felt the mountain had been defaced with the images of their conquerors (e.g., Presidents Washington, Jefferson, Roosevelt, and Lincoln). It was during this time that AIM made it their policy to go anywhere they were invited to help. In November 1970, they went to **Plymouth Rock** to join local American Indians during the 350th anniversary of the colony's establishment. AIM members showed up to a re-creation of the original Pilgrim village carrying signs, beating drums, and singing songs. They walked three or four miles to the village dining hall, where people were eating a turkey dinner. The AIM members turned over tables and then headed out to a replica of the *Mayflower* to throw all of the mannequins overboard, scaring tourists off the ship. Means gave a speech about the true story of Thanksgiving, explaining to the crowd that the colonizers would have starved to death if it had not been for the generosity of American Indians. Later in the dark of night, Trudell painted Plymouth Rock blood red.

The first national AIM convention took place in St. Paul, Minnesota, in 1971. Means claimed the BIA was condemning AIM members as militants. In February 1972, AIM was asked to go to Gordon, Nebraska, to assist with the investigation of the murder of Raymond Yellow Thunder (Oglala Sioux), who was stripped from the waist down and made to dance in front of 200 people at the local American

---

4　They settled for $35,000 12 years later. The settlement allowed the baseball team to continue to use the mascot.

Legion before he was beaten to death by two men who were the sons of a wealthy local white rancher. The brothers were charged with second degree manslaughter, but the members of AIM worried that the men would never serve a day in prison. AIM members moved in on the city and brought attention to all of the crime and corruption within Gordon. In the end, a federal grand jury investigated the crime against Yellow Thunder, and his murderers were sentenced to prison. This event brought national attention to AIM.

In October and November 1972, AIM members organized and took part in the Trail of Broken Treaties, which would end in the U.S. capital just days before the presidential election. AIM members wanted to share a list of demands with government officials. Caravans began in Seattle, San Francisco, and Los Angeles. There were stops at 33 reservations along the way to pick up people. The four-mile caravan arrived in Washington, D.C., in early November. The place they were supposed to stay was full of rats, so they headed to the Bureau of Indian Affairs (BIA) headquarters and asked to meet with authorities to discuss the demands. The authorities stalled, and the occupiers took over the BIA and declared it a Native American embassy. By the second day of the occupation, there were 700 AIM supporters in the BIA headquarters. They secretly made copies of documents showing that the BIA was taking oil and natural gas from American Indian land. Louis Bruce (Mohawk), the commissioner of Indian Affairs, sided with AIM. The occupation lasted for 6 days until the White House agreed to set up a task force to consider the list of demands. After they left, the federal government and the media accused AIM members of trashing the BIA building. Deloria critiqued AIM for tarnishing the reputation of American Indians. He believed AIM's leaders were narcissists who should have focused on feeding their followers rather than enhancing their public images.

The year 1973 was another busy one for AIM. There were 79 AIM chapters, including eight in Canada. In February, AIM members went to Custer, South Dakota, to offer help with another murder investigation. This situation was similar to the one in Nebraska with Yellow Thunder. This time, Wesley Bad Heart Bull (Oglala) was killed in front of his mother by Darald Schmitz, a white man, who stabbed him seven times in a bar. Schmitz was charged with second degree manslaughter and was immediately released on bail. AIM asked for a meeting with the county attorney. He would only meet with four representatives, and he refused to change Schmitz's charge to murder. While the meeting was in progress, more protestors tried to get in the courthouse, which resulted in a riot during which tear gas canisters were thrown and two police cars were torched and gutted. Twenty-two people were arrested that day, including 19 American Indians. In the end, Schmitz was acquitted of murder and never served a single day in jail. The mother of Bad Heart Bull served 5 months for "riot with arson."

AIM members are probably most famous for the 1973 takeover of Wounded Knee. They felt Richard Wilson, chairman of the Oglala Lakota Sioux, was a puppet of U.S. government agencies, in particular the BIA. AIM members wanted to see the **Pine Ridge Reservation** under the leadership of traditional Oglala Lakota Sioux people. They felt the traditional ways were being threatened, and by the time of this siege, they were willing to risk their lives to save it. The government reacted with a show of force and surrounded Wounded Knee with weapons and agents. Gunfire was often exchanged during the 71-day takeover. During this time, Marlon Brando refused to accept his Oscar for *The Godfather* as a show of solidarity with his friends at Wounded Knee. The siege finally ended on May 8, 1973, when the government promised to hold hearings regarding the Fort Laramie Treaty of 1868. All totaled, two American Indians were dead, 500 were arrested, and there were 185 federal indictments against AIM members and supporters.

Many AIM members were tied up in court after the siege of Wounded Knee. It took until 1978 for another major event to happen. The Longest Walk was organized to protest anti-Indian legislation that was considered annually by Congress. AIM members believed the legislation did not honor treaties and threatened sovereignty. One issue of concern was that the Indian Health Service was sterilizing a large percentage of American Indian women of childbearing age. AIM members said the women were tricked into signing release forms. The walk began in February at Alcatraz. Unfortunately, the media no longer seemed interested in AIM and would not cover the walk. In July, ally Marlon Brando joined the marchers in Washington, D.C. Brando's participation increased media coverage. In the end, there were 80,000 marchers, and U.S. President Jimmy Carter met with representatives from the walk. AIM threatened to file a $300 million damage suit on behalf of American Indian women who had been tricked into sterilization. This threat forced the government to put a moratorium on that program.

After the Longest Walk, AIM really fizzled. Means went to prison in 1978 for rioting in South Dakota 5 years earlier, and Banks went on the lam when he was found guilty of similar charges. Trudell's family was killed in a suspicious house fire, causing Trudell to seek asylum with the Canadian government. All three men have passed away in the past decade—Means in 2012, Trudell in 2015, and Banks in 2017.

Women's Liberation (1963–1977)

During World War II, men were off to war, and women were asked to work in their vacated jobs, where it was reiterated that the jobs were temporary and a service to the country. Many women went to work in the aviation industry, thanks in no small part to the **Rosie the Riveter** campaign. After the war, the men reclaimed their jobs as promised, and women were sent back home. As a result of the GI Bill and easy mortgage credit, many families became middle class and could make it on the husband's salary alone. They could also afford modern conveniences, such as washing machines and frozen meals, that made the life of a housewife less taxing. Middle-class American women, who had enjoyed a little taste of independence while working outside the home, had to be convinced that they were needed at home full-time. Television shows such as *Father Knows Best and Leave it to Beaver* created the impression that once women were married and had children, they had little reason to leave the house. Women were convinced that the good life was the stay-at-home life. If a married woman did work outside the home, she often kept it a secret so her husband would not appear inadequate. For the most part, everything went as planned until the early 1960s, when the first wave of the **Baby Boom generation** started high school. Most of their mothers were still in their prime, and with no small children, housework did little to keep their interest.

In 1963, Betty Friedan authored the book *The Feminine Mystique, which* spoke to the boredom of mostly white middle-class housewives. Friedan had surveyed her Smith College classmates during their 15th class reunion and found that most of them were not using their degrees and were quite unsatisfied cooped up in their nice homes. As a result of the popularity of her book, Friedan was a speaker in high demand around the country. By 1966, the **National Organization for Women** (NOW) was founded with Friedan as president. Other smaller, more temporary groups also formed. They were more radical and antihierarchical than NOW; one of the best-known groups that followed this model was New York Radical Women. Together, NOW and the smaller groups made up a movement commonly referred to as the **women's liberation movement**.

Much like civil rights organizations before them, NOW formed a legal committee and took their fight to the courts. In one of the cases, Lorena Weeks of Georgia took on Southern Bell Telephone and Telegraph Company. In 1964, Weeks had followed with great interest the passing of the Civil Rights Act by the U.S. Congress. The legislation prohibited discrimination against an individual based on race, color, national origin, religion, or sex. It also created the **Equal Employment Opportunity Commission** (EEOC). Weeks knew she had the backing of the law when she decided to move from a clerk's position to a job that would allow her better pay and better hours. The new position would require her to make sure routing equipment was functioning properly. As she expected, the management at Southern Bell rejected her application and said the job was only open to men because it required the ability to lift 30 pounds without assistance. Weeks, who could easily lift 30 pounds, complained to the EEOC and filed a legal appeal in 1967, which was handled by a NOW lawyer. The Fifth Circuit Court of Appeals, in a decision that has been quoted again and again, found in favor of Weeks in 1969.

It was also during this time in the 1960s that a sexual revolution took place. In 1960, the birth control pill was approved as contraception. Two years later, Helen Gurley Brown published the book *Sex and the Single Girl*, which sold two million copies in 3 weeks and inspired a movie of the same name starring Natalie Wood, Tony Curtis, Henry Fonda, and Lauren Bacall. Brown encouraged women to be financially independent and to experience sexual relationships without marriage. By 1965, six and a half million women had prescriptions for the pill, which is credited for allowing women the freedom to pursue careers that required long-term commitments, since they could now control their fertility.

By 1967, consciousness-raising groups were forming at the University of California-Berkeley and then in neighborhoods around the country. Women, often finding each other through advertisements in leftist newspapers, would gather to talk about expressing anger, orgasms, abortions, sexual assault, economics, and a number of other issues. Tips for forming CR groups and potential topics for group discussion were printed in feminist publications. Younger women from the Baby Boom generation, including lesbian women and women of color, found the movement. Baby Boomers had been trained in civil rights movements, where they had first realized that women were treated like second-class citizens—even amongst social justice activists. The younger women wanted more than antidiscrimination laws, and this caused conflict within the women's liberation movement at times. For example, the younger generation wanted to take up sexuality as a cause, which did not please NOW founder Betty Friedan, who was convinced there was a lesbian conspiracy to take over the organization. She referred to lesbians as the "Lavender Menace." Pauli Murray, a co-founder of NOW, left the organization because she felt it was only advocating for professional white women.

Three important demonstrations took place at the end of the decade: the Miss America demonstration in 1968, the *Ladies' Home Journal* sit-in during March 1970, and the Women's Strike for Equality in August 1970. One of the events most bastardized by the media was the Miss America demonstration in Atlantic City. The first official public demonstration by women's libbers, the plan was to protest the objectification of women at the Miss America pageant by burning fashion-torture items such as hair curlers, stockings, high-heeled shoes, fashion magazines, and girdles, but the plan never came to fruition because the city officials refused to give the demonstrators a permit to light their bonfire. Instead, the women threw the torture items in a barrel but did not burn them. A reporter for the *New York Post* wrote that there was a bra burning, and that story has stuck ever since.

The other demonstrations took place in 1970. In March, there was a sit-in by 200 women at the office of the editor in chief of the *Ladies' Home Journal*. The protesters had a list of demands, which included free child care for employees, the abolishment of advertisements that degraded women, and one issue of the magazine to be put out by women in the movement. After 11 hours and a smaller meeting with 12 of the protestors, the male editor in chief agreed to pay the women to put together an eight-page supplement. Five months later, in August, NOW sponsored the Women's Strike for Equality on New York City's Fifth Avenue. The event, which was held on the 50th anniversary of the passing of the 19th amendment, was more of a march than a strike and was the largest gathering of women since the fight for women's suffrage. There were thousands of sister demonstrations across the country.

Gloria Steinem, whose name is synonymous with women's lib, became recognized as a feminist leader in 1969 after she published an article about the movement in *New York* magazine. Not long after the article was published, she went on a speaking tour with Dorothy Pitman Hughes, a child welfare advocate from New York City. Steinem and Hughes often critiqued Friedan and other pioneers for leaving women of color and lesbian women out of the conversation. In 1971, Steinem and Hughes co-founded *Ms. Magazine*. Women's liberation began to get attention from Hollywood, where it was discussed on *Meet the Press*, *The Dick Cavett Show*, *The Tonight Show*, *60 Minutes*, and *The Merv Griffin Show*. Terms such as "sexist" and "sexism" were coined and used frequently.

There were three important battles regarding women and the law in the early 1970s. They included the Equal Rights Amendment (1970); Title IX (1972); and *Roe v. Wade* (1973). The ERA, authored by suffragist Alice Paul in 1923, asked that female pronouns be inserted in addition to the existing male pronouns within the U.S. Constitution to reflect that *all* people are created equal and given the same protections, rights, and responsibilities under the law. It took 50 years, but the amendment finally passed both houses of Congress. In 1972, the ERA was left to the states for ratification, and 30 states ratified the amendment by 1974. Only eight more states were required for the amendment to become law. It was endorsed by both U.S. President Gerald Ford and First Lady Betty Ford. The ratification of the amendment looked like a sure bet. Then Phyllis Schlafly, a conservative activist, got involved. She and her supporters argued that the ERA, among other things, would allow for fully funded abortions and gay and lesbian rights, require all able-bodied women to be drafted into military duty, and end single-sex education and organizations. As a result, not only was she able to stop more states from ratifying the ERA, she actually got five states to rescind their earlier ratifications. To this day, the ERA has still not been ratified.

The Entire Text of the Equal Rights Amendment

Section 1. *Equality of rights under the law shall not be denied or abridged by the United States or by any State on account of sex.*

Section 2. *The Congress shall have the power to enforce, by appropriate legislation, the provisions of this article.*

Section 3. *This amendment shall take effect two years after the date of ratification.*

Feminists did achieve victories with Title IX and *Roe v. Wade*. Title IX, sponsored by two female legislators, is a federal law that bans sex discrimination in schools that receive federal funds. It is not a law aimed specifically at sports, even though it often gets interpreted that way. By 1980, there were 30 different national women's collegiate championships, compared to none in 1970. With *Roe v. Wade*, the Supreme Court ruled in a 7–2 decision that any attempt to interfere with a woman's right to abortion during the first 3 months of pregnancy was a violation of her constitutional right to privacy.

Steinem said that the most important event about which nobody has ever heard happened in November 1977 in Houston, when 2,000 delegates and 18,000 observers from 56 countries met for the 3-day **National Women's Conference**. Five years earlier, the United Nations had declared that 1975 would be the International Women's Year. In response, three female lawmakers wrote legislation that would allow for every state and territory to send women to a national convention to set an agenda for U.S. American women. Congress delayed and slashed the budget, but it was finally approved. Twenty-six issues that emerged during the state conferences were brought to the national meeting. One of the most debated planks regarded lesbian rights. Betty Friedan spoke in favor of the amendment after spending the previous decade trying to keep the "Lavender Menace" out of the women's movement. Many caucuses (e.g., Asian American, Hispanic, Black, American Indian, and Alaskan Native) took place before and after the main sessions. The minority plank they created was accepted by acclamation by all 2,000 delegates. Not to be outdone or ignored, a counterconference led by Phyllis Schlafly took place across town.

Infighting within the movement, disappointment related to the failure of the ERA, and people's belief that women had "arrived" and no longer needed feminism helped put an end to the women's liberation movement. Over the next few decades, people advocated for women's rights, but the force of a large-scale movement had dissolved.

Gay and Lesbian Rights (1951–1979)

World War II was a turning point for gay men and lesbian women, who often came from small U.S. American towns and cities where they kept their sexuality a secret. Once in the military, they often met other people who were attracted to the same sex. After the war ended in 1945 and the soldiers returned, many of them chose to live in large U.S. American port cities rather than move back to their oppressive small towns. The former GIs took jobs in the government and military. Although most of these state and federal employees kept their sexuality a secret, members of the legislature became suspicious, and in 1950, a Senate subcommittee launched an extensive closed-door investigation that led to the publication of a special report, *Employment of Homosexuals and Other Sex Perverts in Government*. The subcommittee reported that gay men and women were unsuitable for government work and were a security risk because they could easily be blackmailed by foreign governments.

As a result of the report, the government went on fishing expeditions, actively seeking the names of men and women who identified as gay or lesbian. People were detained and questioned about their sexuality and consequently lost their jobs or were kicked out of the military. It was during this time that two organizations were founded, the Mattachine Society (in 1950) and The Daughters of Bilitis (in 1955).[5] Early on, gay and lesbian organizations published their own magazines and newsletters and mailed them to subscribers throughout the nation. They wanted to create a network of communication for gay and lesbian communities. The post office, backed up by the FBI, refused to mail some of the publications

---

5   Unfortunately, the division of men into Mattachine and women into DOB was reflective of the sexism of the 1950s. In fact, many of the women involved in all these movements were also involved in women's liberation. Dolores Huerta, a Chican@ labor rights organizer, fought sexism within her own community. She kept tallies of all the sexist things uttered at organizing meetings and then, at the end of the meetings, would tell her male counterparts how many sexist remarks they had made. Once their consciousness was raised, the sexist remarks all but disappeared—at least when the men were in the company of Huerta.

because it deemed them obscene. The case of *One, Inc. v. Olesen* made it all the way to the Supreme Court in 1958, where it was decided that *One* could continue to publish its content. It was the first Supreme Court case to involve anyone from the LGBTQ+ communities. It was a victory for free speech and the movement.

Figure 3.1 Stonewall Inn, site of the 1969 Stonewall Riots, in New York City.

Throughout the 1960s, more branches of Mattachine and Daughters of Bilitis (DOB), as well as new organizations, were established throughout the United States. The groups organized pickets, including one in front of the White House in 1965 protesting the government's treatment of people who were gay or lesbian in the military or who otherwise worked for the government. A big turning point in the movement occurred in the summer of 1969 during a police raid of the Stonewall Inn, an LGBTQ+ bar in Greenwich Village in New York City. Police Raids had happened for decades, but on this night, people fought back. It was a younger generation who was tired of playing nice. They were bored with pickets; they wanted to fight. Marsha P. Johnson, a self-identified drag queen, has been named as one of the first to resist arrest that night. Johnson's close friend Sylvia Ray Rivera, another self-identified drag queen, took action by throwing a bottle at the police. Their actions began 3 days of rioting that attracted national media attention. One year later, more than 15,000 people participated in a march to commemorate the event. Stonewall marked the beginning of a shift in how lesbian, bisexual, gay, and trans people saw themselves increasingly as an oppressed minority group.

Much like with the women's liberation movement, there was also a generational divide with the movements for gay and lesbian rights. After Stonewall, radical activists formed the Gay Liberation Front (GLF) and the Gay Activists Alliance (GAA). GLF had no officers or membership rolls. They held consciousness-raising sessions and decided everything by consensus. Members of the GAA, who opted for parliamentary procedure in lieu of consensus, led a campaign to have sexual orientation added to the list of protected categories in New York City's human rights ordinances in 1971. During the same time, members of Mattachine and DOB lobbied the **American Psychological Association** (APA) to have homosexuality removed from its list of mental disorders. They did a number of things to make this happen, but the one they are best known for occurred in 1972, when they hosted a panel at the APA national conference that featured a disguised APA member who was gay. In 1974, the APA removed homosexuality from its list of mental disorders and formed a National Gay Task Force.[6]

The 1970s was a busy time in the political arena for people who identified as gay or lesbian. In 1974, Elaine Noble became the first out gay person to be elected to public office when she joined the Massachusetts House of Representatives. In the same year, a bill was introduced in the U.S. House of Representatives proposing that the categories of "sex, sexual orientation, and marital status" be added to the 1964 Civil Rights Act. The bill did not pass, but it was a victory in that it was the first time gay civil rights legislation was introduced at the federal level. In 1977, Harvey Milk, a small business owner, was the first openly gay man elected city supervisor in San Francisco. Milk was instrumental in promoting a boycott of the union-busting Coors Beer Company and in defeating Proposition 6 (aka the Briggs Initiative), which would have required the dismissal of any schoolteacher who was gay. He also led protests when gay rights laws were appealed in Miami, Florida, and Wichita, Kansas. He believed that people who were gay or lesbian should come out to their families and friends and that coming out would allow gay and lesbian communities to gain rights. Milk was seen as a leader in the movement, and it was a tragedy when he was murdered by a fellow city supervisor after serving only 11 months in office.

In October 1979, gay and lesbian communities held their first march on Washington with more than 100,000 participants. Unfortunately, there was an epidemic in the gay community that would soon divert the activists' attention. In 1981, AIDS was first identified, and everything had to be put on hold while the health epidemic was addressed.

---

6   The Gay and Lesbian Alliance Against Defamation (GLAAD) has put "homosexual" on its list of offensive terms and in 2006 persuaded The Associated Press, whose stylebook is widely used by many news organizations, to restrict its use of the word.

Review

The 20th century was a time of great political unrest in the United States. Ethnic minorities with a heightened social justice orientation, including activists who identified as Black, Mexican American, and American Indian, made public stands and organized against their oppressors, especially in the courts and in public marches and rallies. Women and members of the LGBTQ+ communities, who would not be denied their rights because of their sex or their sexuality, held public demonstrations, published newsletters, and passed around books that made them feel less isolated. The movements gathered strength and allies and experienced many successes with legislation, litigation, and cultural shifts.

However, the movements were not without challenges. Generational differences led to fracturing of larger organizations, all of the movements mentioned in this chapter (with the exception of women's liberation) were critiqued for being male dominated, and both women's liberation and gay and lesbian rights movements were accused of being **white centric**. Many of these 20th-century movements have also been implicated for **classism**. Consciousness-raising is a never-ending concern for people who fight for social justice.

Discussion Starters

1. The author stated that the histories of many groups have received inadequate coverage in our history books. What do you remember about the coverage of these movements from history classes that you have taken? How do you think such movements should be covered in history classes?

2. This chapter focused on the 20th-century civil rights movements for people who were Mexican American, Black American, American Indian, women, and members of the LGTBTQ+ communities. What do you know about the current status of civil rights for these communities? Where did you learn that information?

3. Would you have made different choices for inclusion of communities in this chapter regarding 20th-century social justice activism?

4. Generational differences amongst activists in a movement often threatened the cause. What could have been done to improve relationships?

5. The activist movements of the 20th century lasted for a considerably shorter time than the movements of the 19th century. What do you think contributed to the abbreviated time frames?

6. What can today's activists learn from the social movements of the 19th and 20th centuries?

Further Reading/Viewing

Akers, C. G. (2016). *The inspiring life of Texan Héctor P. Garcia*. Charleston, SC: History Press.

Banks, D., & Erdoes, R. (2004). *Ojibwa Warrior: Dennis Banks and the rise of the American Indian Movement*. Norman, OK: University of Oklahoma Press.

Brownmiller, S. (1999). *In our time: Memoir of a revolution*. New York City, NY: Random House, Inc.

Carroll, P. J. (2003). *Felix Longoria's wake: Bereavement, racism, and the rise of Mexican American activism*. Austin, TX: University of Texas Press.

Collins, G. (2009). *When everything changed: The amazing journey of American women from 1960 to the present*. New York, NY: Little, Brown and Company.

DuVernay, A. (Director). Winfrey, O., Gardner, D., Kleiner, J., & Colson, C. (Producers). (2014). *Selma* [Motion picture]. London, UK: Cloud Eight Films.

Faderman, L. (2015). *The gay revolution: The story of the struggle*. New York, NY: Simon & Shuster.

France, D. (Director). (2017). France, D., Reed, K., & Teodosio, L.A. (Producers). *The death and life of Marsha P. Johnson* [Motion picture]. New York, NY: Public Square Films.

Gutiérrez, J. A. (1998). *The making of a Chicano militant: Lessons from Cristal*. Madison, WI: The University of Wisconsin Press.

King, M. L. (1958). *Stride toward freedom: The Montgomery story*. Boston, MA: Beacon Press.

McKenzie-Jones, P. R. (2015). *Clyde Warrior: Tradition, community, and Red Power*. Norman, OK: University of Oklahoma Press.

Means, R., & Wolf, M. J. (1995). *Where white men fear to tread: The autobiography of Russell Means*. New York, NY: St. Martin's Griffin.

Olmos, E. J. (Director). Esparza, M., & Katz, R. (Producers). (2006). *Walkout* [Motion picture]. New York, NY: HBO Films.

Rosenberg, R. (2017). *Jane Crow: The life of Pauli Murray*. New York, NY: Oxford University Press.

Steinem, G. (2015). *My life on the road*. New York, NY: Random House.

Van Sant, G. (Director). Jinks, D., & Cohen, B. (Producers). (2008). *Milk* [Motion picture]. New York, NY: Focus Features.

Wilkerson, I. (2010). *The warmth of other suns: The epic story of America's great migration*. New York, NY: Random House.

X, M., & Haley, A. (1965). *The autobiography of Malcolm X*. New York, NY: Grove Press.

Yarsinske, A. W. (2004). *All for one and one for all: A celebration of 75 years of the League of United Latin American Citizens (LULAC)*. Virginia Beach, VA: The Donning Company Publishers.

Appendix: Timeline

1892—Homer Plessy, a man of mixed race, is arrested in Louisiana for sitting in a railroad car for white passengers.

1896—The Supreme Court rules in *Plessy v. Ferguson*, making "separate but equal" doctrine the law of the land for the next 60 years.

1909—NAACP is founded in New York City.

1929—League of United Latin American Citizens (LULAC) is founded in Corpus Christi, Texas, bringing together the Order of Sons of America, Knights of America, and League of Latin American Citizens.

1939—World War II begins.

1943—Zoot Suit Riots take place in Los Angeles.

1945—World War II ends.

1947—The Ninth Circuit Court of Appeals hands down its decision regarding *Mendez et al. v. Westminster School District of Orange County*, ruling that students of Latin descent are white.

1948—American GI Forum is founded in Corpus Christi, Texas.

1949—A funeral home in Three Rivers, Texas, refuses to have a wake in the funeral home for Felix Longoria, a Mexican American soldier who died during World War II.

1950—A Senate subcommittee publishes a special report entitled *Employment of Homosexuals and Other Sex Perverts in Government*.

1950—Mattachine Society is founded in Los Angeles.

1954—The Supreme Court rules in *Hernandez v. Texas*, unanimously declaring that Mexican Americans are entitled to equal protection under the 14th Amendment.

1954—The Supreme Court rules in *Brown v. Board of Education of Topeka*, striking down "separate but equal" as law.

1955—Emmett Till, 14 years old, is lynched in Mississippi for talking to a white woman.

1955—Rosa Parks refuses to give up her bus seat to a white man, beginning a year-long Bus Boycott in Montgomery, Alabama.

1955—Daughters of Bilitis is founded in San Francisco.

1955—Vietnam War begins.

1956—Indian Relocation Act is put into place.

1957—Southern Christian Leadership Conference is founded in Atlanta. Rev. Dr. Martin Luther King, Jr. is selected as the first president.

1957—The Little Rock Nine partnered with the local NAACP to desegregate Central High School in Little Rock, Arkansas.

1958—The Supreme Court rules in *One, Inc. v. Olesen*, stating that the post office must mail newsletters from gay and lesbian organizations.

1960—Ruby Bridges, a kindergartener, helps desegregate schools in New Orleans.

1960—Jacqueline Kennedy records a campaign advertisement in Spanish for John Kennedy's U.S. presidential campaign and Viva Kennedy Clubs are formed throughout the United States.

1960—Student Nonviolent Coordinating Committee is founded in Raleigh, North Carolina.

1960—The birth control pill is approved as a contraceptive.

1961—National Indian Youth Council (NIYC) is founded by Clyde Warrior (Ponca) and Melvin Thom (Pauite).

1962—Helen Gurley Brown's book *Sex and the Single Girl* is published.

1963—King pens *Letter from Birmingham Jail*.

1963—Medgar Evers, field secretary for Mississippi's NAACP, is shot in front of his family home in Jackson, Mississippi.

1963—The March on Washington for Jobs and Freedom takes place and King gives his *I Have a Dream* speech on the steps of the Lincoln Memorial.

1963—Betty Friedan's book *The Feminine Mystique* is published.

1964—Members of NIYC and actor Marlon Brando stage a fish-in at the Puyallup River in Washington to protest a treaty agreement that was not being honored.

1964—Civil Rights Act is passed.

1965—March from Selma, Alabama, to Montgomery, Alabama, takes place after the death of Jimmie Lee Jackson.

1965—The Voting Rights Act is passed.

1965—A picket occurs outside the White House protesting the government's treatment of people who are gay or lesbian.

1965—Malcolm Shabazz (formerly known as Malcolm X) is assassinated.

1966—The term "Red Power" is coined by Clyde Warrior (Ponca).

1966—The National Organization for Women is founded with Friedan as president.

1967—Women's consciousness-raising groups begin to form.

1968—10,000 high school students in East Los Angeles participate in a walkout to protest the treatment of Mexican American students.

1968—La Raza Unida is founded by José Ángel Gutiérrez.

1968—The American Indian Movement is founded by George Mitchell (Ojibwa) and Dennis Banks (Ojibwa) in Minneapolis, Minnesota.

1969—Students in Crystal City, Texas, participate in a walkout to protest the treatment of Mexican American students.

1969—Occupation of Alcatraz Island takes place.

1969—The Fifth Circuit Court of Appeals rules that Southern Bell cannot discriminate against employee Lorena Weeks based upon her sex.

1969—Gloria Steinem publishes an article about the women's liberation movement in *New York* magazine.

1969—Police raid the Stonewall Inn.

1969—Both the Gay Liberation Front and Gay Activists Alliance are founded in New York City.

1970—Mexican Americans protest the disproportional numbers of deaths of Mexican American soldiers in the Vietnam War.

1970—AIM members join three Lakota women to occupy Mount Rushmore.

1970—AIM members join local American Indians to riot and protest at Plymouth Rock during the 350th anniversary of the colony's establishment.

1970—Sit-in at the offices of the *Ladies' Home Journal.*

1970—Women's Strike for Equality takes place on New York City's Fifth Avenue.

1970—The Equal Rights Amendment fails to become ratified.

1971—First national AIM convention takes place in St. Paul, Minnesota.

1971—Alcatraz occupants are removed by the U.S. federal government.

1971—Steinem and Dorothy Pitman Hughes co-found *Ms. Magazine.*

1972—La Raza Unida has a national convention in El Paso, Texas.

1972—AIM members go to Gordon, Nebraska, to assist with the investigation of the murder of Raymond Yellow Thunder (Oglala Sioux).

1972—AIM members organize and take part in the Trail of Broken Treaties, ending in Washington, D.C., and occupying the headquarters of the Bureau of Indian Affairs.

1972—Title IX becomes law.

1973—AIM members go to Custer, South Dakota, to assist with the investigation of the murder of Wesley Bad Heart Bull (Oglala).

1973—AIM members take over Wounded Knee, insisting that it be under the leadership of traditional American Indian people and not a puppet of U.S. government agencies.

1973—The Supreme Court rules in *Roe v. Wade*, stating that it is a violation of a woman's constitutional right to privacy if there is any attempt to interfere with her right to an abortion during the first 3 months of pregnancy.

1973—The United States pulls out of the Vietnam War.

1974—The American Psychological Association removes homosexuality from its list of mental disorders and forms a National Gay Task Force.

1974—Elaine Noble becomes the first out gay person to be elected to public office.

1975—Vietnam War ends.

1977—National Women's Conference takes place in Houston.

1977—Harvey Milk is the first openly gay man elected city supervisor in San Francisco.

1978—The Longest Walk, protesting anti-Indian legislation, takes place.

1978—Russell Means (Oglala/Lakota) goes to prison for rioting in Custer, South Dakota.

1979—Gay and lesbian communities hold their first march on Washington with more than 100,000 participants.

FIGURE CREDITS

Activists have a common language, but it is important that the vocabulary is never used to isolate other people interested in the work.

CHAPTER 4

The Language of Experienced Activists

T WENTY-FIRST-CENTURY SOCIAL JUSTICE activism certainly comes with its own language. Specific words are meant to convey specific messages, but it is pretty easy to become overwhelmed by words and philosophical conversations when you are with experienced activists. Remember, they were all novices once as well. They have learned the language by reading books and articles, attending meetings and class sessions, and co-constructing meaning with other activists. You will as well.

Below is a primer of more than 40 words and phrases most commonly used by people committed to social justice. This shared language allows activists to evaluate society and social practices to identify areas for potential activist intervention. If someone says something you do not understand, ask

Table 4.1 **Social Justice Vocabulary**

Able-Bodied Privilege	Heteronormativity	Political Correctness
Activism	Homogenous	Postfeminism
Advocacy	Ideology	Postracial
Allies	Institutional Discrimination	Privilege Guilt
Assimilation	Intersectionality	Savior Complex
Choice Feminists	Kyriarchy	Social Justice
Cisgender	Marginalizes	Social Movement
Co-Opting	Microaggressions	Spectacle
Consciousness-Raising	Misogynistic	Systemic
Cultural Appropriation	Objectify	Tokenism
Cultural Erasure	Oppressive	Triggering
Entitlement	Othering	White Fragility
Ethnocentric	Paradigms	White Guilt
Feminism	Patriarchy	White Privilege
Hegemony	Person-First Language	Woke

them for an explanation (or you can look it up later). Language should never be used to isolate another person. A competent communicator will ensure that their audiences understand their messages.

Let's begin with the concept of the **patriarchy**. People who operate from a patriarchal perspective (or **ideology**) make the rules and dictate norms, especially when it comes to sex and gender. They hold the power and are dominant in patriarchal systems. They operate as the **hegemony**—experiencing authority and control over everybody else. They are also **misogynistic**—believing that women's work is making dinner and taking care of children, while men's work is mowing the lawn and having a career outside the home. Within this perspective, a man may have a sense of **entitlement** when it comes to available leadership positions and may also expect immediate respect from anyone they encounter. The dominant patriarchal discourse is that men are better elected officials than women because they are less emotional and more decisive. Additionally, the notion that marriage should be between a man and a woman is perpetuated by this ideology. This is referred to as **heteronormativity**. To expand on the notion of patriarchy, the term **"kyriarchy"** was introduced in the early 1990s to better encompass concepts such as social class, ability status, sexuality, and race.

Some people will look to white, straight, **cisgender** (a person born into a body that is in sync with their gender), middle-to-upper-class males and declare that they *are* the patriarchy in the United States, but that is not necessarily true. Neither the patriarchy nor the kyriarchy is a group of people; they are guiding sets of principles. Because these principles are used to make laws, decide media representations, and establish cultural norms, they are **systemic** and not something simply embodied by individuals. John Lewis, a Freedom Rider, was never angry with the individuals who physically attacked him and his colleagues during the rides; he was mad at the system that produced them. People and systems who value patriarchal and kyriarchal ideologies take a top-down approach to the world and believe their approach is *the* correct way to handle things. They tend to be **ethnocentric**, believing their cultural norms are superior to other people's cultural norms. Their goal is **cultural erasure** and to make people more **homogenous**, espousing the same values, goals, and ideas of the dominant culture—a process that is referred to as **assimilation**. This was the goal of the American Indian boarding school movement described in the last chapter.

The ethnocentrism of the dominant group benefits people who think like the hegemony (or are willing to assimilate) but certainly **marginalizes** (pushes to the outside) others who do not fit into the ideals of the patriarchy or kyriarchy and have no desire to assimilate. Anyone who is not heterosexual will be marginalized because heterosexual is "normal," by which all other sexualities are judged. In other words, heterosexuality is the center lane, whereas everything else is sent to the margins. A woman who calls out sexism on the job will also likely be marginalized because a patriarchal mindset has made people believe women are inferior to men. Again, men are the norm by which everything else is judged. This marginalization can be the result of **microaggressions,** when people intentionally or unintentionally communicate messages that are demeaning. Examples of microaggressions include telling a person who is Black that they do not act like a *normal* Black person or leaving a middle-aged coworker out of a conversation about Snapchat because it is assumed they know nothing about the social media platform.

Marginalization can also be the result of **institutional discrimination**, which occurs when society and its institutions, through unequal selection or bias, discriminate against groups of people. Like microaggressions, institutional discrimination can be intentional or unintentional. University professors may practice institutional discrimination by holding all their office hours during the same time as athletic practices or by writing exam questions that assume all students come to them with similar prior experiences. When people in leadership at an organization are made aware of institutional discrimination, they may take action to eradicate it, but it is crucial that they not engage in **tokenism** by including only a small number of marginalized people at the table who are not really heard or taken seriously. It is just a symbolic effort. Instead, marginalized people should be involved and heard. It is not a matter of simply inviting them to the dance: they should be able to choose the venue, pick out the music, and dance.

Constant marginalization leads to **othering**, where a person is made to feel like an outsider or the "Other" (with a capital O). In 2015, gay couples in Rowan County, Kentucky, were othered when a county clerk refused to issue marriage licenses despite the Supreme Court decision earlier in the year that legalized marriage for all people. Heterosexual couples in the county were given the licenses, while same-sex couples were told to leave the courthouse. Constant pressures from patriarchal or kyriarchal **paradigms** are suffocating to those who will not or cannot subscribe to the norms. Outsider status can cause people to question their own sanity and approaches to life. It can also cause a person to internalize an inferior status. It can be difficult for people to discuss othering experiences, as it can cause **triggering** or emotional distress related to a particularly traumatic experience. Triggering is most often associated with survivors of crime, particularly sex crimes.

Figure 4.1 A government official in Rowan County, Kentucky, refuses to issue a marriage license to a gay couple in 2015.

Feminism offers an alternative to patriarchal and kyriarchal ideals. While feminist scholars and activists in the 1960s and 1970s acknowledged a woman's multiple identity categories, they focused their energies on fighting for equality centered solely on biological sex. Women of color (WOC) theorists brought attention to the intersections of assigned sex, sexuality, race, religion, politics, class, ability, etc. This is referred to as **intersectionality**. It is from this era that the term "kyriarchy" was coined. During the 1980s and 1990s, WOC scholars argued singular identity categories limited social justice theories (and application of those theories) and that the complications of the lived experience should not be considered simply from the perspective of gender or assigned sex. For example, a person who is Black, heterosexual, Buddhist, cisgender, and permanently in a wheelchair should not be put into separate identity categories. She must be considered holistically by considering places where the "categories" intersect (or weave together) to create the tapestry of her lived experience.

People informed by feminism do not want people informed by the patriarchy or kyriarchy to make the rules by which we are all expected to live. These rules are **oppressive** to marginalized people who do not have the ability or desire to operate under the patriarchy. Some definitions of feminism center on the notion of choices by oppressed people. For example, a woman staying home with children is a feminist act to **choice feminists** as long as she had the choice to stay home. If patriarchal norms caused her to feel like she *had* to stay home, then her staying home would not be a feminist act. Other examples include women who use their bodies to make money, whether as a Hooter's waitress, as a dancer at a men's club, or as a sex worker. Again, choice feminists would say these women are feminists as long as they freely made informed choices about their work.

Feminists who are critical of choice feminism make the point that people often do not have real choices as a result of the overt and covert racism, sexism, ableism, ageism, etc. within our society. They want it acknowledged that restaurants such as Hooter's exist because some people like to **objectify** women by looking at them as body parts and that women work in these places because (a) they have learned to value attention for their appearance and/or (b) the tips are good, and they have to raise their children in a country where childcare is very costly. Choice feminism is just one of dozens of types of feminism. **Postfeminism** is the false notion that feminism is no longer necessary because equality has been achieved for everyone. Relatedly, some people also believe that we are **postracial** and that racism is no longer a problem in the United States, which is laughable, considering the recent activity of white nationalists (see Chapter 7 for more information about WN).

Consciousness-raising occurs when a person becomes aware of things such as patriarchy, kyriarchy, marginalization, othering, feminism, oppression, and objectification. At first, people may not even know what to label these things but become aware of these concepts through reading, watching films, or having conversations. Perhaps this is where you are on your journey. Once a person becomes aware, there is no unknowing. In other words, there is no going back to a state of ignorance once a social justice consciousness has been raised. You can either choose to ignore what you know, deny the oppression, or do something about the oppression. A raised consciousness also requires people to acknowledge their privileges.

There are many types of privilege. Probably the most acknowledged and written about is race privilege, often referred to as **white privilege**. In most of the United States, appearing to be white has advantages that are taken for granted by the people who most benefit. There are many positive assumptions about white people: they are educated, they are law-abiding, and they are upwardly mobile. Scholar Brittney Cooper believes that white privilege makes the advantage of white people invisible while simultaneously making hypervisible the "poor choices" of people of color. Other types of privilege, such as class privilege, complicate the notion of white privilege. If a person appears to be poor and white, they may be referred to as "white trash" or "trailer trash," and it will be assumed that they are not well educated, law-abiding, or upwardly mobile. There is also **able-bodied privilege**. There are places people with disabilities (no matter their race or class) simply cannot be, whether it is the second floor of a building with no working elevator or a public event with no sign language interpreter. But with all other characteristics being equal (i.e., class, ability, sexuality, etc.), whiteness prevails in the United States.

When racial inequality is pointed out to a person who is white, they may respond with discomfort and defensiveness. This response is referred to as **white fragility** and is used as a means of control and dominance by white people who do not want to be confronted about their racism. These people are often the same ones who bemoan **political correctness** (commonly abbreviated as PC), which is the use of language and policies to better include members of marginalized groups. For example, **person-first language,** in which a person is put before their descriptor ("girl with a visual impairment" instead of "visually-impaired girl"), may be considered over-the-top PC by a person experiencing white fragility, when in reality, it is simply valuing a person more than their condition or other adjective related to race, sex, class, religion, etc. The concept of person-first language originated in disability studies.

As a person's social justice consciousness becomes raised, they may experience **privilege guilt**. This is often referred to as **white guilt**, since many able-bodied heterosexual white people tend to experience it and write about it. People with white guilt will think back through generations of their families and all the bad deeds their ancestors must have done, particularly with regard to people of color. This exercise tends to conjure up guilt about situations beyond a person's control. Living in this guilt is not productive for anybody, whether they are privileged or oppressed. It is far more productive for people of privilege to think about their current personal roles in oppression and marginalization and what they can do to speak with and amplify the voices of those who have been othered by the majority. They can put aside the guilt and empathize with the struggle and act as **allies**[1] (friends and other supporters of the marginalized and oppressed), fighting against the very oppression from which they benefit.

People experiencing privilege guilt often make three common mistakes: (a) trying to act as savior of all oppressed people; (b) making a spectacle of oppressed people; and (c) adopting the culture of oppressed people. The **savior complex** (aka superhero complex, messiah complex) occurs when a well-meaning (usually white) person expects a pat on the back for their ally work and/or speaking *for*

---

[1]   Recently, people have started to refer to allies as accomplices or coconspirators, emphasizing the importance of being bold when fighting beside marginalized folks.

oppressed people, rather than acting as an ally. Recently, a number of Hollywood movies have been critiqued for their promotion of a "savior." One such movie is *Green Book* (2018), which won the Academy Award for Best Picture and is based on the real-life relationship of famous pianist Don Shirley, a Black man, and his driver and bodyguard, Tony Vallelongo, an Italian American. The entire film, which takes place in the early 1960s, is told from the perspective of Vallelongo, while Shirley's character, the more accomplished of the two, is the supporting character. Throughout the movie, Vallelongo treats Shirley like he is helpless, and in one scene, he even teaches Shirley how to eat fried chicken so he can be more in touch with his Black culture. In another scene, Vallelongo speaks for Shirley when he is apprehended by a police officer. It is *always* oppressive when marginalized people are silenced, even if it is by privileged people telling their stories *for* them. The best actions a privileged person can take are to listen, practice humility, and call out oppression when nobody else can or will.

Another common novice mistake is to treat the "Other" like a **spectacle**. It is perfectly acceptable for a person who is not a member of an American Indian tribe to attend a publicly advertised powwow, but it is not acceptable for that person to walk around like they own the place or treat the event like a zoo exhibit—staring and taking photos. Again, the visitor should practice humility and remember that they are a guest in what may be a very sacred cultural ritual or space. When a person takes on a culture that is not their own, this is often referred to as **cultural appropriation** or **co-opting**. Kylie Jenner, a white female celebrity, has been accused of co-opting Black culture and fashion and has been called out by Black celebrities for both her appropriation and her refusal to use her fame to bring attention to police brutality against Black men.

People who care about equality for all and are willing to advocate for that equality are considered **"woke"** and committed to **social justice**. They desire to educate and change the world through advocacy and activism.[2] **Advocacy** is the act of lending support to a cause or action that is often less confrontational than activism. **Activism** requires direct action (e.g., strike, street march) by a group or individual who wants to see change. A **social movement** occurs when many activist events are coordinated to focus on one issue over a long period of time. #BlackLivesMatter is an example of a modern-day social movement. As you read in Chapters 2 and 3, there are many examples of progressive activism and social movements throughout the history of the United States.

---

2   The terms *advocacy* and *activism* are used interchangeably throughout this text.

Review

Well-meaning people have fought for social justice in the United States for hundreds of years, and during that time, they have discovered a shared vocabulary to express their ideologies and concerns and to work with allies who empathize. In this chapter, we have explored more than 40 words and phrases used by modern activists. The language helps us better understand and articulate oppression, its causes and consequences, the oppressors, and possible solutions.

Discussion Starters

1. Have you ever been around somebody you felt was isolating others with their language? Describe the experience. Did anybody try to correct it?

2. Social justice activism is often critiqued for being too academic and elitist. How might the language we use contribute to that critique? Is the language necessary to communicate a message?

3. How do the concepts in this chapter relate to the information regarding social movements discussed in Chapters 2 and 3?

4. What words and phrases would you like to see added to this chapter?

Further Reading

Combahee River Collective. (2015). A Black feminist statement. In C. Moraga & G. Anzaldúa (Eds.), *This bridge called my back* (4th ed., pp. 210-218). Albany, NY: SUNY Press.

Cooper, B. (2018). *Eloquent rage: A Black feminist discovers her superpower.* New York, NY: St. Martin's Press.

Crenshaw, K. (1991). Mapping the margins: Intersectionality, identity politics, and violence against women of color. *Stanford Law Review, 43*(6), 1241-1299. doi: 10.2307/1229039

Diangelo, R. (2018). *White fragility: Why it's so hard for white people to talk about racism.* Boston, MA: Beacon Press.

Hardiman, R., Jackson, B., & Griffin, P. (2007). Conceptual foundations for social justice education. In M. Adams, L. A. Bell, & P. Griffin (Eds.), *Teaching for diversity and social justice* (pp. 35-66). New York, NY: Routledge.

Jensen, R. (2005). *The heart of whiteness: Confronting race, racism and white privilege.* San Francisco, CA: City Lights Publishers.

McIntosh, P. (2003). White privilege: Unpacking the invisible knapsack. In S. Plous (Ed.), *Understanding prejudice and discrimination* (pp. 191-196). New York, NY, US: McGraw-Hill.

In 2017, workers remove a statue of Confederate General Robert E. Lee in New Orleans.

CHAPTER 5

Personal Turning Points for Social Justice Activists

MOST PEOPLE DO NOT WAKE UP one day and proclaim, "I am now an expert on Topic X and will declare myself an activist from this day forward." In fact, it is estimated that less than five percent of movement sympathizers will ever take action. The activist journey is a choice and often happens over the course of months or even years after an initial conscious-ness-raising. Actions may start out small—signing an online petition or calling out a person for racist language on Twitter—but will often graduate to some-thing more involved—such as calling a member of Congress or participating in a march. This activism journey and the choices for action are discussed in more depth in the next chapter.

In short, activism occurs as a result of a person being pushed so far that they have no other choice but to react. The convert clearly sees the oppres-sion and privilege that surrounds them and believes they must do everything possible to achieve social justice. It is at this moment that there is potential for transformation and an opportunity to move beyond political passivity. This moment of clarity is referred to as a **turning point**, and in this chapter, we will explore dozens of people's "Aha!" moments (aka turning points). You may remember that in Chapter 3, we read that Rosa Parks's turning point was the murder of Emmett Till just 5 months before Parks refused to give up her seat on the bus.

Activists choose to take *active* roles as societal citizens—not only pointing out problems but also taking the extra steps of identifying and advocating for solutions. Committed activists inspire others while sacrificing personal com-fort to make contributions to the greater good through collective action. It is not convenient to be an activist: it takes time and dedication, and, as you will read in Chapter 10, it can result in loss of friendships, reputation, and health.

If a person waits to become an expert on a cause or activism in general, they will never feel completely ready. As you will see reflected in the stories below, activism requires on-the-job training.

In this chapter, we will explore both the consciousness-raising moments and turning points for famous and little-known activists in social justice movements dedicated to racial and ethnic equality, judicial reform, education reform, women's rights, environmentalism, LGBTQ+ rights, and disability awareness. The people in this chapter were chosen for inclusion because of their compelling stories related to their turning points. If the activist was living at the time this book was published, their Twitter handle follows their name to encourage you to follow and interact with the activists you most admire. While neither the list of activists nor social justice causes is exhaustive, these stories will hopefully inspire and encourage you on your journey to social justice.

Table 5.1 **Activists Included in Chapter 5**

LaDonna Brave Bull Allard	Anita Hill	Jillian Mercado	Judy Shepard
Erin Brockovich	Jazz Jennings	Janet Mock	Eunice Kennedy Shriver
Marva Collins	Coretta Scott King	Wes Moore	Karen Silkwood
Patrisse Khan-Cullors	Mayor Mitch Landrieu	Sister Helen Prejean	Gloria Steinem
Paulo Freire	Lilly Ledbetter	Cecile Richards	Bryan Stevenson
Vice President Al Gore	Viola Liuzzo	Ed Roberts	George Takei
Temple Grandin	Clara Luper	Fred Rogers	Malala Yousafzai

Racial and Ethnic Equality

This section focuses on the turning points for activists who dedicated their lives to racial and ethnic equality, including Clara Luper, Coretta Scott King, Viola Liuzzo, and Mayor Mitch Landrieu. The backgrounds of these folks are quite different from each other—they are Black and white, men and women, politicians and housewives, wealthy and working class, from the North and the Deep South—but they all had one goal in mind: equality for all.

For 41 years, **Clara Luper** (1923–2011) was an educator, spending most of career teaching high school social studies in Oklahoma City. She was a leader of the local **NAACP** (read more about the national organization in Chapter 3) and organized a youth council at her school. In 1958, when Clara was in her mid-30s, she took the members of the youth council to New York City for the NAACP convention. Both she and the students enjoyed the freedoms of the city, where they could eat at a restaurant of their choice, sit anywhere in a movie theater, and drink from a water fountain without looking for a sign granting them permission to do so. This experience was a turning point for both her and her students. Clara, who had been inspired by the nonviolent approach of the Montgomery Bus Boycott of the mid-1950s, supported the members of the local youth council when, upon returning from New York, they voted to stage a sit-in at the segregated lunch counter at Katz Drug Store on Main Street in Oklahoma City. It was one of the earliest of many sit-ins during the U.S. Black civil rights campaign of the 1950s and 1960s. The protestors were doused with condiments and harsh words as they silently sat at the counter and were eventually escorted out by law enforcement. The students returned a second time, but by then, white sympathizers had petitioned Katz management to serve people who were Black. The management conceded and, after the third sit-in, **desegregated** all of their stores—which included locations in four states. Clara would go on to participate in the 1963 **March on Washington** and the protests in Selma are discussed in Chapter 3. All totaled, Clara was arrested 26 times fighting for civil rights.

As a teen, **Coretta "Corrie" Scott** (1927–2006) would meditate for hours in the woods near her Alabama home. She instinctively knew she was destined for something bigger than herself. When she was 15 years old, racists burned her family home to the ground; she saw the tragedy as preparation for her future. Like many Black teens in the Deep South, Scott attended a segregated high school—Lincoln Normal School—where she remembered her white teachers (many of whom were **Quakers**) for being kind and showing an interest in her. In fact, it was the Quakers who facilitated a turning point in her life when they introduced her to the concept of nonviolence and peace activists such as Bayard Rustin, whom she initially met when she was in the ninth grade. (Many years later, Rustin would become a mentor to her husband, Rev. Dr. Martin Luther King, Jr.). The leadership at Antioch College in Ohio took an interest in Lincoln graduates, including Coretta. While a student at Antioch, she was active in the NAACP, a race relations committee, and a civil liberties committee. After 6 years at Antioch, she left to attend graduate school in Boston, where she met King. Many people think of Coretta simply as the widow of MLK. That would be a mistake. She was an activist before she met him, during their time together, and after his death. While they were married, she acted as an organizer and manager during the U.S. Black civil rights movement, openly protested the **Vietnam War**, advocated for LGBTQ+ communities, and had an appointment with the **United Nations**. After her husband's death, she single-handedly led the 14-year effort to build the King Center in Atlanta. She had the vision, the ability to raise millions of dollars, and the organizational skills to make it happen.

In March 1965, **Viola Liuzzo** (1925–1965), a housewife and married mother of five, watched Selma protestors get beaten by police on her television screen. A white woman from Detroit, she was well aware of the indignities suffered by Black folks, thanks to her close friend and family housekeeper, Sarah Evans, a Black woman. In fact, both Viola and Sarah were members of the local NAACP; however, Viola had never participated in any civil rights protests. After witnessing the beatings on television, she attended a march and rally at Wayne State University, where she heard Selma participants speak. That day she decided she had to go to Selma. She put a few clothes in a shopping bag and asked Sarah to take care of her family. Unfortunately, Viola never returned home. Members of the **Ku Klux Klan (KKK)** shot her driving down the highway between Selma and Montgomery on March 25. Her passenger was Leroy Moton, a young Black civil rights worker. They were transporting marchers between Montgomery and Selma.

In 2018, two-term **Mayor Mitch Landrieu** (@MitchLandrieu) of New Orleans received the **John F. Kennedy Profile in Courage Award** for the courage he displayed when he had three figures honoring Confederate heroes and one monument dedicated to the **White League** removed from city spaces. During Mitch's research about the statues, he learned they had been erected as political weapons by people who mourned the Confederacy's loss of the Civil War, or—as the mayor learned in school—"The War Between the States." Mitch, a white man, was heavily influenced by his white parents during his childhood: they lived in a racially diverse working-class neighborhood; his dad was also mayor of New Orleans who fought for Black civil rights; and he had witnessed his mother stop their car when he was a child to help a Black woman who was passed out in the street. All of these moments made an impression on him, but no moment was more life changing than when Mitch's childhood friend and well-known musician, Wynton Marsalis, asked him to remove the statues from the city in time for the tricentennial celebration slated for 2018. Marsalis explained to his friend that many Black folks, including music legend Louis Armstrong, had left New Orleans because they never felt welcome. That conversation in a New Orleans coffee shop was a turning point for Mitch.

Judicial Reform

The United States has only five percent of the world's population but a quarter of the world's prison population. Furthermore, people of color are overrepresented in U.S. prisons. While people identified as Hispanic make up 16% of the nation's population, they make up 30% of the prison population. The odds are even worse for Black folks, who make up 12% of the nation's population but 33% of the prison population. This section focuses on the turning points for both lawyers and activists who have dedicated much time and energy to social justice and the judicial system: Wes Moore, Sister Helen Prejean, Bryan Stevenson, and Patrisse Khan-Cullors.

Wes Moore (@iamwesmoore) grew up in Baltimore, Maryland. In early 2000, another Wes Moore from his large neighborhood (whom he did not know) was arrested for a serious crime that caused him to be sentenced to life in prison without the possibility of parole, while the first Wes Moore was completing his undergraduate education at Johns Hopkins University and had recently been named a Rhodes scholar. Both Wes Moores grew up in the same neighborhood, were raised by single mothers, were the same age and ethnicity, but one of them landed in prison and the other ended up an academic hotshot. The Rhodes scholar wanted to know why. The two of them eventually became pen pals. What the Rhodes scholar found was that both of them had needed help as preteens. They were both committing minor crimes (e.g., tagging property with graffiti, putting smoke bombs in lockers) and struggling in school. One of them got the help he needed, and the other one did not. The Rhodes scholar's mom sent her son to military school when he was 12 years old. He had grandparents who helped co-parent. The inmate Wes Moore did not get out of the neighborhood, but he did drop out of school, fathered a child at 16 years old, and got involved with the family business of dealing drugs. Both Wes Moores believe that expectations matter. When people expect good things from a person, that person will often not want to disappoint their supporters. The Rhodes scholar believes that higher education and the implantation of critical thinking, understanding consequences, and building a social network of fellow college graduates will save people from committing crimes and going to prison.

Sister Helen Prejean (@helenprejean) is a Catholic nun who started her career teaching religion and English in a junior high school in New Orleans. She prayed for the poor and admittedly left it to God to take care of them. She thought of herself as a nun, not an activist or a social worker. Sister Helen believed it was God's will for the poor to organize to help themselves. Her turning point came in 1980 at a conference where she heard Sister Marie Augusta Neal make the claim that poverty is not God's will for anyone and that social justice is the job of Christian people. After that conference, Sister Helen moved to a government housing project to live amongst people who were Black and poor. It was during her time at the housing project that she was asked to write to men on death row. She did, and today, she is a world-renowned advocate for abolishing capital punishment in the

United States. Susan Sarandon's character in the feature film *Dead Man Walking* (1995) was modeled after Sister Helen and won Sarandon the Academy Award for Best Actress.

At the age of 21, **Bryan Stevenson** (@eji_org) started law school at Harvard University. He felt out of place because the coursework was disconnected from his goal to work on race and poverty issues. Then he found a 1-month intensive course on race and poverty litigation that included a mandatory internship. Bryan chose to do the internship at the Southern Prisoners Defense Committee. There, he was told to visit Henry, a death row inmate, to let him know they did not have a lawyer for him yet but he would not be executed in the next year. Bryan did not believe the message was very comforting, but, to Bryan's great surprise, Henry was thrilled with the news. He and Bryan began to visit. They were completely lost in conversation for nearly 3 hours, which upset the guards, who had told them they could visit for only 1 hour. As a result of their anger, the guards were rough on Henry—putting his restraints on tight and shoving him. Henry reacted in a way that was completely unexpected for Bryan—he calmly began to sing a gospel hymn as he was led away. Bryan admits that in that moment, his life and career were completely altered by Henry's display of human potential, redemption, and hopefulness. It was a turning point. Bryan eventually founded the **Equal Justice Initiative,** and he and his staff have won reversals, relief, or release for more than 125 wrongfully convicted prisoners on death row.

When **Patrisse Khan-Cullors** (@OsopePatrisse) was 16 years old, her older brother Monte did not fulfill his promise to pick her up from dance class. His absence concerned her because she had witnessed the police make unprovoked demands of boys in her neighborhood to lift their shirts and pull their pockets inside out. She worried that her brothers and their friends were sitting targets. After dance class, she took the bus home and learned that Monte had been incarcerated for attempted robbery. Their mother searched for him in the prison system for 2 months after the arrest. When she finally found him, the family learned that he had experienced a mental breakdown (as a result of a diagnosed schizoaffective disorder) and was consequently hearing voices when he was initially imprisoned. He was also beaten black and blue. This turning point caused Patrisse to become an advocate for judicial reform and eventually led to her cofounding #BlackLivesMatter (see Chapter 7 for more about BLM). She desires a prison-free world where people are held accountable and feel safe. She would like to see a portion of the money currently used for law enforcement and prisons to be directed toward social programming—giving marginalized people access to food, education, mental health resources, etc. She wants people like her brother Monte to thrive rather than simply survive.

Education Reform

This section focuses on education reform, from early childhood education through secondary education and adult education. Fred Rogers was a recent college graduate who became a pioneer of children's television programming. Marva Collins, tired of the poor quality of education in inner-city Chicago, opened up a school in her home. Malala Yousafzai was a teen who advocated for her rights and the rights of her peers. Finally, no section about education reform would be complete without the inclusion of the compelling story of Paulo Freire, a man who believed people in the middle class had to commit "class suicide" to work authentically with people who were historically oppressed.

When **Fred Rogers** (1928–2003) was in college, television made its debut, and he was very disturbed by the medium. He did not like the slapstick comedies that he felt robbed people—particularly children—of their dignity. The discovery of television programming became a turning point in his career, and as a result, he put his seminary plans on hold and decided to make television programs for children. The initial show, *The Children's Corner,* looked nothing like ***Mister Rogers' Neighborhood***, which was later loved and embraced. Instead, it was a show hosted and produced by Josie Carey that depended a lot on film—fragile film that would often break. When that would happen, Fred (whose face rarely appeared on the show) would bring out his puppet Daniel Striped Tiger. Daniel became a fan favorite and was later a regular in the Land of Make Believe on *Mister Rogers' Neighborhood*. Fred, who grew up in a home where he was not allowed to express emotions, was very concerned about very young children's ability to express themselves and wrote more than 900 scripts and 200 songs that were positive and focused on early childhood. Fred, who completed graduate studies in child development, was an advocate for quality children's television programming and guaranteed that the future of television would include shows positively focused on early childhood development. He was awarded a **Presidential Medal of Freedom** in 2002.

In 1975, **Marva Collins** (1936–2015)—disappointed with the quality of education in inner-city Chicago—withdrew $5,000 from her teacher retirement account and began a preparatory school for children in her impoverished West Side neighborhood. She believed every child was teachable and that eliminating behavioral challenges and loving students unconditionally were necessary for children to learn. While employing the **Socratic pedagogical method** (sometimes referred to as simply the Socratic method) and often speaking in Latin, Marva would frequently refer to her students as "brilliant" or use similar compliments. Her students, most of whom were elementary aged, were expected to read a classic book (e.g., Bronte, Shakespeare, Emerson) every 2 weeks and write a composition daily. Marva ultimately built three schools and an institute for training teachers in the Marva Collins way. She also traveled the globe giving workshops and advocating for high expectations for all students—no matter their race or economic status. Today, many of Marva's former students are police officers, attorneys, business owners, and educators.

Figure 5.1 Malala Yousafzai speaking at a Nobel Peace Prize Ceremony.

In 2012, when **Malala Yousafzai** (@Malala) was 14 years old, she was shot in the head on her way home from the school her father had founded, which she attended. Malala was a well-known figure in her country of Pakistan, having blogged for the British Broadcasting Corporation (BBC) for years speaking out about her belief that all girls should be educated. Malala miraculously survived the 2012 shooting, addressed the United Nations 2 years later, and won a **Nobel Peace Prize** at 17 years old. She had been inspired from an early age by her father and his humanitarian work. Her turning point came when she was 4 and a half years old and her father defiantly enrolled her in school. (Malala's mother was illiterate and went to school for only 1 year when she was 6 years old). During Malala's childhood and adolescence, her father would have her sit with him when he met with visitors to their home. He was proud to have a daughter and did not hide her, unlike many other Pakistani fathers who hid their daughters.

Brazilian **Paulo Freire** (1921–1997), the person often given credit for bringing **critical pedagogy** to the academies of the United States in the late 1960s, spent 15 years in exile from his home country as a result of his belief that every person, no matter their class or political persuasion, had a right to be literate. It was a notion with which not everyone in his government agreed; hence, half the country was illiterate. A turning point for Paulo regarding access to education came when his father died when Paulo was 13 years old; in turn, Paulo got behind in school. By the time he entered the equivalent of sixth grade in 1937, he was 16 years old. His classmates were 5 to 6 years younger than him and from a higher socioeconomic class. About this time, his brother began to work outside the home and could financially provide for the family in a way that allowed Paulo to eat better food. Paulo instantly noticed an improvement in his ability to concentrate, and his grades also improved. He discovered a passion for language, literacy, and teaching. By the time he was in his mid-20s, he worked for the Social Service of Industry in Brazil, where he helped working-class people get services (including good nutrition) and overcome barriers. This job, which Paulo held for nearly a decade, shaped the rest of his life. Forever an advocate of the working class, he believed educators should have a central role and great influence on social reconstruction. He felt traditional teacher-focused classrooms killed the curiosity and creativity of students. He believed students should have the tools to critique their current situations and the ability to work with a community of like-minded individuals to improve it.

Women's Rights

This section focuses on turning points in the lives of women's rights activists Cecile Richards, Gloria Steinem, Anita Hill, and Lilly Ledbetter. Their work has focused on many areas, including reproduction, women's health, harassment, and pay equity. Some of these heroines had activism modeled for them as children and were anxious to get involved themselves; others were more reluctant activists. No matter how they arrived at their activism, all four of them have made an incredible impact on the quality of life for women, particularly in the United States.

When **Cecile Richards** (@CecileRichards) was just 13 years old, she wore an armband to her junior high school to protest the Vietnam War. Her principal did not approve, but her mom (Ann Richards, who would go on to be governor of Texas) was completely supportive of her. Shortly after wearing the armband, Cecile started an environmental club with her friends. She had experienced a turning point and was ready to use her energies. Many years later, in the fall of 1975, Cecile began her undergraduate education at progressive Brown University in Rhode Island, where, during her first year, she stood in solidarity with university janitors and librarians who were on strike. She felt conflicted about the privilege and "contradiction of life" at Brown and spent the spring semester of her sophomore year in Washington, D.C., where she interned for an agency that focused on **Title IX** and women's equity (read more about these efforts in Chapter 3)—both hot-button issues in the 1970s. She lived in a group house and attended congressional hearings. After the internship, she returned to Brown, started a food cooperative, and fought against **South African apartheid**. Although Cecile saw organizing as a passing phase for many Brown students, it wasn't just a phase for her. After graduation, she went to work for **labor unions** and became best known for the 12 years (2006–2018) she spent fighting for women's health as the president of Planned Parenthood.[1]

In August 1963, **Gloria Steinem** (@GloriaSteinem) worked as a freelance writer publishing celebrity and style pieces. She was not the feminist activist we know today. She had read that the Rev. Dr. Martin Luther King, Jr. and colleagues had organized the March on Washington, but she decided not to attend because she did not have an assignment to cover the event. She believed it would be much easier to watch the march on television. For reasons Gloria still cannot explain, she decided at the last minute to attend the march in person, and at that historic event, she met a woman who would change her life's entire trajectory. Mrs. Greene walked next to Gloria as they made their way to the Lincoln Memorial, where the stage was set for the speakers. Mrs. Greene, who had worked in Washington, D.C., during President Harry S. Truman's administration a decade before, asked Gloria why there weren't more women on the speaking platform. Specifically, Mrs.

---

1 Planned Parenthood is a nonprofit organization probably best known for abortion referrals and services, but they provide many more health services, including birth control, emergency contraception, pregnancy testing, Pap tests, STD testing and treatment, abortion referral and services, HIV services, patient education, and other general health services for both men and women.

Greene wanted to know who would tell Black women's stories. Until that very moment, Gloria hadn't even noticed the lack of females on the stage. Furthermore, she herself was in the habit of giving her story suggestions to men in meetings because she felt people took men more seriously. Gloria's conversation with Mrs. Greene was a turning point. She gives Mrs. Greene the credit for teaching her to stand up for herself and other women.

An increased awareness of sexual harassment is often attributed to **Anita Hill** (@AnitaHillMovie), a sexual harassment survivor[2] who reluctantly testified before a judicial committee in the early 1990s on international television. She had worked for Supreme Court nominee Clarence Thomas a decade earlier at the Department of Education and then the **Equal Employment Opportunity Commission (EEOC)**, where he pressured Anita for dates and discussed pornography in front of her. When Thomas was announced as a Supreme Court nominee in 1991, Hill, a law professor, consulted with her closest friends to ask their opinions about coming forward with her experiences. She decided to just wait for the Federal Bureau of Investigation (FBI) or another government entity to come to her if warranted during their investigation. When they finally did, she told them about the sexual harassment, but only after she was promised the comments would be kept confidential and she would not need to publicly testify. That promise was not kept: she did have to publicly testify, and she was scrutinized across the country as someone who was either making up the allegations or taking pleasure in the attention from Thomas. While Thomas was (narrowly) confirmed to the Court, complaints of sexual harassment to the EEOC increased after Anita's testimony, and she has spent the past decades raising consciousness regarding sexual harassment in the workplace.

In March 1998, **Lilly Ledbetter** (@Lilly_Ledbetter) had worked at Goodyear for nearly 20 years and was 1 year from retirement eligibility when she received an anonymous note in interoffice mail that would forever change her life. The handwritten note listed salaries for Lilly and three of her male colleagues, all four of them tire managers hired in the same year. The males' salaries were all within a thousand dollars of each other; she made nearly 40% less than any of them. This information was a turning point for her. She filed an EEOC complaint, and they gave her a right-to-sue letter in 1999. Four years later, a jury awarded Lilly nearly $4 million in damages, but Goodyear filed an appeal, and the case went all the way to the Supreme Court in 2006. She lost because the majority opinion from the Court was that she should have complained about her lower pay much earlier

---

2   The term "survivor" rather than "victim" is used to signify that Anita Hill is triumphant and has taken control by sharing her story and advocating for the rights of other survivors.

than 1998—even though she did not know her pay was lower prior to receiving that anonymous note in her mailbox. Lilly spent the next couple of years lobbying for equal pay on Capitol Hill, and in early 2009, President Barack Obama signed the **Lilly Ledbetter Fair Pay Act of 2009** as one of his first actions as president. Since 2008, Lilly has traveled the globe telling her story.

Environmentalism

As witnessed in this section, environmentalists come from many backgrounds (blue-collar workers, scientists, investigators, politicians, concerned citizens, etc.) and serve many functions (**whistleblowers**, policy makers, agitators, etc.). Below are the turning points for Karen Silkwood, Erin Brockovich, U.S. Vice President Al Gore, and LaDonna Brave Bull Allard (Lakota/Dakota).

Karen Silkwood (1946–1974) was the only female in her Texas high school chemistry class in the 1960s. She attended college for a short time but quit after she met a man and had children. After 7 years in a troubled relationship, she moved to Oklahoma (sans the ex and her three children) and took a job as a lab analyst checking plutonium pellets at Kerr-McGee, an energy company that ceased operations in 2006. Just 3 months after she started working at the plant, some employees went on strike, and she joined them. The strike was a bust, but as a result of the strike, Karen was asked by other members of her labor union to investigate safety conditions at the plant and to serve on the bargaining committee. When Kerr-McGee got behind schedule on a government contract, Karen noted that they got sloppy with safety and that employees were exposed to radiation. In fact, radiation was found throughout Karen's apartment, and she tested positive for **plutonium** in her lungs. As a result of related stress, Karen lost 21 pounds from her 115-pound frame and began taking Quaaludes for depression. When the national leadership of the union informed her that the plutonium exposure put her at risk for cancer, she was shocked and scared. This news was a turning point for her. She made plans to meet with a journalist from *The New York Times* to blow the whistle on Kerr-McGee. On the way to that meeting, Karen had a fatal car accident. Crime scene investigators suggested she had fallen asleep at the wheel, but there were skid marks, evidence she had been rear-ended, and a missing binder of documents that held all the information she had planned to share with the reporter. In time, Kerr-McGee settled out of court with her family.

Environmentalist **Erin Brockovich** (@ErinBrockovich) takes pride in being called a rebel. Her family and a beloved teacher expected good things from her, but most people did not. Fulfilling the majority's prophecy, she did not do well in college and spent most of her time socializing and partying. During her 20s, her life was a series of unfortunate events, including divorces, poverty, and bouts of anorexia. At the end of her second marriage, she met a therapist who encouraged her to give voice to her inner self by talking out loud when she was alone. That was a turning point for Erin, then a single mom of three children. By the early 1990s, Erin was in her early 30s and a legal assistant in East Hollywood, California. Ed Masry, one of the partners in the firm, asked Erin to organize a box of documents. As she did, she learned about a case that would change her life. The decision makers at Pacific Gas & Electric (PG&E), which operated a pumping station located in Hinkley, California, were being accused of allowing the local water supply to be contaminated with chromium-6 (C6), a chemical linked to cancer that was used to keep pipes from rusting. Erin learned that PG&E had recently bought residential properties around the Hinkley plant and had bulldozed the houses. While many of the residents gladly sold their homes, some residents grew suspicious and came to Masry's law firm. Ed and Erin (who was eventually named lead investigator) interviewed people in Hinkley and heard about their miscarriages, nosebleeds, skin rashes, digestive disorders, and cancer diagnoses. In 1995, Ed filed suits against PG&E for 634 families. PG&E decided to settle for $333 million, of which Erin received $2.5 million. A Hollywood movie entitled *Erin Brockovich* (2000) starred Julia Roberts as Erin and won Roberts the Academy Award for Best Actress.

Former U.S. Senator and Vice President **Al Gore** (@algore) had a life plan, and it included being president of the United States (POTUS). More than anything, he wanted to utilize the role to magnify his concerns regarding the environment. In 1976, Al, a newly elected representative from Tennessee's 4th District in the U.S. House of Representatives, held the first national congressional hearings on climate change. In 2000, he got very close to becoming POTUS when the tie-breaking decision was left to the state of Florida, and their very close vote was contested. The Supreme Court of the United States ruled against Al and gave the presidency to George W. Bush. It was the second time that Al had lost this coveted office. When it happened 12 years earlier in 1988, he started writing his best-selling book *Earth in the Balance: Ecology and the Human Spirit* (1992). While working on the book, he put together the slideshow that would eventually be used in the documentary *An Inconvenient Truth* (2006), which won an Academy Award for Best Documentary Film. Al's turning points regarding the environment date back to the 1960s, when his mother would discuss Rachel Carson's book **Silent Spring** (1962) at the dinner table, and a few years later, when, as a student at Harvard University, he took a class with Roger Revelle, one of the first scientists to measure carbon dioxide in the atmosphere. In 2007, he won the Nobel Peace Prize. Today, he travels the world talking about climate change and regularly holds training events to teach others how to deliver a similar message.

LaDonna Brave Bull Allard (@ladonnaallard2) had her turning point late in life, when she was a grandmother acting as the tribal historian and genealogist for the **Standing Rock Sioux Tribe**. During this time, people began to organize against a pipeline (dubbed the Keystone[3] pipeline) that would run from an oil field in western North Dakota to southern Illinois, right under the water supply and through the ancient burial grounds of her tribal land. Before the pipeline proposal, LaDonna (Lakota/Dakota) had never considered herself an activist, but four things motivated her turning point: (a) she and her people believe that "water is life" and annually go 4 days without water to remind themselves of the importance of the gift; (b) she loved her tribal land and had many memories associated with it; (c) her son and ancestors was buried on the land; and (d) she was the closest landowner to the proposed pipeline. When she heard a meeting had been called at the end of March 2016 that would include people who fought the Keystone pipeline, she attended and volunteered her land as a camp. Five days later, the first four water protectors set up at Sacred Stone Camp, which was completely run on green energy. LaDonna started livestreaming and posting on social media to ask for help. Over time, participation increased, getting up to 15,000 campers by the end of 2016. People would come to pray and drink water, and they would bring water from all over the world to put in the river to help it heal. LaDonna constantly reminds everyone that she follows the young people (who have always referred to her as "Auntie" or "Grandma"). She believes the youth are fulfilling the prophecy of the **Seventh Generation** to heal their people. Although her Sacred Stone Camp was closed in early 2017, other camps have sprung up around the world with similar goals. LaDonna continues to travel the world visiting camps and speaking about environmental issues and indigenous rights.

LGBTQ+[4] Rights

Much time has been spent elsewhere in this book discussing LGBTQ+ rights (see Chapter 3 for a thorough discussion of the gay and lesbian movements of the

---

3   Keystone was a name given by a pipeline official who referenced the keystone as the last but most important piece when building a bridge. He believed the pipeline would provide an important "bridge" between oil producers and their markets.

4   The "LGBTQ" part is formed based on the following terms: lesbian, gay, bisexual, transgender, and queer. The plus symbol allows for a clearer representation of people who are lesbian, gay, bisexual, transgender, queer, questioning, intersex, gender nonconforming, pansexual, asexual, straight allies, etc.

mid-20th century), but a few people's stories and turning points are so inspiring that they needed their own space in this chapter. Janet Mock, George Takei, and Jazz Jennings have lived experiences as representatives of LGBTQ+ communities. Judy Shepard is an ally—the mother of Ryan Shepard, a man who was killed for simply being gay.

Janet Mock (@janetmock) is a journalist and trans advocate specializing in trans media representations who grew up mostly in Hawai'i with her often absent mother. At the age of 4, she knew she had been born with the wrong body and struggled for years with when, how, and if to communicate her trans identity. At the age of 13, she met a girl named Wendi who would become her best friend. Assigned male gender at birth, Wendi was unabashedly a girl who had plans to start hormone treatments the day she turned 16 years old. Wendi's courage gave Janet courage, and she would often use Wendi's extra estrogen pills to aid her own physical transition. During this time, Janet began spending time at her school's teen center because it provided support for LGBTQ+ youth. She said the center, and one social worker in particular, provided a turning point. With the encouragement of the social worker, she became a teen mediator and trained other teens to do the same. Today, Janet is one of the most recognizable faces of the trans community.

Today, actor and activist **George Takei** (@GeorgeTakei) is a social media sensation with millions of followers on Facebook, Twitter, and Instagram. He educates his followers about **Japanese American internment camps** in the United States, immigration, LGBTQ+ rights, and a number of other social justice issues about which he is passionate. He wasn't always so open about his thoughts about social justice, though. It wasn't until 2005 that George, who had been with his partner, Brad, nearly 20 years at the time, came out as a gay man. His turning point occurred when California Governor Arnold Schwarzenegger vetoed the state's gay marriage bill. George watched the protestors on the evening news and knew he had to come out and own his Truth. He and Brad married in 2008.

From a very early age, **Jazz Jennings** (@JazzJennings_) knew her assigned sex of male at birth did not match how she felt inside. She repeatedly told her parents that she was not a boy, and they reluctantly allowed her to dress more feminine around their house. At her fifth birthday party, she had a "coming out" where she wore a girl's one-piece bathing suit. After that party, her parents never asked her to dress like a boy again. In April 2007, at the age of 6, Jazz was featured on the national news program 20/20 in an interview with Barbara Walters. At that time, trans children had not been featured much in the national media, and little Jazz won over many viewers' hearts and minds and would do so again when Walters interviewed her when Jazz was 11. Jazz's mom started TransKids Purple Rainbow, a foundation for trans youth and their parents, and Jazz would often speak on panels with her but was hesitant to become a public figure. When Jazz was in the seventh grade, her mom received an email via the foundation from a mother whose trans child had recently committed suicide. That correspondence was a turning point for Jazz, and at that moment, she dedicated herself to advocacy and voluntarily became a public face and a voice for trans children. Since her pre-teen years, she has starred on the reality show *I Am Jazz,* won many awards from national organizations (e.g., **GLAAD, the Trevor Project**, ESPN), and has been named to many prominent lists, including *Time's* 25 Most Influential Teens in 2014 and 2015.

Judy Shepard (@WYOJudyShepard) and her husband, Dennis Shepard, received a call in October 1998 very early in the morning. They lived in Saudi Arabia at the time for Dennis's job. Their 21-year-old son Matthew, who attended college in Wyoming, had been **pistol-whipped,** tied to a fence post, and left for dead—all because he was gay. Judy and Dennis founded the Matthew Shepard Foundation on December 1—Matt's birthday—just 6 weeks after his murder. Their website features resources for the LGBTQ+ community, and Judy became a very popular speaker on college campuses, where she changed many lives with "mom hugs." Matt's death was a turning point. Before his death, the Shepards had not been involved in advocacy work of any kind. In 2009, the staff at the Matthew Shepard Foundation celebrated when a **hate crimes bill** was signed into law. Both Judy and Dennis encourage allies to be involved in the fight for equality.

Disability Awareness

Nearly 57 million of the 326 million people in the United States are classified as disabled. Diagnoses include anxiety disorder, rheumatoid arthritis, autism, lupus, diabetes, vision loss, dyslexia, spinal cord injury, and hundreds more. People without diagnoses are really just temporarily abled, as everybody is one accident or screening away from a disability. As it is often pointed out, people who are disabled (or "differently abled") are in a marginalized group that anyone can become a part of at any time. This section focuses on the turning points for disability activists Ed Roberts, Eunice Kennedy Shriver, Temple Grandin, and Jillian Mercado.

At the age of 14, **Ed Roberts** (1939–1995) contracted polio and was confined to an **iron lung**. For the next 3 years, he had to phone into high school. By the time he was a senior, he could attend classes in a wheelchair but came close to not graduating because he was not included in the required courses of driver's education or physical education. When it came time for college, Ed was determined to live independently, but first, he had to fight for aid because California's Department of Rehabilitation thought college was a bad investment for people with his medical condition. When he started attending the University of California in Berkeley (the first person with significant disabilities to do so), he had to live in the university's hospital because it was the only residential space on campus that could handle his 800-pound iron lung. Ed taught himself to drive his power wheelchair in 1 day so he could be alone with his girlfriend. From that moment on, he saw himself in a new light. He was independent. It was a turning point. After earning both a bachelor's and a master's degree, Ed was appointed by Governor Jerry Brown in 1975 to be the director of California's Department of Rehabilitation—the very department that had discriminated against him years before. Ed, a co-founder of the World Institute of Disability and winner of a MacArthur Genius Grant, helped fight for the **Americans with Disabilities Act of 1990** signed by President George H. W. Bush.

The fifth of nine children, **Eunice Kennedy Shriver** (1921–2009) was born 11 months after women won the right to vote in the United States (see Chapter 2 for information about U.S. women's suffrage). She was raised in the shadows of her brothers, and her career was ignored by the father she idolized. Her oldest sister, Rosemary, was sent to a boarding school for children with intellectual disabilities at the at the age of 11 and given a **lobotomy** in 1941 at the insistence of her father and without the knowledge of her mother. The surgery left 23-year-old Rosemary incapacitated; she was committed to an institution until she died of natural causes at 86 years old. In 1962, after Eunice's father suffered a stroke that left him mute and partially paralyzed, Eunice went public with an article in the *Saturday Evening Post* about Rosemary's institutionalization. Up to that point, their father had given the press many partially true explanations regarding the absence of his oldest daughter from public life. Eunice, who was 20 years old at the time of the lobotomy, harbored guilt for allowing her dad to keep her sister out of public life for 20 years. She was also quite angry and spent the rest of her life trying to make up for what had happened to Rosemary. Eunice had her brother Ted, a senator, add $10 million in funding for "a program of recreational and physical recreation for mentally retarded and physically handicapped youngsters" to federal disability law, and in 1968, she funded some games through a Chicago parks program. She took those games international, and they became today's Special Olympics. On its 50th anniversary, there were one million athletes in 172 countries with more than one million coaches and volunteers. Eunice was awarded a Presidential Medal of Freedom in 1984.

One of the most famous modern academics is **Temple Grandin** (@DrTemple-Grandin). While her terminal degree is in animal science and she is a renowned expert on livestock handling, she is best known as a person living with autism and for having the ability to explain her cognitive processes to general and academic audiences. In a TED Talk from 2010, she explained how many (but not all) people with autism think in pictures. For example, when the word "steeple" is used, a person who is not autistic may think of one very generic steeple. Instead, Temple will think of every steeple she has seen in her life in a sort of slideshow fashion. Ever since Temple was very young, she dreamed of having a machine that would surround her and provide enough pressure to give her relief—like a big hug. William Carlock, her high school science teacher, encouraged her to build a prototype based on cattle equipment during her senior year. Lying in the machine and applying pressure helped her control her aggression and accept human affection. When she went to college and people doubted the validity of the machine, William encouraged her to perform satisfaction experiments using college students. That project and her ongoing relationship with her high school teacher were turning points.

In early 2014, **Jillian Mercado** (@jilly_peppa) made a big impression on the fashion industry when she became the face of Diesel Clothing. A well-known fashion blogger, she had been in a wheelchair since the age of 12 and was an unlikely candidate to be in a national mainstream fashion campaign. She was found through an open casting call, and as a result of her work with Diesel, she was signed with an international modeling agency. Since then, she has modeled for Nordstrom, Beyoncé, and Target, and her images have appeared in Times Square. Jillian grew up in New York City and was often disappointed with the depictions of models in wheelchairs—usually images of able-bodied people positioned in wheelchairs for health care advertisements. These advertisements were a turning point for her, and she was determined to see better depictions of people like herself on television, in print advertisements and fashion shows, and on billboards. She earned a degree from a fashion institute and worked behind the scenes in the fashion industry, including many times as a volunteer for **New York Fashion Week**. She hopes her work as a model will help change people's minds about how they view people with disabilities. She has worked with the United Nations and other entities to spread her message of diversity, inclusivity, safety, and accessibility.

Review

In this chapter, we have learned about 28 remarkable activists within seven different causes. They are from all over the world; some are living, and some are not; many of them witnessed models of advocacy in their childhood, but many others did not. They are all alike in that they saw a problem and did something about it. They experienced empathy. When turning points happened in their lives, they took notice and were determined to work toward positive outcomes that would advance social justice, even when it was difficult. They challenged their own abilities and made sacrifices for things bigger than themselves. It is likely that they did not recognize their turning points as they were occurring, and it is only through reflection and time that they can see the influences on their social justice consciousnesses and social justice orientations.

Perhaps you have recently experienced a turning point and are contemplating your own reaction. In the next chapter, we will explore both social justice causes and potential actions. Are you ready to be one of the less than five percent who will take action and make a difference? Do you recognize the privilege and oppression that surrounds you? Have you been pushed far enough?

Discussion Starters

1. Whose turning points most inspired you? Why?

2. Which person's turning point most surprised you? Why?

3. Identify a turning point in your lived experience. How did it change your thinking and your subsequent actions?

4. Whose stories and/or what additional causes would you add to this chapter?

Further Reading/Viewing

Baumgardner, J., & Richards, A. (2005). *Grassroots: A field guide for feminist activism*. New York, NY: Farrar, Straus, and Giroux.

Brockovich, E. (2002). *Take it from me: Life's a struggle but you can win*. Boston, MA: McGraw-Hill.

David, L., Bender, L., & Burns, S. Z. (Producers). Guggenheim, D. (Director). (2006). *An inconvenient truth* [Motion picture]. Beverly Hills, CA: Participant Media.

Jennings, J. (2016). *My life as a (transgender) teen*. New York, NY: Random House.

Khan-Cullors, P., & bandele, a. (2018). *When they call you a terrorist: A Black Lives Matter memoir*. New York, NY: St. Martin's Press.

King, C. S. (2017). *My life, my love, my legacy*. New York, NY: Henry Holt and Company.

Klandermans, B., & Oegema, D. (1987). Potentials, networks, motivations, and barriers: Steps towards participation in social movements. *American Sociological Review, 52(4)* 519-531. doi:10.2307/2095297

Landrieu, M. (2018). *In the shadow of statues: A white Southerner confronts history*. New York, NY: Viking.

Ledbetter, L. (2012). Grace *and grit: My fight for equal pay and fairness at Goodyear and beyond*. New York, NY: Random House.

McNamara, E. (2018). *Eunice: The Kennedy who changed the world*. New York, NY: Simon & Schuster.

Mock, F. L. (Producer & Director). (2014). *Anita: Speaking truth to power* [Motion picture]. New York, NY: First Run Features.

Mock, J. (2014). *Redefining realness: My path to womanhood, identity, love, & so much more*. New York, NY: Atria Books.

Moore, W. (2010). *The other Wes Moore: One name, two fates*. New York, NY: Random House.

Neville, M., Ma, N., & Capotosto, C. (Producers). Neville, M. (Director). (2018). *Won't you be my neighbor?* [Motion picture]. New York, NY: Focus Features.

Prejean, H. (2006). *The death of innocents: An eyewitness account of wrongful executions*. New York, NY: Vintage Books.

Richards, C. (2018). *Make trouble: Standing up, speaking out, and finding the courage to lead*. New York, NY: Touchstone.

Ricketts, A. (2012). The *activists' handbook: A step-by-step guide to participatory democracy*. New York, NY: St. Martin's.

Saines, E. G. & Ferguson, S. (Producers). Jackson, M. (Director). (2010). *Temple Grandin*. [Motion picture]. New York, NY: HBO Films.

Shepard, J. (2009). *The meaning of Matthew: My son's murder in Laramie, and a world transformed*. New York, NY: Penguin.

Steinem, G. (2015). *My life on the road*. New York, NY: Random House.

Stevenson, B. (2014). *Just mercy: A story of justice and redemption*. New York, NY: Random House.

Thione, L. (Producer & Director). (2016). *George Takei's Allegiance*. [Motion picture]. Greenwood Village, CO: Fathom Events.

Yousafzai, M. (2013). *I am Malala: The girl who stood for education and was shot by the Taliban*. New York, NY: Little, Brown and Company.

Figure Credits

People gather in Ferguson, Missouri, in 2015 to mark the one-year anniversary of the shooting death of Michael Brown, Jr. by a police officer.

CHAPTER 6

Choosing a Cause and Taking Action

We cannot seek achievement for ourselves and forget about progress and prosperity for our community ... Our ambitions must be broad enough to include the aspirations and needs of others, for their sakes and for our own.
—César Chávez, co-founder, United Farm Workers

ALICE WONG IS a disability activist, media maker, and consultant. Having been in a wheelchair for the majority of her life, she feels she must constantly remind people that her life (and the lives of other disabled folks) have value and are not the tragic experiences often depicted in movies, on television, and in other media. She spreads this positive, **paradigm**-shifting message with public talks, social media, blog posts, podcasts, and through her work with Disability Visibility, a project she founded and directs in partnership with StoryCorps, a national oral history organization. Activism informs Alice's every day. In fact, activism should inform everybody's every day.

We should all live as activists directed by our passions—whether it is advocating for a public education free of discrimination at a meeting with the school principal or showing support for clean water by attending a city council meeting. In this chapter, we will recognize the necessity of a personal values statement in identifying specific causes and actions to attain social justice in our communities and look at ways to organize to have the greatest impact.

Personal Values Statement

A values statement allows for people to understand the top priorities of a business, nonprofit organization, or an individual. For example, the values of YWCA Clark County in Vancouver, Washington, are diversity, teamwork, commitment, service, respect, and empowerment. The people of that organization believe these values are in line with the national mission of the **YWCA USA** to empower women and eliminate racism. Both Clark County and YWCA USA put all their efforts into their shared mission and leave it to other groups and individuals to take on other social justice concerns. The YWCA finds other issues to be important, but its leaders must focus their limited resources on the things that they are most qualified to handle. Their values, and consequently the mission, are the reason they exist.

Just like organizations have stated values, so should people. While there are many social justice concerns in the world, it is best to hone personal time, talents, and energies to just a few. In Chapter 5, you read about dozens of activists who dedicated much time and attention to their causes. Each of their journeys was driven by their values. Clara Luper valued fairness and equality and believed that anybody of any race should be served at a lunch counter. Mayor Mitch Landrieu valued responsibility and service and had to bring down racist statues in his city to stay true to his values. Sister Helen Prejean values compassion and wants to see an end to capital punishment. Lilly Ledbetter values equity and consistency and believes in equal pay for equal work.

Table 6.1 **Common Values of Social Justice Activists**

Honesty	Respect	Accountability	Humor
Fairness	Diversity	Sustainability	Confrontation
Justice	Service	Compassion	Creative
Empathy	Freedom	Liberty	Teamwork
Responsibility	Protection	Equality	Commitment
Opportunity	Democracy	Trust	Education
Cooperation	Empowerment	Community	Stewardship
Consistency	Appreciation	Common Good	Transparency

A budding or experienced activist needs to pay attention to current events. This is best achieved by listening to people most affected via conversations, national news programming, reputable newspapers, Twitter feeds, Google alerts, books, documentaries, etc. It is also important to fact-check information by looking at multiple sources regarding the same story. When you do this research, common themes will emerge. Ask yourself a few questions about these themes: What value(s) constantly come up for me when looking at these sources? In other words, what value(s), when violated, make(s) me the angriest? Is it freedom? The common good? Opportunity? Whatever the values are, they should show up in your personal values statement.

A personal values statement does not need to be lengthy. In fact, a sentence or two focused on a value or values—not specific causes—is perfect. A person's causes (discussed in the next section) are more temporary than a person's values. Values drive causes, not the other way around.

Personal Values Statement (Example)

I will commit my time and resources to the common good, even when it means I have to make a personal sacrifice.

The statement above makes it clear that this person believes in putting societal needs above their own needs. For example, if there is a need in the community for better schools, even though this person does not have children of their own, they willingly pay higher property taxes or make a donation to the school for the betterment of the community. The common good is this person's driving value.

What about you? Consulting the list of values above or contributing your own, what value or values are most important to you? How important is/are the value or values to you? Draft your values statement in the box below.

```
Your Personal Values Statement:



```

In the future, when tough decisions have to be made about where to spend time and resources, revisit your values statement. It will not only help you make decisions regarding activism; it can also guide you when it comes to relationships, career decisions, financial investments, etc. For example, if empathy is an important value to you, then you would not want to be in a relationship with someone who is tough on people going through difficult times. You also would not want to work for or invest in a company that is dismissive of international labor conditions.

Identifying Specific Social Justice Causes

Now that your core values have been declared, it is time to expand upon your social justice journey by identifying specific social justice causes. Si Kahn, the founder of **Grassroots Leadership**, was a young activist and organizer in the U.S. Black civil rights movement as a member of the **Student Nonviolent Coordinating Committee** (SNCC). He used his experience to advise activists and organizers to remain positive, work to help others gain confidence, and share a united belief that a better world is possible. Kahn recommends that people stay focused on their values while learning about themselves, each other, history, justice, community, and friendship. His primary desire is to see activists love the struggle for justice and not simply endure it. In short, he wants social justice crusaders to be passionate and not simply work from a sense of obligation—like some people do as a result of privilege guilt (described in Chapter 4).

In 2018, the National Society of Leadership and Success, an honor society made up of university students, surveyed 3,500 of its members about their willingness to participate in activism. Almost 59% of the respondents said they would publicly protest for a cause about which they were passionate. They listed their top causes as affordable education, race relations, gun-related issues, workplace gender equality, and climate change.

DeRay Mckesson found his passion for community organizing while watching television in his living room. It was August 2014, and he had followed the racial unrest and protests in **Ferguson**, Missouri (a suburb of St. Louis), pretty closely via Twitter. The protests were a result of the shooting death of 18-year-old Michael Brown, Jr. by a police officer. DeRay noticed the television footage about the protesting did not match what he saw on the social media pages of the protestors. (Perhaps DeRay had a value of consistency). Right then, he decided he wanted to get involved. He asked for vacation time from his job with the Minneapolis Public Schools and immediately drove 9 hours to St. Louis, a city he had never visited before. He attended meetings, marches, protests, and trainings to learn more about Ferguson's issues and the community. When DeRay's vacation time ran out, he quit his job in Minneapolis and stayed in the St. Louis area for more than a year. Recently, his podcast, *Pod Save the People,* was ranked in the Top 5 on the iTunes podcast chart.

Both Si and DeRay, though born 40 years apart, found similar passions for the causes of race relations, but there are a number of other social justice causes about which a person can be passionate. See below for a nonexhaustive list. Mark your favorite cause(s) and add any that are not included. In order for an item to be on the Social Justice Causes list, it must center on ending oppression of the marginalized (one of the three components of a "social justice orientation" discussed in Chapter 1). Focusing on your personal values statement, narrow your list of social justice causes to two or three (preferably overlapping). More than three, and the work could seem overwhelming.

Table 6.2 **Find Your Social Justice Cause(s)**

Environment	Beauty Standards	Homelessness	Prison Reform
Sexual Orientation	Domestic Violence	Animal Rights	Bullying
International Education	Poverty	Violence Against Women	Arts Education
	Equal Pay		Gun Control
National Security	Gender Identity	Slut Shaming	Reparations
Health Care	Religious Persecution	Economic Inequality	Affordable Education
Immigration	Capital Punishment	Sex Education	Anti-War
Ageism	Ableism	Corporate Responsibility	Human Trafficking
Labor Rights	Pro-Choice	Race Relations	
Foster Care	Indigenous Rights	Food Safety	

Actions and Goal Setting

Randy Shaw, an attorney and author, has spent most of his career fighting for tenants' rights in Berkeley, California. He believes the two biggest mistakes made by activists are (a) letting themselves get distracted by their opponents and (b) allowing their opponents to frame the issues. Instead, goals (and ultimately the agenda) should be guided by the people most affected by the oppression. For example, it was the migrant farmworkers who made the decisions regarding the Delano Strike (see Chapter 2) and not Robert Kennedy, although he turned out to be a great ally. Kennedy could not make the decisions because he had never lived the experience.

Saul Alinsky, who wrote one of the earliest books for community organizers, was best known for his ability to organize large groups of people. Like Shaw, he strongly believed that every activist should know what specific outcome they want as a result of their actions. In this next section, we will explore specific examples of activism, the importance of understanding oneself and one's community, and activist goal setting.

Examples of Activism

Once a social justice cause(s) is/are identified, it is time to take action. After all, as freed slave and activist Frederick Douglass famously wrote in a letter to an abolitionist associate: "Power concedes nothing without a demand." Those words were written in 1849 but are just as true today. Actions taken by an activist can range from high-risk, such as breaking an unjust law, to something considerably more low-risk, such as sharing a news article on a personal social media page. Even then, that so-called low-risk action can feel pretty high-risk if the post upsets a beloved relative or causes a confrontation with a coworker at the proverbial watercooler. Activism looks different to everyone, depending upon where they are on their social justice journey.

In the next few pages, specific ideas for action are shared. They graduate (albeit subjectively) from low-risk to high-risk. It is important to recognize that an action does not have to be high-risk to be legitimate or effective. Within a social movement, it is best to take multiple actions with varying levels of risk. Doing so allows each person to find their own place to contribute. Additionally, the variety keeps the oppressors guessing the next move and lets them know the movement and its supporters are strong and supported and have longevity. Kahn encourages movement leaders to help new activists gain confidence by initially inviting them to perform low-risk actions and to gradually build their confidence to take part in more high-risk activities.

DIALOGUING—MEETING AT THE PUB AND MIX IT UP AT LUNCH DAY

In July 2009, noted race scholar Henry "Skip" Louis Gates, Jr. was arrested in his home when he was mistaken for an intruder in what appeared to be a result of racial profiling. At the suggestion of former U.S. President Bill Clinton (a friend of Gates), Gates, who is Black, invited James Crowley, the white police officer who arrested him, to meet at a local pub to discuss what had happened. At that meeting, Crowley explained to Gates that his goal every day was to return home to his spouse, and because two suspects had been reported to 911, the officer feared the entire time he was questioning Gates that the other suspect would come from elsewhere in the house and shoot him. That explanation moved Gates (who must value empathy), who reported in 2016 that he and Crowley had become good friends and saw each other often.

Having a conversation with a person who appears to have a dramatically different ideology than your own can be intimidating. There is the understandable concern that the conversation will not go well or be very productive. (See Chapter 7 for tips on dialoguing). It is important to start these uncomfortable conversations early in one's life. In 2001, the Southern Poverty Law Center started a project called Mix It Up at Lunch Day for schoolchildren at all grade levels. The goal was for the children to sit in new seats in their school cafeterias, meet new people, cross cultural boundaries, and build a culture of inclusivity and acceptance. The official Mix It Up Day is held annually at the end of October, but many organizations made up of adults (including college, university, and civic organizations) are holding their own Mix It Up events throughout the year. You could organize such an event in your community.

....

Research shows that Mix It Up programming works. According to a survey of Mix organizers, the program produces powerful results:

- *97% said students' interactions were positive during Mix It Up at Lunch Day.*

- *95% said Mix It Up at Lunch Day prompted students to interact with people outside their normal social circles.*

- *92% said Mix It Up at Lunch Day increased awareness about social boundaries and divisions within school.*

- *83% said the event helped students make new friends.*

- *79% said students have heightened sensitivity toward tolerance and social justice issues as a result of Mix It Up.*

- *78% said students seem more comfortable interacting with different kinds of people as a result of Mix It Up.*

Source: Mix It Up Survey conducted by Quality Education Data, 2008

....

VOTING AND CAMPAIGNING

One of the simplest but most crucial ways to fight for social justice is to cast a ballot as an informed voter, but there are other ways to contribute to campaigns as well (e.g., volunteering to register voters, being a poll worker on Election Day, and/or working on a campaign). During the acceptance speech of newly elected U.S. President Barack Obama in 2008, he gave a great amount of credit for his underdog victory to the millions of volunteers and organizers who worked for his campaign. During his successful reelection bid in 2012, more than two million people volunteered for Obama's campaign. They registered 1.8 million new voters. Howard Dean, a former politician and chair of the Democratic National Committee during Obama's initial victory, said Obama's campaign was the best he had ever witnessed in politics. Admittedly, much of that success had to do with the management and development of campaign volunteers.

Figure 6.1 Former U.S. President Barack Obama meets with campaign volunteers during his 2012 reelection bid.

Volunteering for a campaign is as simple as reaching out to the local party headquarters or a specific campaign by phone, email, a website, or social media. There are opportunities for people with all different skill sets—including phone and text banking, entering data into spreadsheets and databases, canvassing neighborhoods, helping plan or execute events, and organizing yard signs. These patriotic actions are especially important to activists who value freedom, liberty, and community. In 2016, Bronx citizen Alexandria "Sandy" Ocasio-Cortez worked as an organizer for the U.S. presidential campaign of Bernie Sanders. Sanders lost his election bid, but in 2018, Alexandria (also known as AOC) became the youngest woman ever elected to the U.S. Congress when she challenged a 20-year incumbent. She was inspired to run for office by Sanders and actions of activists such as Mari Copeny (see her story below) in Flint, Michigan, and Ladonna Brave Bull Allard (see Chapter 5) at the Standing Rock Indian Reservation in North Dakota.

LETTER WRITING

In 2016, when Mari Copeny was just 8 years old, she wrote a letter to President Obama asking to meet him or First Lady Michelle Obama while Mari was visiting Washington, D.C., for a congressional hearing about the status of water in her hometown of Flint, Michigan. Mari was already a well-established activist in Flint, having participated in marches and rallies to bring attention to the dangerous levels of bacteria and lead in the city's water supply. She spoke to the people of her community and understood their needs. Her local nickname was "Little Miss Flint." President Obama wrote back to Mari and let her know that he planned to visit Flint within a couple of weeks to meet with her. After visiting Flint, the president authorized an expenditure of $100 million dollars to repair Flint's water system.

SOCIAL MEDIA—PETITIONS AND CUSTOMER REVIEWS

In 2012, McKenna Pope was a 13-year-old in New Jersey when she found her 4-year-old brother, Devyn, attempting to cook a tortilla on a lightbulb. She asked her mom to buy him an Easy-Bake Oven for Christmas. At the store, they found that the ovens came in limited colors of purple and pink and that the boxes had pictures of girls but no boys on them. McKenna (who likely valued fairness) did not feel that Hasbro, the company that makes the ovens, was very inclusive of all their potential customers. She interviewed her brother about the problem and put the video on a petition website, along with a detailed letter to the company stating specifically the outcome she and her brother desired. The petition received 46,000 signatures within a month, and Hasbro added ovens in black, silver, and blue to their inventory.

Not all social media activism ends as positively; sometimes activists fail with their campaigns. Thousands of **Amazon** customers attempted to humiliate the BIC Corporation shortly after its release of the BIC for Her pen in 2012. The pen's packaging promised a "thin barrel to fit a woman's hand," and much like the problematic Easy-Bake Oven, the pens were available solely in purple and pink. They also cost significantly more than similar pens from the same company. The customer reviews were scathing and sarcastic, calling out the sexism of the company and the irrelevance of the product. It became national news, and talk show host Ellen DeGeneres was uncharacteristically critical of the company. It appeared BIC had a real crisis on its hands, but the company never publicly responded to the backlash and continues to successfully sell the product on Amazon all these years later.

Amazon Reviews for BIC for Her

I wrote down this review actually using this product, but my husband had to type it out for me, as I have no idea how to use any form of technology other than a blender.

AnnaGram, August 29, 2012

I recently purchased these for my wife as a novelty item, knowing full well that most women do not know how to read and therefore have very little use for a pen specifically for ladies. Much to my surprise, she picked it up very quickly and within a few short hours was able to draw simple shapes and was starting to make letters.

PapaJohn, November 28, 2013

I gave these to all of the men in my office, and they all received pay cuts a few weeks later! Thanks, BIC for helping me to bridge the pay gap.

Jessica, April 10, 2015

EDUCATING OTHERS—CORRECTING HARMFUL LANGUAGE, AUTHORING, AND SPEECHMAKING

Being an activist can be as simple as influencing conversations. Harmful language is used both intentionally and unintentionally every day. "Gypped" is short for "gypsy" and is used to mean to cheat or swindle; "jewed" is used to mean to bargain; "lame" is used to mean something is boring or not worth the time; "sold down the river" is used to mean betray; and the "peanut gallery" is used to signify a place for hecklers. All these words and phrases are problematic when their origins and evolutions are considered.

"Gypsy" was a slur word used for Eastern European Romanis, who throughout history have been stereotyped as a group of swindlers. The word "jewed" is a verb derived from the adjective Jewish; Jewish people have been stereotyped as hagglers. "Lame" was synonymous with the term "disabled" for many years. To use the word "lame" to describe a situation implies that people with physical disabilities are boring or not worth the time. There are also words in the common **vernacular** that make light of mental health (and should also be stricken from your vocabulary), including "crazy," "insane," and "hysterical." Finally, "sold down the river" and "peanut gallery" are both linked to the history of Black folks in the United States. Slaves who were seen as problematic were often "sold down the river" to plantations with harsher conditions; the "peanut gallery" was the upper balcony reserved for Black audiences in segregated theaters. It is an activist move to raise the social consciousness of conversational partners. They cannot unknow once they know, and perhaps, in turn, they will educate their other conversational partners about harmful language.

Authors have agendas, and many times their agendas have a social justice focus. Harriet Beecher Stowe (see Chapter 2) was an abolitionist who wanted to humanize the slave experience for a broad white audience. She used slave narratives that she collected and information from anti-slavery newspapers to write her book *Uncle Tom's Cabin* (1852), which was a best-seller. U.S. President Abraham Lincoln gave her credit for laying the groundwork for the American Civil War. Upton Sinclair (see Chapter 2) was an outspoken socialist who wrote *The Jungle* (1906) at the turn of the 20th century to expose the poor labor and working conditions of Chicago's immigrant community. He spent 7 weeks working in the meatpacking industry to gather information for the book.

In 1960, Elie Wiesel fought to have the first edition of his book *Night*, a semi-autographical account of **the Holocaust**, published. By 1986, his book was extremely well circulated, and he was awarded the **Nobel Peace Prize**. In his acceptance speech, he swore to never be silent when there was human suffering, as he believed that silence benefitted the oppressor. Khaled Hosseini was born in Kabul, Afghanistan, in 1965 and moved to the United States to seek **asylum** with his family when he was a teenager. As an adult in the 21st century, he told the story of Afghanistan and its people by writing best-sellers, including *The Kite Runner* (2003) and *A Thousand Splendid Suns* (2008). Both Wiesel and Hosseini displayed the values of education and opportunity by teaching the world about people who were historically misunderstood.

. . . .

I swore never to be silent when and wherever human beings endure suffering and humiliation. We must always take sides. Neutrality helps the oppressor, never the victim. Silence encourages the tormentor, never the tormented.
—*Elie Wiesel (1986)*

. . . .

In 1981, Rayna Green (Cherokee) gave a speech at a conference on education equity for an audience that was primarily made up of American Indian women. Green was unhappy with museum policies regarding the collection of indigenous bones and other objects. In the speech, she used humor to suggest that they create a Museum of the Plains White Person and include the bones of **John Wayne**, a food display made up of plastic exhibits of white bread, mayonnaise, peanut butter, and a reconstructed McDonald's, and dance exhibits from the last living white people. She made her speech available in essay form, and it has been making the rounds in classrooms and reading circles ever since.

In 1959, Lorraine Hansberry's play *A Raisin in the Sun* debuted on Broadway. It starred a nearly all-Black cast and tackled fair housing practices by depicting a Black family attempting to move into an all-white neighborhood. The play was nominated for four **Tony Awards**, including Best Play. It had two Broadway revivals, one in 2004 and again in 2014, when it won the Tony for Best Revival of a Play.

Eve Ensler, a survivor of childhood sexual abuse, became an advocate against gender-based violence as an adult. She interviewed her female-identifying friends and friends of friends (200 people in total) about their experiences with sex and gender-based violence and, in 1996, performed *The Vagina Monologues* for the first time as a one-woman show in her native New York City. Today, her monologues are performed annually throughout the world, including on thousands of college campuses. The proceeds from the performances are used to benefit local crisis centers and other resource centers.

Movies have also been used as activist statements. Filmmaker Spike Lee is well known for spending the past 3 decades producing and directing confrontational films that deal directly with race, racism, class, and a number of other political issues. One of his earliest films, *Do the Right Thing* (1989), focuses on a Brooklyn neighborhood's racial tension that culminates in tragedy when a police officer kills a man from the neighborhood. The film was criticized for having the potential to cause Black audiences to riot. Lee thought the criticisms were outrageous and racist. In 2018, Lee directed *BlacKkKlansman*, a film based on the memoir of a Colorado police officer who was Black and went undercover via phone conversations as a potential recruit for the KKK. Although the film is set in the early 1970s, it is juxtaposed with modern events, including recent acts of police brutality and rallies led by **white nationalists**.

Like Eve Ensler, artist Veronica Castillo of San Antonio also has a desire to end gender-based violence but does her advocacy work with ceramic and clay sculptures. She is a fourth-generation Tree of Life artist. Her father, who won the **National Prize for Arts and Sciences** in Mexico, modernized the Tree of Life art form to depict the everyday, which was different from the work of his parents, who depicted traditional Catholic scenes in their art. Veronica uses her trees to advance social justice. One of her most famous pieces, *El Arbol de la Muerte: Maquilando Mujeres* (*The Tree of Death: Factory Women*), addresses the brutal murders of hundreds of women in the border town of Ciudad Juarez, Mexico, many of them poorly paid factory workers.

Sally Roesch Wagner, a women's studies academic, had concerns that not all women's stories were included in those told about the U.S. suffrage movement.

In particular, she worried that the stories of **Matilda Joslyn Gage** and the women from the **Haudenosaunee Confederacy** (see Chapter 2) had been left out. In response, Sally wrote books about the women, but she also gave lectures and public talks with Haudenosaunee women and sometimes in period costume as Matilda Joslyn Gage. Sally's lectures and performances can be found on YouTube.

CHARITY WORK—CARE PACKAGES AND PRODUCT DRIVES

Sometimes it may feel that the quickest or least frustrating path to a solution is to just provide it rather than wait for a larger entity to respond. For example, some people help the homeless by carrying a few care packages in their cars—sealable plastic bags full of snack bars, applesauce, crackers, canned meat, socks, money, deodorant, hand wipes, etc. They give away the packages as they encounter people who need them. While this charity work is admirable, activism requires a willingness to get to the root of injustice, challenge system oppression, and transform social structures. Think of charity work as a temporary solution and the other actions listed here as more permanent or systemic.

The winter holidays were approaching, and Ashley Arevalo of Corpus Christi, Texas, wanted to do some good for her community. She looked around the Internet and found information about Kotex's Period Pledge, a national drive to collect feminine products for women in homeless shelters. Within a month of starting a **GoFundMe** campaign and posting on her Facebook page, Ashley surpassed her $1,000 goal and was able to donate 7,472 period products to local shelters. Since that drive, she has expanded her activism by establishing a local period organization and lobbying her local university through petitions, media interviews, and meetings to offer free period products in campus restrooms. Ashley and her colleagues are looking for permanent solutions by getting to the root of injustice, challenging systemic oppression, and transforming social structures.

BOYCOTTING AND BUYCOTTING

When a company's values or practices do not line up with a person's values, then a boycott is often a good solution. Certainly, well-orchestrated boycotts have been successful throughout history: the 1955 **Montgomery Bus Boycott** (see Chapter 3) resulted in desegregation of the city's buses; the 1965 Delano grape boycott (see Chapter 2) forced growers to bargain with laborers; and the 2015 boycott of school merchandise at the University of Missouri (see Chapter 7) helped force the resignation of the university's president. In recent years, there have been calls for boycotts of many companies, including Walmart, Cracker Barrel Old Country

Store, Wendy's, Lowe's, Chick-fil-A, and Hobby Lobby. None of the boycotts appear to have done much damage to the companies' bottom lines.

Instead, some activists are turning their attention to buycotts (which is similar to the charity work described above if it doesn't lead to systemic change)—deliberately purchasing products or services to show support for a company's policies rather than boycotting to show lack of support. For example, companies that use one-for-one purchasing models (e.g., TOMS shoes, Bombas socks) have experienced success. Their products tend to be more expensive than competitors' products, but people are willing to pay the higher prices because a matching or similar product is given to someone in need. Additionally, entertainment is an area that has benefitted from buycotts. In 2017, both *Wonder Woman* and *Black Panther* were unexpected hits at the box office and pulled in new audiences for action films who wanted to see a powerful all-female cast in *Wonder Women* and/or, in the case of *Black Panther*, a cast made up predominantly of people of color.

LEGISLATIVE PROCESS—SPONSORING, FILIBUSTERING, AND PRESSURING

As an elected official or a private citizen, it is possible to influence the legislative process. Patsy Mink, a member of Congress from Hawaii, was a sponsor and champion of **Title IX**—legislation that required equality for women and men in education. Title IX has now been in place for nearly 50 years. Wendy Davis, a Texas state senator, staged an 11-hour filibuster in 2013 to stop a vote on an anti-abortion bill. During the 11 hours that she spoke, she was not allowed to eat, drink, use the restroom, sit, or lean against her desk. Her performance gained a national audience when it was livestreamed on social media, and the brand of tennis shoes she wore was a top seller on Amazon in the days after her performance.

Members of United We Dream, an advocacy group constituted of many undocumented youths, are given the credit for the **presidential executive order** that resulted in the Deferred Action for Childhood Arrivals (DACA) policy in 2012. The group flooded the White House and the Department of Homeland Security with phone calls, walked the halls of Congress, laid down in front of federal vans in Arizona to stop the deportation of immigrants, and staged a hunger strike at the headquarters of U.S. President Barack Obama's reelection campaign in Colorado. Many of the youth of this movement were inspired by the **U.S. Immigration Reform Protests of 2006,** which, on 1 day, involved protests in 140 cities and 39 states in the United States.

Legislative action does not just have to take place at the state and national levels. In fact, many colleges and universities have student governments that allow for the passing of resolutions and referendums that are then forwarded to local administrators and other decision makers. In 2019, the students at Georgetown University, led by the GU272 Advocacy Team, voted 2-to-1 to institute a **reparations** fund for descendants of the 272 slaves who were sold in 1838 to pay off the school's debt and sustain it financially. If the referendum is put into practice, students will pay a fee of $27.20 every semester to be placed into a fund to be controlled by five descendants of the 272 slaves and five current GU undergraduate students.

MARCHES/VIGILS/WALKOUTS

Upset about the election of Donald J. Trump to the U.S. presidency and the defeat of **Hillary Rodham Clinton**, women immediately began to create social media pages inviting people to join them in Washington, D.C., for a protest march. Their efforts were combined, and on January 21, 2018 (the day after the inauguration), half a million people participated in the Women's March on Washington, and millions more marched in other cities across the world. They wanted to send the message that they were prepared to fight for women's rights, immigration reform, healthcare, the environment, and a number of other issues they feared would be under fire with a new presidential administration.

On Valentine's Day in 2018, a school shooting took place at Marjory Stoneman Douglas High School in Parkland, Florida. Seventeen people were killed, including students and teachers. In the aftermath of the shooting, students began to organize using the hashtag #Neveragain. Their goal was to make their school shooting the very last school shooting ever. Initially, there were candlelight vigils held by local churches and organizations. A handful of student leaders organized a field office at one of their houses to handle phone calls from the media. The students did interviews and reached out to politicians. They organized a nationwide walkout for 1 month after the shooting, and then 39 days after the shooting, they hosted March for Our Lives in Washington, D.C.—the biggest youth-led protest since the **Vietnam War**. March for Our Lives inspired Swedish climate activist Greta Thunberg, then in the ninth grade, who refused to attend school on Fridays so she could protest for reduced carbon emissions. In turn, her activism inspired millions of other schoolchildren around the globe to organize for the environment.

In February 2018, a state bill to increase education spending in Oklahoma failed in the state's House of Representatives. Frustrated at the very low teacher pay in the state (#50 in the United States), the **Oklahoma Education Association (OEA)** announced that a teacher walkout would happen on April 2, 2018 if the bill did not pass. The legislation failed, and the Oklahoma Teacher Walkout began on the planned date and lasted 9 days at the Capitol in Oklahoma City. The protestors wanted a $10,000 raise for every teacher over the course of 3 years, which was

$4,000 more than each of them had been promised earlier in the legislative session. The Oklahoma Senate and House adjourned on April 12, 2018 without making appropriations for the $10,000 raises. As a result of the walkout, 65 OEA members ran for the legislature in 2018, and 22 of them won their seats.

PROTESTS

DeRay Mckesson compares protests to storytelling—a way to use bodies, words, and art to talk about pain and to demand justice. He admits that sometimes people are not ready to hear about the pain because they are not even convinced that there is a problem. Direct actions, when carried out well, can help grow public support. William Nathan Mathis, a 74-year-old peanut farmer from Alabama, is one such protestor who won a lot of public support. He showed up at a political rally for Judge Roy Moore, a man who had referred to members of LGBTQ+ communities as "perverts." These comments upset William, whose lesbian daughter had committed suicide years earlier. He made a protest sign and pretended to be a Moore supporter to get close to the rally. He stood alone and quietly held his anti-Moore sign, which included a photo of his daughter from high school. William received attention from reporters, and his remarks on video were watched millions of times online.

In 2019, students and faculty at the University of South Carolina protested when a selection committee, whose makeup was 82% male, named four finalists for the presidency who were all men. After more research, the protesters learned that the larger pool of 11 semifinalists was also made up of men only. When the board of trustees met to decide the sole finalist, protesters were nearby, chanting, "We want answers." In the end, the board decided to name an internal interim president and to reopen the search for a university president.

ACTS OF DEFIANCE

Acts of defiance as activism have been around a long time. During temperance, Carrie Nation (see Chapter 2) took it upon herself to destroy saloons with hatchets. During women's suffrage, Susan B. Anthony (see Chapter 2) decided to vote, although she had no legal right to do so. The tradition continues today. In late 2014, 25-year-old Loujain al-Hathloul was arrested when she tried to drive into Saudi Arabia from the neighboring United Arab Emirates (UAE). While there is no law against women driving in Saudi Arabia, the traditional ban—related to a strict system of behavior that restricts women from acting without the guidance and approval of a male guardian—is enforced by the police. A few weeks after the initial arrest, Loujain was transferred to a terrorism court over comments she made on social media prior to her drive from the UAE to Saudi Arabia. Ultimately, she was detained for a total of 73 days.

Below is a list of actions that have been utilized by activists, organizers, and agitators for centuries. Take the time to score your willingness to perform these actions for the social justice cause(s) closest to your heart. There are no right or wrong answers. It is just an opportunity to take a personal inventory.

Think about the cause most important to you. What are you willing to do to persuade others to think more like you when it comes to that cause? (On a scale of 1–5, 1=highly unlikely, 2=unlikely, 3=unsure, 4=likely, 5=highly likely).

_____ Write a letter to the editor

_____ Attend a public meeting

_____ Support strikers

_____ Have a conversation with a naysayer

_____ Post personal feelings on social media

_____ Make a short video and post it

_____ Create art and display it

_____ Sign a petition

_____ Go to jail

_____ Donate money or products (charity)

_____ Attend a vigil

_____ Post reviews about a controversial product or company

_____ Boycott a business or product

_____ Support a business or product

_____ Write academic papers

_____ Make a presentation to a local group

_____ Start a club

_____ Volunteer for a nonprofit

_____ Write or call legislative reps

_____ Participate in a march

_____ Participate in a protest

_____ Canvas a neighborhood

_____ Write a letter or email to a decision maker (company executive politician)

_____ Correct another person's harmful use of language or attempt at a joke

Understanding Your Community

Most activists do their advocating in the geographic area in which they live and are most knowledgeable about the people, cultures, geography, stakeholders, influencers, media, etc. From time to time, they may also visit communities that are a little less familiar—such as the state capital, the headquarters of a company, or the scene of a shooting or other crime. Some activists even choose to relocate to bigger cities to dedicate their lives to causes.

Once such example is Shelby Knox, the subject of a 2005 award-winning documentary at the **Sundance Film Festival** that depicted her at the age of 15 taking on her Texas public high school to demand sex education that expanded beyond an abstinence-only approach. After high school, Shelby moved from Lubbock, Texas, to New York City because she felt she could do more to fight for women and gender representation in media if she was in an entertainment hub surrounded by like-minded feminists. Since moving to New York, Shelby has worked closely with **Planned Parenthood** and Gloria Steinem (see Chapters 3 and 5) and served as the director of women's rights organizing for **change.org**. She now travels internationally as a speaker regarding youth activism, feminism, and media representations of women.

No matter the geographic location, it is important for activists to have answers to the following questions about themselves and their communities: (a) What are personal barriers to my activist agenda?; (b) Who are some potential collaborators for this work?; and (c) How do I handle naysayers and cynics?

WHAT ARE PERSONAL BARRIERS TO MY ACTIVIST AGENDA?

It is likely that you have given some thought to why you cannot or should not be an activist. Commonly identified personal barriers include financial and family responsibilities, no similar-minded peers, lack of movement leaders or organizers, a dislike of politics, fear of verbal confrontations by naysayers, and family ideology. For every one of these concerns, there is a response. Financial and family responsibilities? Depending upon the particular situation, possible solutions could include making a rally a family affair, doing advocacy work from home, and/or spending less money on eating out or entertainment. As mentioned earlier in the chapter, activist work should inform a person's everyday life. There will never be a perfect time or scenario for a person to enter into advocacy, but it is important to take an inventory of perceived personal barriers and to be confident that they can be managed. Activism requires commitment.

WHO ARE SOME POTENTIAL COLLABORATORS FOR THIS WORK?

Two of the common personal barriers listed above include lack of similar-minded peers and lack of leadership. No one is expected to lead a movement right away. It is best to get some experience with activism first. Review social media and local news outlets for like-minded people with comparable passions. Look for folks who are doing charity work, holding rallies, having public meetings, etc. It is very likely that they may be part of a group—such as a local LGBTQ+ center, a YWCA, or a local church or university. Respond. Attend their meetings. Take a friend who has similar interests. Volunteer and see where things go. (See Chapter 9 for tips on how to be an effective group member).

How do I handle naysayers and cynics?

Just like there will be great opportunities for collaboration and making new friends, there will also be those people who oppose your passions and your advocacy work. It is easy to be flippant and dismissive of cynical strangers, but it is much more challenging to handle a naysayer when it is a family member or a close friend. If you have a history of a healthy relationship with the critic and they really seem to care about you, then be patient with them. It is important that you follow your passion, be consistent in the advocacy, answer any questions they have, and engage in thoughtful dialogues about social justice. (See Chapter 7 for specific tips for dialoguing with naysayers and cynics). If your relationship with this person has always been toxic, then it is not likely going to change now that you have taken a stance on an issue about which they disagree. It may be best to distance yourself from this individual, either temporarily or permanently.

#ActivistGoals

Once passions, actions, geography, and collaborators and naysayers have been identified, it is time to set some goals. Be very specific with the plan. For example, if the environment is a passion, what is it specifically about the environment that is of the most interest to you? Is there too much plastic in the ocean? Is water too scarce? Do we need less dependence on oil? Considering geography, if you live near a coast and enjoy the beach, it might be a natural fit to choose the first option—too much plastic in the ocean. Once a specific problem is identified, it is time to consider possible solutions.

Keep the solution pretty narrow and go after the decision makers who can make it happen. If the problem is too much plastic in the ocean, then what is the solution? Maybe ask consumers and retailers to use reusable bags instead of plastic bags? That would be a long-term goal. A short-term charitable goal could include a beach cleanup. If contact with collaborators has not already happened, that should be an immediate action. If that contact has already been made, then the next action would be to present the idea of a beach cleanup to the group and to begin discussions regarding a long-term campaign to remove plastic bags from a local grocery store chain.

Passion:	*Environment*
Problem:	*Too much plastic in the ocean*
Short-Term Goal:	*Participate in a beach cleanup*
Long-Term Goal:	*Petition largest local grocery store chain to stop using plastic bags*
Personal Action:	*Seek out a local group interested in the environment*

Review

Getting started with activism work can be overwhelming, but this chapter has broken it down for you. Start with your values. What are the values most important to you? These will guide you in many decisions you make in life. Then think about your passions (e.g., equal pay, ageism) as they relate to social justice. How do those passions relate back to the values? Do they make sense? What actions are you willing to take for your passions? They can range from low-risk—such as starting an online petition—to something high-risk—such as an act of defiance. Make a specific plan, set short- and long- term set goals, and find collaborators. You are ready to be an activist.

Discussion Starters

1. What are the values you identified as most important to you? How do they specifically relate to your passions?

2. If you've read Chapters 2 and 3, comment on the actions you believe have been most effective historically in ending oppression for the marginalized. Least effective?

3. What separates charity work from activism?

4. Referring to your scores at the end of the chapter, what actions are you most likely to take for social justice? Least likely? Why?

5. When should personal barriers stop a person from pursuing activist work?

Further Reading/Viewing

Blum, J., Lee, S., Mansfield, R., McKittrick, S., Peele, J., & Redick, S. (Producers). Lee, S. (Director). (2018). *BlacKkKlansman* [Motion picture]. New York, NY: 40 Acres & A Mule Filmworks.

Cullen, D. (2019). *Parkland: Birth of a movement.* New York, NY: Harper Collins.

Hosseini, K. (2003). *The kite runner.* New York, NY: Riverhead Books.

Hosseini, K. (2008). *A thousand splendid suns.* New York, NY: Riverhead Books.

Jobin-Leeds, G., & AgitArte. (2016). *When we fight we win!: Twenty-first-century social movements and the activists that are transforming the world.* New York, NY: The New Press.

Kahn, S. (2010). *Creative community organizing: A guide for rabble-rousers, activists, and quiet lovers of justice.* San Francisco, CA: Berrett-Koehler.

Kilk, J., Lee, S., & Ross, M. (Producers). Lee, S. (Director). (1989). *Do the right thing* [Motion picture]. New York, NY: 40 Acres & a Mule Filmworks.

Lipschutz, M., & Rosenblatt, R. (Producers). Lipschutz, M., & Rosenblatt, R. (Directors). (2005). *The education of Shelby Knox.* New York, NY: Incite Pictures.

McKenna, E., & Han, H. (2014). *Groundbreakers: How Obama's 2.2 million volunteers transformed campaigning in America.* New York, NY: Oxford University Press.

Mckesson, D. (2018). *On the other side of freedom: The case for hope.* New York, NY: Viking.

Sanford, A. A. (2018). Classroom ideas for promoting social justice: Encouraging student activism in intercultural and gender communication courses. *Journal of Communication Pedagogy, 1*(1).

Shaw, R. (2013). *The activist's handbook: Winning social change in the 21st century* (2nd ed.). Berkeley, CA: University of California Press.

Wagner, S. R. (Ed.). (2019). *The women's suffrage movement.* London, England: Penguin Classics.

Wiesel, E. (2006). *Night.* New York, NY: Hill and Wang.

Figure Credits

Student protesters at the University of Missouri react to the news of the resignation of the university president.

CHAPTER 7

Convincing Others

Considerations for Dialogue[1]

*When someone is cruel or acts like a bully, you don't stoop to
their level. ... When they go low, we go high.*

—Michelle Obama, speech at the Democratic
National Convention, July 2016

A COMMON BARRIER FOR would-be activists is fear of a verbal confrontation with a person with whom they disagree. Whether the naysayer
is a familiar person or a stranger, it is natural to envision situations in which
a speaker will be caught off guard, freeze and forget what they wanted to
say, be verbally outmatched, and/or have to deal with someone who is angry.
Brené Brown, a social work professor who has received national attention
for her research regarding vulnerability and shame, believes most people in
the United States have sorted themselves into friend groups that are **homogeneous**. In other words, we choose to be with people who look most like
us, share the same political and religious values, and enjoy the same hobbies.

One would assume that people who share so many likenesses would have
no trouble engaging in **dialogue**, even on tough issues such as religion or
politics. Surprisingly, that is not what Brown found in her research. Instead,
she observed that even amongst homogenous friend groups, there is fear of
disagreement. Therefore, people hold back on tough conversations and bite
their tongues when they see injustice, and that lack of dialogue is a problem.
Without critical dialogue, critical consciousness-raising cannot occur. Without consciousness-raising, there will be no societal or systemic corrections

---

1   Segments of this chapter were previously published in Sanford, A. A. (Spring
2018). Confrontation and avoidance: Alternatives to civil discourse. *Dean and Provost,*
19(8), 4–5.

of injustices. In other words, social justice will stall if we choose not to talk to one another about our differences.

Dialogue, when done well, allows for focused conversations and has the goals of increased understanding, addressing problems, and questioning thoughts and actions. Activist actions (e.g., letter writing, petitioning, marching) can be avoided or halted if people on all sides of an issue are willing to engage in dialogue and find solutions. There are many examples throughout this book of when dialogue failed. Repeatedly within labor movements, workers made their demands known to management before and during strikes. Shirtmakers at the Triangle Shirtwaist Factory (see Chapter 2) lost their lives because management refused to dialogue with them. In Chapter 3, Chican@ students in Crystal City, Texas, tried to speak with their administration about their concerns and proposed solutions. The students felt dismissed and staged a walkout. Activism has consequences for people who choose to engage (read more in Chapter 10), but many of the negative consequences can be avoided if all sides will take the time to dialogue with one other.

In this chapter, we will explore multiple dialogic approaches (including avoidance), the opinion continuum, common fallacies people employ when disagreeing, conversational vulnerability, how to handle naysayers/cynics, and common power imbalances people experience when engaged in dialogue.

Approaches to Dialogue

In the fall semester of 2015, a group of student activists at the University of Missouri blocked then-University President Tim Wolfe's car during a homecoming parade. They were protesting what they believed to be his (non)response to reported incidents of racism on campus. Ten days later, students from the group Concerned Student 1950 (named for the year when Black students were initially admitted to the university) sent a list of eight demands to the president's office, including an increase in Black personnel at the university, a hand-written apology and resignation from Wolfe, and more staff for social justice centers on campus. Although Wolfe continued to engage in ongoing dialogues with the students and regularly released well-crafted statements, the students' demands were not met. In response, a **coalition** formed, and one high-profile student leader went on a hunger strike; other students boycotted university merchandise, dining services, and ticketed events; and student athletes on the football team refused to play. Nearly a month after the homecoming protest, Wolfe resigned.

In the spring of the same year, a video was released on social media showing fraternity members at the University of Oklahoma (OU) singing a racist song.

Within 24 hours, then-University President David Boren[2] told the fraternity they had 2 days to vacate their campus-owned property. He reacted quickly to insure justice. Boren did not have to be told why the song was racist or need to be otherwise convinced that the racist act was a problem. He took action and was quickly praised for it.

Two university presidents at similar universities during the same academic year took two radically different approaches to displays of racism involving their campus community. Boren took quick action; Wolfe did not, and that decision ultimately cost him his job and reputation. Boren likely engaged in dialogue with trusted advisers, but unlike Wolfe, student groups did not have try to convince Boren that **systemic** racism existed and needed to be addressed. There are many ways people can (or cannot) engage in conversations about potentially controversial topics, including avoidance, traditional **rhetoric**, invitational rhetoric, passive resistance, and confrontational rhetoric. Each of these concepts is explored below—including some further analysis regarding the dialogic approaches attempted by stakeholders at both Mizzou and OU during these high-profile events.

Avoidance

Avoidance occurs when a person does not want to approach or otherwise deal with a controversial topic. Avoiders who come from marginalized groups regularly endure **microaggressions** and not-so-microaggressions and never say a word—such as the international teaching assistant whose students constantly tell her they cannot understand her or the student of color who did not get a bid from any fraternity at his **predominantly white institution**. Quite frankly, many marginalized people are tired of explaining racism, sexism, homophobia, etc. to people who have never experienced it; therefore, they just stay silent. Additionally, many of people of color, including American Indians, Latinx, African Americans and other Black folks, Asian Americans, and Jewish Holocaust survivors and descendants, have unresolved **historical trauma** that has resulted in cumulative emotional and psychological wounding across generations. As a result, many people who identify with these cultures do not trust people who look like their oppressors and are not necessarily interested in dialoguing with them.

It is also worth noting that there are privileged folks who also avoid controversy, but they tend to practice avoidance because they selfishly benefit from the **status quo** and/or fear dissent will cost them friendships or standing in their communities. Privileged people who identify themselves as allies owe it to marginalized

---

2   David Boren retired in June 2018 after serving 23 years as president of the University of Oklahoma.

Table 7.1 **Approaches to Dialogue**

	Defined	Goals	Common Initiators/Rhetors	Critiques
Avoidance	Do not talk about controversial topics	No change; status quo; comfort; sanity	People who are privileged and benefit from the status quo; people who are marginalized and are fatigued, fearful, or traumatized	Reinforces systems of privilege and oppression
Traditional Rhetoric *Patriarchal Rhetoric; Aristotelian*	At least one of the participants believes they should persuade the other to believe like they do	Persuasion; desire to control and dominate	Privileged white, masculine communicators	Not everyone wants or needs to change; women and ethnic minorities have little access to the public sphere where these conversations occur
Invitational Rhetoric *Dialogic Civility; Compassionate Inquiry; Civil Discourse*	Telling stories and asking questions so the parties can understand each other more	Understanding; creation of relationships of equality	Feminists and other marginalized people	Doesn't account for life-threatening situations; assumes shared interest and power amongst participants; requires civility
Passive Resistance *Respectability; Sly Civility*	Racial minorities behaving in ways that are considered respectful by white majority populations	Want change as a result of good behavior; does not want confrontation	Older generations; conservatives; people of color who feel accepted by privileged folks	Shows too much deference to the oppressive majority; doesn't challenge systemic racism
Confrontational Rhetoric *Uncivil Tongue; Counterpublic; Incivility*	Assertive, in-your-face communication that requires people to deal with the issue immediately	Safety; fairness; being understood when they historically have not	People of color engaged in Black Lives Matter and related social justice movements	Rude; violent; does not subscribe to white civility standards

communities to speak up when they witness injustice, especially if the people most affected are struggling with historical trauma.

Traditional Rhetoric

Of the people who are willing to engage in dialogue about tough topics, many will converse (or debate) using the lens of traditional rhetoric, which has an end goal of persuading others to think like the **rhetor**. Traditional rhetoric dates to the fourth century B.C., when Greek philosopher Aristotle articulated the basics of the art of rhetoric, which includes three modes of persuasion: *ethos* (character of the speaker), *pathos* (emotional influence of the speaker on the audience), and *logos* (logic of the argument). Aristotle believed persuasion could occur only when one or more of these modes were utilized effectively by the speaker. Admittedly, a skilled rhetorician can use their talents for good or bad purposes (think cult leaders). The biggest obstacle with traditional rhetoric is that it often falls short of dialogue because (a) the other person in the discussion/debate is viewed as a mere spectator and (b) the goal of the rhetorician is to be *the* winner at the end of the exchange. In traditional rhetoric, winning is valued more than increased understanding.

Invitational Rhetoric (Civility)

In the 1990s, an alternative to traditional rhetoric was formally introduced to the academic community by communication scholars. The alternative was labeled "invitational rhetoric," and it is grounded in the principles of equality, immanent value, and self-determination. Participants are expected to enter a conversation with no desire to persuade or be persuaded. While the traditional Aristotelian model looked like debate, the invitational model resembled more of a conversation, with people telling stories and asking questions with the objective of understanding each other more. It is as **feminist** as the traditional model is **patriarchal**. It was meant to provide a mode of communication for women and other marginalized groups to use in their efforts to transform systems of domination and oppression. The traditional model discussed above tends to occur in places (e.g., corporate board rooms, golf courses) where women and other marginalized populations do not have the same privileged access.

Like all models of rhetoric, invitational rhetoric does have its critics. Namely, it has been critiqued for valuing civil interactions over civil rights. It does not allow enough space for conflict that can lead to **paradigmatic** shifts. Historically, civility can be viewed as a tool utilized by dominant groups to silence the marginalized. Black and Brown anger is seen as unreasonable and something that must be corrected. When people write or talk about the superiority of the civil discourse present in invitational rhetoric, their arguments often come across as patronizing to folks on the margins who have regularly been talked over, ignored, and brushed off. It hardly seems fair that the privileged get to make up the rules of "civility" for **Others** to follow.

Passive Resistance (Respectability)

Just as civility is used by white folks to police the language and actions of people of color, passive resistance (or respectability) is used by people of color, particularly people from Black communities, to police each other. This sort of Black-on-Black policing goes back more than a century to a time when Black aristocrats promoted a philosophy of "racial uplift" to prove to white people that Black people were actually human and not animals. With either civility or respectability, the end goal is the same: make sure the people in the majority are comfortable.

During the Black civil rights movement of the mid-20th century, when **John Lewis** was in his early 20s, he was on a panel with Thurgood Marshall, who made it clear that the **Freedom Rides** John Lewis and his contemporaries planned were dangerous and a waste of time. Not surprisingly, Marshall, a lawyer who would eventually become a U.S. Supreme Court justice, believed freedom should be achieved through the courts and not on the streets. Respectability popped up again during the civil rights movement when Claudette Colvin was rejected for the more wholesome Rosa Parks to be the face of the **Montgomery Bus Boycott** (see Chapter 3). Nearly a year before Parks refused to give up her seat on the bus, Colvin, 15 years old, had done the same and was also jailed. Members of the movement did not embrace Colvin as their poster child, though; she was too loud, too poor, too young, and too dark-skinned. She also became pregnant not long after her arrest, and leaders believed she would not be viewed as *respectable* by the white community.

In May 2004, **Bill Cosby**, then still a beloved comic and star of *The Cosby Show*, gave a speech in Washington, D.C., at an **NAACP**-sponsored event meant to celebrate the 50th anniversary of the *Brown v. Board of Education of Topeka* decision. In his infamous speech, Cosby scorned other Black folks for "not holding up their end of the deal." He told them to pull up their pants, give their children names that were more acceptable to white people, and clean up their use of English. Fifteen years later, in 2019, former U.S. President Barack Obama participated in a town hall in Oakland, California, where the audience was made up of young men of color. Near the end, one of the attendees asked Obama (the first Black person elected to the U.S. presidency) how he would expand upon the

Figure 7.1 Freedom Riders arrested in 1961 after a sit-in at a segregated airport restaurant in Florida.

"narrow" definition of masculinity so many in the audience had been taught. He advised them to be kind, dependable, and compassionate. Like Cosby, he also critiqued the appearance of young men of color. He did not tell them to pull up their pants, but he did advise the men in the audience to quit wearing "eight-pound" gold chains and to never **"twerk"** with multiple women.

Confrontational Rhetoric

More recently, **Millennial** activists have completely rejected respectability politics (or passive resistance) and are focused on the confrontational rhetoric put forth by #BlackLivesMatter (BLM), abolitionist Frederick Douglass, Black civil rights activist Malcolm X, politician Maxine Waters, academic Cornel West, hip-hop artist Tupac Shakur, and musician Tef Poe (who said he cannot appreciate another person's humanity if they do not acknowledge his). West, an Ivy League scholar who is well known for his cultural and political commentary, said in a *60 Minutes* interview in 2016 that he uses **hyperbolic** language to bring attention to a state of emergency. During the interview, West said, "All of that rage and righteous indignation can lead one not to speak politely sometimes."

Since the #BlackLivesMatter hashtag was first used in 2013 as a response to the killing of **Trayvon Martin** in Florida, it has been used more than 100 million times. BLM has shut down highways and taken over political rallies. They inconvenience people to force a conversation about systemic racism and to illustrate the inconvenience of being a person of color in the United States. Maxine Waters, a well-respected U.S. representative from California, said in a 2017 podcast, *Never Before with Janet Mock,* that she believed BLM disrupts "business as usual" and "a separation of the politics of getting along." Waters, 79 years old at the time of the interview, said she admired the way the BLM movement confronts systemic racism in ways that are more direct and confrontational than what was utilized during the U.S. Black civil rights movement. Waters employs confrontational rhetoric in her political work. In June 2018, she vocally supported people who had confronted political appointees of U.S. President Donald Trump (e.g., Scott Pruitt, Kirstjen Neilsen, Sarah Sanders) in restaurants. The protesters yelled at the appointees, asked them to leave restaurants, and made statements that caused the Trump supporters to feel uncomfortable. In a public appearance, Waters encouraged attendees to cause a scene anytime they encountered a Trump appointee.

People who engage in confrontational rhetoric are not interested in persuasion: they are interested in justice. They do not believe a person or an institution needs to agree with them to enforce the law or insure safety for a person of color. This concept is something David Boren at the University of Oklahoma understood very well. He was confrontational in how he dealt with the fraternity men. At the University of Missouri, the students were engaged in confrontational rhetoric while President Wolfe teetered between traditional and invitational rhetoric. The students wanted immediate action, much like what happened at OU, but they did not get it.

Karen Lee, a publicist for the late hip-hop legend Tupac Shakur, gives an example that illustrates the generational struggle with respectability politics within the Black community. Shakur, who was in his early 20s, gave a public lecture in 1992 to the Malcolm X Grassroots Movement in New York in which he used confrontational language and cursed when discussing systemic racism. An older lady in attendance privately asked him to change his language because she found it offensive; in other words, she wanted him to be respectable. Shakur replied to her that his language was not any more offensive than the world her generation had left him. Bishop T. D. Jakes, a contemporary middle-aged Black preacher with a cult-like following and prescriber of respectability, admits that he longs for the days when Black children had role models like Rosa Parks and **Medgar Evers**. He specifically was not impressed with Shakur.

Confrontation is often a starting point for Millennial social justice activists. It is the jolt to get the attention of the decision makers. If they are heard and some meaningful action is taken quickly, they may take a seat at the table and discuss the future. This shift has been modeled by BLM, whose members have recently spent less time closing down highways and more time partnering with lawmakers and attorneys to move their agenda forward. But if people are ignored or placated with never-ending conversations, excuses, and futile actions, then chances are that confrontational activists will continue to disrupt.

Opinion Continuum

Undoubtedly, you have had—and will continue to have—many opportunities to interact with people regarding your thoughts on controversial issues. Potential conversational partners include family members, friends, mentors, colleagues, and even strangers. Some of them will share your positions on issues, but many will not. Additionally, some people will have no opinion at all on topics about which you feel a great deal of passion.

People's opinions operate on a continuum, and those opinions will fall in different places on different issues during different times in a person's life. For example, 7 years ago, Joe may have strongly disagreed with a woman's right to choose abortion, but then he learned his lifelong friend had an abortion and all the factors that went into her decision. He also saw the movie *If These Walls Could Talk* and a PBS documentary about back-alley abortions. Now he finds himself moved on the opinion continuum. Perhaps in 7 more years, he will find himself an advocate for a women's right to choose, or perhaps he will find that he strongly disagrees again. His position will all depend on his life experiences, including the books he reads, the television shows he watches, and the dialogues in which he engages.

Your approach to dialogue and persuasion should depend somewhat on where you believe the other person (or an audience) is on the continuum. When you encounter people who are *undecided* or *ambivalent* regarding a controversial issue, it could mean that they are (a) apathetic and do not care (and possibly benefiting from the status quo) or (b) interested and waiting to be taught. In these

Table 7.2 **Choosing the Appropriate Rhetorical Approach**

	Avoidance	Traditional	Invitational	Passive	Confrontational
Truth and truths	truths	Truth	truths	Truth	Truth
Other Rhetors' Intentions	Winning	Dialogue, fact sharing, winning	Dialogue and learning from difference	Winning	Winning
Preferred Setting	NA	Face to face	Face to face	Mediated	Public space
Other's Opinion Continuum	Strongly disagree	Undecided/Ambivalent	Undecided/Ambivalent	Strongly disagree	Strongly disagree
Nonverbal Communication	Submissive	Masculine, confident, alpha	Open, interested in the other person	Submissive	Masculine, confident, alpha
Vulnerability	Would rather not	Would rather not	Invites it	Lives it every day	Lives it every day
Downplay Differences	NA	Maybe	Yes	Yes	No
Verbal Communication	NA	Uses "you" language; may get loud	Uses "I" language	Uses "I" language	Uses "you" language; may get loud
Common Fallacies	Red herring	Prone to many fallacies	Emotional appeal	Bandwagon	Ad hominem
Compassion	Maybe	Maybe	Yes	Yes	No
Pacing	NA	Quick	Slow, allowing for reflection	Slow, allowing for reflection	Quick
Ending the Conversation	Constantly negotiated	Need a winner	Dialogue is ongoing	Dialogue is ongoing	Need a winner
Objective(s)	No change; status quo	Persuasion; desire for control and domination	Understanding; creation of relationships of equality	Want change because of good behavior; does not want confrontation	Safety; fairness; being understood when they historically have not

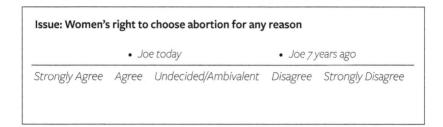

Figure 7.2 Opinion Continuum

rhetorical situations, simply share your thoughts on the controversial issue and see where the conversation goes.

When engaging with people that fall far on the *disagree* end of the continuum, it is best to take an invitational approach during the initial exchange so you can get a very clear understanding of their arguments. *Listen* to their concerns and reasons and present them with facts, avoiding the fallacies discussed later in this chapter. Mindful listening requires that you give all of your attention to your conversational partner, noticing their nonverbal communication as well as the words they share. Let the other person talk without interruption and listen simply to understand their lived experience and thoughts. Ask questions to make sure you understand their lived experiences, positions, and intent. Give the other person supportive nonverbal feedback (e.g., a head nod, leaning forward) and repeat what is said to make sure you understand their point. Hopefully they will provide the same courtesies to you during the interaction. If not, then you certainly have other dialogic choices that do not require you to play nice.

Ultimately, most people want to feel respected and to have the opportunity to share their personal experiences; however, if their discourse is harmful, it might be best to call them out (if you handle it publicly) or call them in[3] (if you handle it privately). If there is a complete lack of empathy and compassion from a conversational partner, then the conversation will likely not progress to become a meaningful dialogue. As mentioned in Chapter 1, there are people who believe in Truth (with a capital T), and they may never budge from their place on the continuum. They are guided by family narratives, laws, and religious texts that are not debatable in their minds. It is very difficult to move them on the continuum, but it is not impossible.

---

3   Recently, social justice activists have promoted calling in rather than calling out, arguing that a call-out culture is counterproductive to social justice and does not allow people to make mistakes while they grow as activists.

The Story of Derek Black

One person who beat the odds was Derek Black, a **white nationalist** (WN) who went to college, made new friends, and changed his entire worldview. The change did not come easily, though; his new friends (and his critics) worked on him for years as he went all over the opinion continuum regarding race and ethnicity. When Derek arrived in Sarasota, Florida, at the New College of Florida in 2010, it was after he had spent many years being homeschooled by his parents, including his WN father, who founded and moderated the popular **Stormfront website**, and his mother, who was the ex-wife of David Duke. In fact, Duke, the former grand wizard of the **Ku Klux Klan**, was Derek's godfather and his dad's best friend. WNs like the Black family and Duke espouse the belief that the IQ scores of white people are superior to the scores of all other races and ethnicities.

New College was everything WN was not. It was liberal and gay friendly, it embraced diversity, and the curriculum and student activities had an emphasis on social justice. Derek's parents, who lived across the state from Sarasota, did not worry about the college changing him, though: his dad confidently boasted on his WN radio show that it was more likely that Derek would recruit the other students to WN and not the other way around. Derek chose New College because it was an honors college, had good history and language programs, and ranked as the most affordable university in the state. He also knew that a degree from a mainstream university would help legitimize him to people who critiqued WN, and he planned to make a life's career as an ambassador for WN beliefs.

From the beginning of his time at New College, Derek could not help but make friends who exemplified everything his family hated. On his first day, he met Juan, an immigrant from Peru. Then he met Matthew and Rose, who were both Jewish. At the beginning of his time at New College, he lived secretly—not letting anyone know about his birthright to white nationalism. He dated Rose and eventually felt so guilty about his secret that he allowed himself to be outed. Most people in the campus community ostracized him once he was out, but Juan invited him for a beer, and Matthew invited him to weekly **Shabbat** dinner. Rose broke up with him, but he soon rebounded and began to date Matthew's roommate Alison, who eventually went undercover to WN conferences with Derek, engaged him in academic debate about the science of race, and sent him journal articles to read.

It was the result of the kindness of Matthew and Juan (who continued to love Derek but rarely discussed WN with him), the calling in from Alison, and the calling out from the greater campus community that eventually changed Matthew's mind and his future. It took 2 years, but Derek publicly rejected WN by sending a letter to the **Southern Poverty Law Center** to be printed in their newsletter. In the process, Derek lost his relationship with his family, changed his name, and went into hiding for a short period. Friends of Derek have relayed to journalists how difficult it was to maintain a relationship with him once they knew he was a WN. They were not sure they could ever change his mind, but their persistence paid off.

Fallacies

Fallacies occur when a rhetor uses faulty reasoning and unsound arguments while trying to persuade another person to believe like them. For example, the belief that people of faith do not care about marginalized people is committing the discursive fallacy of a *hasty generalization*. There are many examples of people of faith showing deep commitment and concern for people on the margins. Jay Bakker, son of televangelists **Jim Bakker** and **Tammy Faye Bakker Messner**, is a preacher and advocate for inclusive Christianity. He embraces marriage equality and LGBTQ+ communities. The Sisters of Mercy—Roman Catholic nuns who vow to alleviate suffering—advocate for women, people in poverty, the homeless, people with disabilities, all races, inmates, and immigrants. Derek Black used *hasty generalizations* when he spoke about people of color.

Another common fallacy—the *slippery slope*—is also used in arguments against social justice. It is a fallacy used to convince listeners that one "wrong" decision will lead to a bad consequence that will lead to an even worse consequence. It promotes an out-of-control domino effect. For example, people against women's suffrage (see Chapter 2) hypothesized that the vote would give women too much freedom, which would cause them to leave their families, and their children would become orphans. During the fight for the Equal Rights Amendment (see Chapter 3), opponents argued that equal rights would require all able-bodied women to be drafted into the military and the end of single-sex education, neither of which were true. Both of these arguments were employed quite effectively to stall both women's suffrage and the ERA.

Many of the activists featured in this book have endured *ad hominem* attacks. Karen Silkwood (see Chapter 5) was painted as a drug addict and bad mother when she blew the whistle on Kerr-McGee. Participants in the women's liberation movement (see Chapter 3) have been referred to as "bra burners" and "man haters" for nearly 50 years. Cecile Richards (see Chapter 5), former president of **Planned Parenthood**, has repeatedly been called a baby killer. Instead of focusing on the issues of environmentalism, equality, and a woman's right to control her body, some people would rather attack the person or people involved in advocacy about the issues.

These three common fallacies as well as five others are described below. You should avoid the use of faulty reasoning when you are engaged in dialogue and make others aware when they do it. Focus on the issues and not dialogic tricks or mind games. Keep your persuasive communication honest if you want to build credibility as a speaker and activist.

Table 7.3 **Common Fallacies Defined**

Common Fallacies	Definition	Example
Hasty Generalization	The assumption that everyone in a group is exactly alike in habits, ambitions, like, dislikes, etc.	Assuming all indigenous nations have traditional regalia that include large headdresses
False Dichotomy	Providing only two choices as if they are the only choices; an either-or proposition	If someone doesn't vote for a woman for president, then they must hate all women.
Red Herring	Distracting from the current discussion by introducing a new, unrelated topic or concern; also called a *non sequitur*	During a discussion about wind turbines, a past heated discussion about fracking is brought up.
Slippery Slope	Arguing that a decision will lead to a bad decision that will lead to an even worse decision, and so on	Gun control will lead to all guns being banned by the government.
Straw Person	Setting up a weak version of an argument from the opposition and knocking it down	When arguing for the legalization of marijuana, the topic of marijuana being a gateway drug is brought up and quickly debunked.
Ad Hominem	Attacking a person instead of their ideas or positions	Discussing a politician's personal life rather than their policies or professional achievements
Bandwagon	Asking someone to join a movement or believe in an idea because everybody else is doing it	Retweeting a cause (without any research) because it is endorsed by a celebrity
Emotional Appeal	Trying to get someone to pity or feel sorry for another person and/or situation	Pretending to tear up when discussing alternatives to fossil fuel

Vulnerability and Cynicism

For many people with newfound social justice orientations, the mere thought of a conversation about women's rights, gun control, or marriage equality with the family **patriarch** at the Thanksgiving table makes their hearts beat faster and their palms sweat. You can always use the avoidance strategy, but if a controversial topic comes up, your silence may be mistaken as an endorsement of a position you do not like. On the other hand, engaging in the conversation could result in confrontation you do not want at a family gathering, not having answers, or feeling embarrassed. Brené Brown, who was mentioned at the beginning of this chapter, believes people must be *vulnerable* (which involves uncertainty, risk, and emotional exposure) to engage in invitational dialogue—the dialogic approach most people will employ at a family meal.

Admittedly, some people are in a constant state of vulnerability because of their marginalized status, but sharing an unpopular opinion, no matter a person's demographics, can make an otherwise privileged person vulnerable. Brown refers to this vulnerability as "the wilderness"—a place where a person may have to stand alone. What if you disappoint Grandpa because you believe your best friend should be able to marry her same-sex partner? How will he react if *you* want to marry a same-sex partner? How will your cousin react? There is *uncertainty* about how Grandpa and your cousin will react to your social justice orientation. Before achieving a raised consciousness, you may have always gotten along with the beloved family patriarch and the cousin who shared a playpen with you, but you have also never expressed an opinion different from theirs. There is also the *risk* of how welcome you will feel at the next family dinner. There is a great deal of *emotional exposure* involved when sharing an opinion for the first time. Will people question your morality or perhaps your salvation, if you belong to a religious family?

In an ideal situation, vulnerability requires boundaries, trust, and mutual sharing (not oversharing) with people who have earned it. This type of environment may not adequately reflect your family's Thanksgiving table. Perhaps there is no safe place for you to be vulnerable because nobody else is willing to be vulnerable with you. People who are not willing to be vulnerable have a need for the uncertain to be certain; they operate from the very ends of the opinion continuum and are nearly impossible to persuade. They tend to have the attitude of "I'm right, you're wrong. Shut up." They also tend to be extremists and *cynical* about other people's experiences and opinions. Unfortunately, many people's automatic response to an opinion that is different from their own is to be cynical. They may put the idea down verbally or nonverbally and belittle the person expressing the idea. They do not want to do the hard work of seeking answers with others to complex communicative problems. People from all over the political spectrum are guilty of cynicism. Even progressives can be so righteous in their concerns about social injustice that they trample over others with different views. When we are convinced we have gotten somebody figured out, we tend to shut down and stop listening.

Cynics will yell from the sidelines, be quick-witted, and belittle people with differing opinions. These are people who prefer traditional rhetoric over an invitational approach. They do not like to collaborate with others because their solutions are the only ones that make sense to them. They may have valid points, but nobody listens to them. They tend to highlight differences, which just leads to isolation. If you find yourself in a relationship with a family member who is a cynic, you may find yourself having to make some rhetorical (and perhaps life) decisions. Should you avoid the conversations altogether to maintain the relationship (and your emotional well-being), even though that person may not have anyone else in their life to offer an alternative truth? Should you play nice and engage in an invitational approach to just try and understand each other, even though you take the risk of the other person flipping the script and turning it into a winner-takes-all conversation? Should you just take charge and try traditional or confrontational rhetoric, even though it may cost you the relationship? Is the other person just too toxic to be in your life and it is just time to cut them loose?

....

Sawubona (Saw – ah – bōn – uh)

The Zulu people of South Africa employ the greeting "Sawubona" ("We see you"), which can be used as an invitation for vulnerable dialogue and exploration of why the dialogic partners are on the earth at the same time. The ultimate question for each person is "How do I have to be as a human being for the other person to be free?" The "we" in the statement incorporates not only the people present but also their ancestors and the divinities; the word "see" establishes commitment to an intense presence in the moment. The other person or persons must acknowledge the greeting with "Yabo sawubona" ("I see you seeing me") to engage in the discourse.

....

Power Imbalances, Culture, and Competence

Outside of family and close friends, there are many instances in which conversational partnerships may feel out of balance because of perceived or real power differences. The potential conversational partner may be your teacher, work supervisor, religious counselor, or medical doctor. It may feel like that other person can control many things that matter, including grades, employment, eternal salvation, finances, or health. Involving these people in a dialogic situation can feel risky and leave you vulnerable. This power differential has the potential to impede or delay constructive dialogue. It can be particularly tricky when that other person asks you to engage in controversial conversations, which is very likely when considering the teacher-student relationship.

In these conversations, it is probably best to commit to keeping the conversation going. This commitment is invitational, requiring an open mind, asking questions, listening, and showing respect to conversational partners. However, if it appears the person is abusing their power, again, some important rhetorical and life decisions will have to be made. In these situations, it is important to calm yourself by focusing on your breathing and taking three to five deep intentional breaths. Try to place yourself on the sidelines and take a look at the discussion. Then you have to make the decision to reengage, change your approach, or leave the conversation—at least for the time being.

On the other hand, perhaps you are the person with the real or perceived power. If so, come to the conversation with the intent to learn from the other participant. The perspectives articulated during the dialogue should not affect the person's grade, salary, promotions, or anything else controlled by you. If a person is punished for honestly expressing an opinion, they are likely to withdraw from future conversations and/or not be honest about their positions. Neither of these responses will enrich dialogue.

As a person committed to equality and social justice, it is important to be considerate of other people's cultures and lived experiences when engaging in dialogue. For example, a conversational partner may have been raised in a culture in which **collectivism** is valued, and it would be considered a sign of bad character for that person to deviate from what is collectively believed. In these instances, group harmony is valued more than anyone's need to share a contrary personal opinion. It is often difficult for people raised in the United States, who are taught to assert their individual opinions, to empathize with people who were raised to put the collective before individual needs. It is imperative to recognize when this is occurring, to discuss it when appropriate, and not to devalue the other person's cultural experiences. Another intercultural challenge is the use of cynicism. In some cultures, people will exercise what appears to be cynicism about the Other until that person proves trustworthy. In some places, such as the Middle East, trust is earned through a third party, and one must remain cynical until that trust is earned.

People's perception of their competence has been studied by social psychologists David Dunning and Justin Kruger. The researchers found that people with the lowest levels of competence dramatically overrated their abilities. This phenomenon is referred to as the Dunning-Kruger effect, and it was first experimentally observed in 1999 at Cornell University. On the flip side, the most competent people tended to underrate their abilities. When shown proof of competence, the underraters could adjust to be more realistic about their abilities. When shown their lack of competence, the overraters would not adjust; they continued to believe they were more knowledgeable and competent than they were. Kruger and Dunning believed the latter simply lacked the competence to realize how incompetent they really were. You may face this situation when dialoguing with someone. No matter how much you reason with them or provide evidence, it will not matter if that person is overrating their competence.

It is important to be aware of common challenges when attempting to create meaningful dialogue. At times, we will experience a power imbalance with our conversational partner, who may be a boss, a teacher, or a student. When this occurs, we should commit to listening and understanding each other's positions. The subordinates in these relationships should never be punished for expressing honest opinions or concerns. Intercultural differences must also be considered, as it is important to understand the lived experiences of our dialogic partners. This commitment may require some research outside of the dialogic exchange. Finally, it is important to understand that not everybody is aware of their competence levels. Engaging with somebody who does not recognize their level of competence can be frustrating. Try to remain engaged and patient, realizing that you may not ever notice a remarkable change in the other person's approach to the world.

Review

It is expected that you will be nervous about talking with potential conversational partners who may not share your social justice orientation, especially when you initially begin to articulate your thoughts and positions. There are many choices when it comes to dialogue, though. You can choose to stay quiet, particularly if you are a member of a marginalized community who is experiencing fatigue. You could also speak up and engage in traditional rhetoric—which often becomes a give-and-take debate about a Truth in which there should be a winner in the end—or take up invitational rhetoric (also called civil discourse), which allows for storytelling about each person's truth(s) with no "winner." There is also passive resistance—where a person in the minority does what they can to please the people in power—and the opposite response of confrontational rhetoric, where it is more about demanding justice that is due and very little about dialogue.

Whatever approach you take, you need to understand the roles of the opinion continuum and fallacies in persuasion and have a willingness to be vulnerable if you expect others to do the same. Both cynicism and power imbalances will cause you to make both rhetorical and life choices, which may include removing toxic people from your life and/or embracing new cultural approaches (such as those of the Zulu people) in your communicative approaches.

Discussion Starters

1. Examine other rhetorical approaches that could have been used by the students at the University of Missouri and discuss why they should or should not have used alternative methods.

2. Describe some examples of confrontational rhetoric from Chapters 2 and 3 of this book.

3. Why do you think so many would-be activists are fearful of dialoguing with people who disagree with them?

4. What is your biggest fear when it comes to talking with others about your causes?

5. What are some common fallacies you have heard people use?

6. Can you think of examples from current events regarding the rhetorical approaches described in this chapter? Of your examples, which approach was most effective at forwarding their cause?

Further Reading/Viewing

Baily, F., & Barbato, R. (Directors). Baily, F., & Barbato, R. (Producers). (2000). *The Eyes of Tammy Faye* [Motion picture]. Santa Monica, CA: Lions Gate Films.
Bakker, J. (2012). *Fall to grace*. New York, NY: Jericho Books.

Brave Heart, M. Y. (1996). The return to the sacred path: Healing the historical trauma and historical unresolved grief response among the Lakota through a psychoeducational group intervention. *Smith College Studies in Social Work, 68*(3), 287–305. doi:10.1080/00377319809517532

Brown, B. (2017). *Braving the wilderness: The quest for true belonging and the courage to stand alone.* New York, NY: Random House.

Brown, B. (2012). *Daring greatly: How the courage to be vulnerable transforms the way we live, love, parent, and lead.* New York, NY: Gotham.

Cooper, B. (2018). *Eloquent rage: A Black feminist discovers her superpower.* New York, NY: St. Martin's Press.

Dyson, M. E. (2005). *Is Bill Cosby right? (Or has the Black middle class lost its mind?).* New York, NY: Basic Civitas Books.

Foss, S. K., & Griffin, C. L. (1995). Beyond persuasion: A proposal for an invitational rhetoric. *Communication Monographs, 62,* 2–18.

Hoose, P. (2009). *Claudette Colvin: Twice toward justice.* New York, NY: Squarefish.

Keating, A. (2007). *Teaching transformation: Transcultural classroom dialogues.* New York, NY: Palgrave Macmillan.

Lewis, J. (1998). *Walking with the wind: A memoir of the movement.* New York, NY: Simon & Schuster.

Patrick, A. (Producer). (2016, March 20). *60 Minutes* [Television broadcast]. New York, NY: CBS News.

Sanford, A. A. (2014). Feminist students' perceived barriers to feminist activism in the heartland. *Iowa Journal of Communication, 46,* 204–224.

Saslow, E. (2018). *Rising out of hatred: The awakening of a former white nationalist.* New York, NY: Penguin Random House.

Taylor, R. T. (2018). *The body is not an apology: The power of radical self-love.* Oakland, CA: Berrett-Koehler Publishers, Inc.

FIGURE CREDITS

Wilma Mankiller and Charlie Soap celebrating Mankiller's election as the first female chief of the Cherokee Nation.

CHAPTER 8

Leadership Committed to Social Justice[1]

M ANY MOVEMENTS ARE immediately associated with a person or persons, some of whom have been profiled in this book: women's liberation— Gloria Steinem and Betty Friedan; LGBTQ+ rights—Harvey Milk; labor—Lewis Hine and Mother Mary Jones (who famously said "Don't mourn, organize"); Black civil rights—Rev. Dr. Martin Luther King, Jr., and John Lewis; the American Indian Movement—Dennis Banks (Ojibwa) and Russell Means (Oglala/ Lakota); and Mexican American civil rights—Hector P. Garcia and Dolores Huerta. Although each person had a different story, they all had something in common: they organized out of a sense of hopelessness and responsibility. They were not bound or influenced by what others thought, even when naysayers argued that things would never change.

Social movements cannot happen without leadership, whether it comes from one individual or a group of individuals. Besides the leaders mentioned above, there were other leaders—**transformational leaders—**who were instrumental to their causes. One such leader was Bayard Rustin, the principal organizer of the 1963 **March on Washington for Jobs and Freedom** and a key adviser to MLK regarding nonviolence. In the late 1940s, Bayard took part in the Journey of Reconciliation in the Upper South—the event the Freedom Riders would use as inspiration for their bus rides in the Deep South years later. Bayard was considered one of the best organizers and motivators of any civil rights movement and was awarded the **Presidential Medal of Freedom** posthumously in 2013. Bayard has been described as fearless, poised, the life of the party, committed to justice, and willing to put his life on the line for other people. He did not shy away from the more radical elements of the U.S.

---

1   Segments of this chapter were previously published in Sanford, A. A. (Summer 2016). Five suggestions for leaders committed to equality. *The Department Chair, 27*(1), 8–11.

Black civil rights movement; in fact, Bayard publicly debated both **Malcolm X** and **Stokely Carmichael**.

Like Bayard, Bella Abzug was also a fearless organizer. She was instrumental in planning and executing the **National Women's Conference** of 1977 and the 56 state and territory meetings that led up to it. Bella, who always wore a wide-brimmed hat, was one of three female lawmakers who secured funding for the conference and meetings. She also acted as emcee for the national conference and was the mastermind who suggested organizers address the antifeminist protestors by having a *harmless* Girl Scout color guard and First Ladies Lady Bird Johnson, Betty Ford, and Rosalynn Carter kick off the event. It was thought that no one but Bella could handle a crowd that large from the podium. Her fellow feminists have described her as brash but warm, kind, funny, and politically savvy.

In the early 1980s, Wilma Mankiller (Cherokee) led a group of mostly Cherokee people in Bell, a community of just a few hundred people in rural Northeast Oklahoma, to dig a 16-mile water line. Up to that time, about a quarter of the residents lacked indoor plumbing and were left hauling water for daily household use. Mankiller, an employee of the **Cherokee Nation**, wrote grant proposals that resulted in the community receiving a million dollars in private and federal money. Since Wilma had recently returned from California to Oklahoma, she asked another Cherokee Nation employee, Charlie Soap (Cherokee), to join her in visiting Bell residents at their homes and encouraging them to get involved in the project. Wilma has been described as genuine, strong, complex, a go-getter, and a world peace leader. Through her leadership, the community people of Bell experienced *Gadugi*—a Cherokee concept that means "working together to solve a problem." Wilma, who passed away in 2010, became the first modern-day female chief of the Cherokee Nation in 1985, married Soap in 1986, and won the Presidential Medal of Freedom in 1998. She counted legendary feminist Gloria Steinem (see Chapters 3 and 5) and author **Alice Walker** amongst her closest friends.

....

The Pew Research Center (2014) has found that the following characteristics are consistently at the top of people's must-have lists when it comes to leaders they want to follow: honest, intelligent, hardworking, decisive, ambitious, compassionate, outgoing, innovative, and organized.

....

Bayard, Bella, and Wilma were transformational leaders committed to advocacy, equality, and social justice. They led from the middle—not from the top or the bottom of an organizational chart—and believed in the power of interpersonal relationships. They had a desire to work side by side with others and not to simply give directives. Jim Sinegal, co-founder of Costco, is another person who prefers to lead from the middle. In fact, he hardly grants interviews because he does not want to encourage "the CEO as superhero" myth. He has appeared on many lists of most-liked leaders and has received other similar accolades; Costco, which employs more than 200,000 people, has also appeared on the top of lists of best places to work. Leaders like Bayard, Bella, Wilma, and Jim welcome diverse viewpoints and a collective approach to problem solving. They do not believe a person's life can be compartmentalized into work and home; instead, they will express empathy should one of their team members go through a rough time. This type of leadership can be quite effective for leaders engaged in social justice work.

In 1939, Kurt Lewin and colleagues studied decision-making and identified three different styles of leadership: autocratic, democratic, and laissez-faire.

Autocratic—the leader makes decisions without consulting with others.
Democratic—the leader involves people in the decision-making, although the process for the final decision may vary from the leader having the final say to their facilitating consensus in the group.
Laissez-faire—minimizes the leader's involvement in decision-making and allows people to make their own decisions.

In this chapter, we will consider five characteristics of effective social justice leaders and two common challenges faced by these leaders.

Characteristics of Effective Leaders

Social movements need advocate leaders who are committed to having tough conversations, embracing people holistically, empathizing with conditions of the oppressed, valuing people's experiences and contributions, and advancing social causes. A leader who is committed to social justice should embody five characteristics: (a) good communication skills, (b) the desire to call out injustices, (c) a willingness to be vulnerable, (d) the ability to see people as individuals and share power with them, and (e) a need to be involved in the communities in which they live. It is important to remember that leadership is not a title: it is about influence. Perhaps you do not strive to *lead* a movement, but you should certainly strive to work *with* (not *for*) great leaders and to recognize good leadership when you see it.

Good Communication Skills

Fifty years ago, Saul Alinsky, a Chicago-based activist and the subject of Hillary Clinton's senior thesis at Wellesley College in 1969, wrote *Rules for Radicals*, one of the first books for community organizers. In the book, he wrote that the single most important attribute of a leader is the ability to communicate well. Because of the importance and centrality of this leadership skill, communication will be given the most space in the following pages. The following communication tips are expanded upon in the next few pages: value everyone, be wholly present, listen more than you talk, show gratitude, seek feedback, and be a person of your word.

A leader committed to equality views everyone equally—no matter their influence, income, or position in life. When these leaders receive messages via email or voicemail, they do not triage to answer just the most important people, selfishly leaving others to contact them two or three times before receiving a response. An effective, communicative leader will answer all messages and requests in a timely manner (taking a few business days at most); this simple act makes people feel valued. When a sender's email or phone message goes unanswered, it says to them that the receiver thinks their time is more valuable than the sender's time. Granted, a busy political leader may not personally be able to answer a message within a week, but there should be some form of communication to the sender that the message was received. A leader committed to equality does not believe their time is more valuable than anybody else's time, and they certainly do not want to communicate a self-centered persona.

Good communicators are also wholly present when conversing with someone, giving all their attention to the person in front of them. When meeting in their office, an attentive leader limits distractions by turning off their computer monitor, silencing their phones, and/or moving from their desk to a different area of the room. At cocktail parties or receptions, an effective leader does not look over the other person's shoulder, seemingly searching for someone more important. Instead, they work the room, spending a few undivided minutes with as many people as possible. They make eye contact and do far more listening than talking. Erin Brockovich, an environmental activist discussed in Chapter 5, was able to collect the stories of the people of Hinkley, California, because she invested time in them, their families, and their stories. In turn, they trusted her.

Before commenting in a conversation, it is important for a person to decide whether the thought they are holding will contribute to and advance the dialogue. If it will, the person should make the contribution after the other person takes a pause in the conversation, being cautious not to interrupt. If the contribution will not advance the dialogue, the person should continue to listen or ask the other person a question about what they just said. Most people respond well to being asked questions because it communicates that the conversational partner is interested in the speaker's life experiences and opinions. "Leaders" are not just good talkers: they are also good listeners. There is a well-known old teaching attributed to Greek philosopher **Epictetus** about humans having two ears and one mouth because we all should do twice as much listening as talking.

A leader committed to social justice and equality communicates gratitude to the people around them. DeRay Mckesson, a former organizer in **Ferguson**, Missouri, and host of *Pod Save the People*, believes relationships are the *only* constant in organizing (read more about DeRay and his journey in Chapter 6). Activism is often an exhausting, thankless endeavor, and a simple "thank you" may reignite someone's spark. When people feel their work is noticed and makes a difference, they will likely become even more committed to the cause and willing to take on new challenges. There are many ways to show gratitude: (a) keep a stack of thank-you cards and commit to sending one weekly; (b) take someone to lunch or out to coffee; (c) pat someone on the back while they are making a protest sign and let them know the movement needs them; (d) give a thank-you from the stage; (e) mention a great contributor in a newsletter; or (f) have a celebratory party after a victory. These suggestions will not work for everybody. For example, some people do not like to be physically touched, even if it is a pat on the back. Additionally, some people would prefer a private thank-you rather than being called out from a stage or having their name in a newsletter. No matter how an expression of gratitude is accomplished, people need to feel appreciated for the sacrifices they make for a cause or a movement.

A leader committed to social justice seeks and accepts critiques from the people they serve. They periodically check in with trusted mentors and advisers to ask for feedback on their leadership and effectiveness. They take the critiques seriously without becoming defensive, and they constantly reflect on their leadership and how their decisions affect the cause and the people around them. As a leader, it is important to surround oneself with talented, intelligent people. In the **Old Testament**, there is a proverb that reads "As iron sharpens iron, so one person sharpens another." There is no doubt that the pairs mentioned at the beginning of this chapter were examples of iron sharpening iron. Bayard Rustin and Martin Luther King, Bella Abzug and Gloria Steinem, and Wilma Mankiller and Charlie Soap respected each other and sought counsel from one another. It is important to seek feedback from the people you lead, whether with a formal survey, an anonymous comment box, a feedback session, or a casual conversation. Jim Sinegal meets with Costco stockholders regularly, and he and his co-founder take questions from the floor until the stakeholders have nothing left to ask. People need to know that they are heard and that necessary corrections (if needed) will be made.

Finally, a good communicator is a person of their word. If they commit to do something, be somewhere, or get back to somebody, they do it. It was very important for Wilma Mankiller to keep her word to the people of Bell. Initially, she was a stranger to the community, having been relocated by the federal government from Oklahoma to California with her family when she was a young child. When she returned to Northeast Oklahoma as an adult, she was seen as an outsider; worse yet, she was viewed as a bureaucrat because she worked for the Cherokee Nation. The people of Bell had been burned by bureaucrats before, and it was only through Wilma's and Charlie Soap's persistence that the two of them were able to win over the people of Bell and get the much-needed waterline built.

Call Out (or Call In) Injustices

Howard Schultz, Starbucks founder and CEO, believes in acting through a lens of social consciousness. In 2001, Starbucks experienced great economic success, with an ever-increasing profit margin; however, economic profits alone did not equal success to Howard. He became concerned with conservation and fair prices for coffee growers and announced to his board that he had committed the company to purchasing fair trade certified coffee, which came with an increased cost for Starbucks. This temporary decrease in profitability was fine with Howard, who declared that he did not want to sacrifice humanity for profitability.

Second only to communication skills for a social justice leader is the ability to call out—or, alternatively, call in—injustices, even when their group, company, or organization is profitable or successful doing business the oppressive way. Promoting an ethical environment is paramount to effective leadership. "Calling out" (if it occurs publicly) or "calling in" (if it occurs privately) can happen face to face in meetings or other conversations, on social media, in newspapers, with protests, etc. A culture of "calling" is best established when there is a diverse team with diverse opinions and tough conversations are expected and embraced.

To organize for advocacy and give voice to all injustices, leaders must bring together groups of people who are diverse. This diversity is particularly important if a leader embodies privilege (like Howard Schultz)—whether it is based on race, sex, class, ability status, etc. or the intersections of these attributes. When Mayor Mitch Landrieu (see Chapter 5) of New Orleans, a man with many privileges, decided to bring down Confederate statues in his city, he sought the advice and approval of many people from diverse backgrounds, including childhood friends, a former mayor, current city leaders who had supported him in the past, local ministers, a tricentennial committee, and the city council. In order for injustices to be brought forward, people need spaces where they can be honest and vulnerable to share unpopular opinions and personal narratives. Mitch worked to create that environment. After all, no one wants to be met with an eye roll or be verbally dismissed when sharing stories of discrimination and concern.

Tough conversations should be moderated and shifted to maximize participation amongst the participants. If members of a group are consistently in agreement with each other on potential actions or solutions to the injustice, then they have probably fallen into the trap of **groupthink**—where everybody thinks alike and either consciously or subconsciously agrees to avoid intragroup conflict (see Chapter 9 for more information about groupthink). **Homogeny** is not good for groups, as it does not promote creativity or vulnerability, nor does it allow ideas to mature (through debate and collaboration) to a place where people are ready to take action. When groupthink regularly occurs, it is a sure sign that the group needs new members or, at the very least, the group needs to read about and discuss points of view different from their own. This concept was demonstrated by Bayard Rustin, who publicly debated men who did not subscribe to nonviolent approaches like he did. These debates were intellectual exercises that allowed Bayard to carefully consider the opinions of people with whom he ideologically disagreed.

Willingness to Be Vulnerable

As discussed in Chapter 7, vulnerability is emotional exposure, and it looks different to different people. To a person with a more relational leadership style, a feeling of vulnerability can occur when disagreeing with another person or sharing an unpopular opinion with a group. Those actions can leave a person open for disagreement and conflict, two scary propositions for leaders who depend upon relationship building for their effectiveness. On the other hand, some leaders will feel the most vulnerable when admitting they are wrong or when sharing personal narratives in which they are not heroes. These leaders do not want to be viewed as weak and without answers.

For a person like Bella Abzug, who was already an established politician, moderating a large, controversial national convention had to make her feel vulnerable. In fact, some people believe her involvement cost her a political future, as she never won another political election after 1976. Besides Bella, many other people mentioned throughout this book made themselves vulnerable. Lilly Ledbetter (see Chapter 5) was near the end of her career when she took on Goodyear regarding pay equality. In turn, she was painted as greedy and a whiner. Both Janet Mock and

Jazz Jennings (see Chapter 5 for both of their stories), separated by a generation, have publicly shared their journeys to becoming trans women. Jazz, whose family disguised their real names when they participated in their first television interview, went as far as to share her gender reconstruction surgery on her reality television show in 2019. Henry Louis Gates, Jr. (see Chapter 6) is a well-known public intellectual who was nearly arrested for breaking into his own home in what appeared to be a case of racial profiling. Henry made himself vulnerable by extending an invitation for dialogue to the officer who detained him.

Vulnerability, no matter how uncomfortable, is necessary for effective social justice leadership because it allows for conversations to move forward and ideologies to evolve. When deliberating or problem solving with a group, participants need to be introspective regarding personal biases and truths. It is important to speak up, admit mistakes, share fears and concerns, and be willing to change a previously held position. Derek Black's willingness to publicly change his mind about **white nationalism** (see Chapter 7) left him feeling vulnerable and emotionally exposed. In fact, he fought going public for quite a while after telling his friends that he no longer prescribed to WN. His girlfriend, Alison, convinced him that going public was necessary to keep the conversation going. Alison understood that dialogue could not progress without some give and take. In short, when there is less certainty and some ambiguity, there is more to consider and discuss. Progress towards social justice requires vulnerability.

Share Power

It is not necessary or healthy for the same leaders to constantly set agendas and lead conversations for a group. Agenda setting and discussion moderation are tasks that can be easily shared. After all, leaders committed to equality naturally believe that every person has value and should be appreciated for their lived experience, truths, and abilities. They can put this belief into practice by sharing power and practicing humility. Two social justice leaders have done a great job modeling this behavior. LaDonna Brave Bull Allard (Lakota/Dakota) was very active in the fight against the building of the Keystone Pipeline on her ancestral land (see Chapter 5), but whenever she appeared in interviews, she was quick to give credit to the "young people" and to talk about how much they had taught her. President Barack Obama always shared credit for his political success with his campaign staff and volunteers (see Chapter 6). Both LaDonna and President Obama understand the importance of the collective in leadership success.

Two social justice leaders mentioned in this book who were not always successful at sharing power were William Lloyd Garrison (see Chapter 2) and Betty

Figure 8.1 Bayard Rustin, principal organizer for the March on Washington for Jobs and Freedom, goes over plans for the event.

Friedan (Chapter 3). William, a journalist and abolitionist who was white, often felt he knew what was best for other abolitionists. When he told fellow white abolitionists to stop voting because it showed support for the government, he lost members of the anti-slavery society he had founded. His dogged commitment to nonviolence cost him his friendship with freed slave Frederick Douglass. More than 100 years later, Betty Friedan was a leader in the U.S. women's liberation movement and co-founded the **National Organization for Women** (NOW) in 1966. Betty's focus on white, middle-class, **cisgendered**, heterosexual women was a complete turnoff to many feminists, who wanted race and sexuality as components of the feminist platform. Betty's inflexibility cost NOW many members as well as the support of co-founder Pauli Murray.

Outside of the group setting, another good space for the practice of shared power is in the relationships of mentor/protégé, teacher/learner, and leader/follower. These pairings should always be in flux. Relationships are most rewarding when they are synergetic and both participants give and take. Helen Rettig, who wrote a book to encourage and mentor experienced activists, was quick to point out that finding the right mentor can take years—maybe even decades—off the time it takes an activist to succeed. Sharing power is particularly important in mentoring relationships such as that of MLK and Bayard Rustin.[2] MLK, who was 17 years younger than Rustin, valued Rustin's experiences with nonviolence. The first time MLK reached out to him was during the **Montgomery Bus Boycott** when MLK was only 26 years old. Rustin became a big brother to MLK; they respected each other's intellect. Over time, though, their relationship became one of equals, and it is very likely that Rustin even learned a few things from MLK.

How to Find a Mentor

A relationship with a more experienced activist leader can be very beneficial for a person beginning their activist journey. Look for a person you admire and witness their leadership in action as often as possible. Look for formal or informal time alone with them to ask specific prepared questions about their journey, the movement, their leadership, etc. Show them through your actions and words that you paid attention during the discussions. From these interactions, a short- or long-term mentoring relationship could develop.

Community Involvement

Finally, a leader committed to social justice should be just as concerned with finding solutions for their communities as they are about calling out problems. After all, identifying problems does not make a person an activist; finding solutions and acting are necessary. As Chapter 6 explains in greater detail, activism could include writing letters to media editors, attending public meetings and inviting other people through social media posts, presenting workshops, creating art, boycotting businesses and their products, starting social justice activist–oriented organizations, participating in marches, etc.

Solution-oriented leaders committed to social justice should display a desire to volunteer for local nonprofits and, when appropriate to their skill set, run for civic office. Mankiller and Soap were in the ditches digging a path for the water pipe. They did not simply watch from the sidelines or call in from their offices at the Cherokee Nation. They led by example. Harvey Milk (see Chapter 3) was a small business owner in San Francisco who became active in his community because he was concerned about the city policies regarding small businesses, the shortage of funds for public education, and the corruption of the **Watergate scandal**. In time,

---

2   The relationship between Rev. Dr. Martin Luther King, Jr. and Rustin Bayard was strained at times. At one point, Rustin, a gay man, was forced out of the spotlight because a politician had threatened to go to the media regarding his sexuality and the nature of his relationship with MLK.

he ran and won city office and is best known today for his activism as it related to gay and lesbian rights.

In addition to volunteerism and civic responsibilities, if leaders can afford it, they should give monetarily to local nonprofits. During the first 5 years of the new millennium, Schultz committed with Starbucks partners (a term Schultz uses for employees) to donate $47 million to local communities in which their stores were located to support literacy programs, victims of disasters, and environmental awareness. While donations are not necessarily activism, the money can provide temporary relief while activists try to get to the root of injustice, challenge system oppression, and transform social structures.

Leadership Challenges

Even the best social justice leaders face pitfalls. Two common challenges are the self-doubt that comes with the **imposter phenomenon** and taking time for self-care. The imposter phenomenon particularly affects women and people who are historically oppressed—two groups that are naturally drawn to social justice causes. Additionally, people from these historically oppressed groups tend to focus on other people's well-being and very little on themselves and the sleep, nutrition, exercise, and downtime that they need to stay healthy.

Imposter Phenomenon

In the mid-1970s, two psychology professors coined the term "imposter phenomenon" as a way to describe the feelings of doubt that women, straight out of the **women's liberation movement** and new to the college scene, felt in academic environments. The students had very few examples of female college graduate role models in popular culture and even fewer in their personal lives. Additionally, they attended elementary and junior high schools in the 1950s and 1960s, when women were scarcely mentioned in history textbooks. In short, these women had no one to emulate; they knew no one who looked like them and had shared their lived experiences. Instead, these young women were stuck blazing an uncertain trail, all while living in fear of failure and, worse yet, worried that others saw them how they often saw themselves—as frauds who could be exposed at any moment.

Today, 40 years later, women, people of color, and others who are marginalized as a result of class, ability status, sexuality, religion, etc. are still susceptible to imposter feelings, not only in higher education but also in their careers. Academics speculate that 70 percent of *all* Americans—including celebrities—experience imposter feelings at some point in their lives. Celebrities Serena Williams, Tina Fey,

Tracee Ellis Ross, Ryan Reynolds, and Jennifer Lopez have all admitted to feeling like imposters. Many people overcome the feelings after repeated successes, but others do not. These chronic sufferers do not have low self-esteem; they simply experience self-doubt when their success is contrary to what they witnessed in their surroundings growing up. They believe other people are smarter than they are, and furthermore, they do not see their success as something they have earned but rather as a result of extremely hard work or luck. They are unable to attribute their accomplishments to their talents or skills.

This inability to recognize one's own talent can lead to trouble for imposter sufferers, who are often already marginalized as a result of assigned sex, race, class, ability, etc. A leader who feels like an imposter does not have a good grasp of their worth, which can lead to lower pay, unrealistic perfectionism, poor personal relationships (because they never take a break from work), and a denial of previous success, which leads to unhealthy procrastination when given a new project.

There are many steps a person can take to overcome imposter feelings. For example, it is very important to read stories and watch movies about people who look like you and have similar life experiences. After all, we can't be what we can't see. Thanks to the success of the 2016 movie *Hidden Figures*, we all now know that Black women were vital to the Space Race 50 years ago. This depiction on film makes it easier for little girls, particular little girls of color, to better envision themselves in careers related to science, technology, engineering, and math.

Relatedly, we need to share the stories of marginalized folks and right the wrongs of history. When we tell the story of women's suffrage in the U.S., we often tell it with white women as heroes, but as you read in Chapter 2 of this book, there were Black women and men who also fought side by side with the white women. Additionally, the suffragists initially got their models for equality from their American Indian neighbors. We need to include everybody in the telling of the story.

If a person suffers from imposter feelings, it is important that they are surrounded by people (e.g., friends, colleagues, a book club) who will allow them to talk through their self-doubt. Successful women (including women of color) with low to no imposter feelings have trusted mentors and romantic partners who believed in them, encouraged them, and unselfishly celebrated their successes. Finally, it is vital that we draw our own boundaries and teach people how to treat us. Believe someone when they offer you a compliment, especially when it is related to work performance. Know your worth and negotiate for the higher pay, the better title, and the bigger office. Stop people from interrupting you in meetings or infantilizing you by calling you "young lady" or "honey" or "sport" or some other disparaging nickname in a room full of your colleagues. Reinforce good behaviors as well. When a colleague compliments you in front of the boss on an otherwise ignored idea, do the same for your colleague when the time is right. It is up to all of us to create inclusive spaces in which women, people of color, and others who have been historically marginalized feel more valued and less like imposters.

Self-Care

Another common challenge for social justice leaders is taking the time to care for themselves and the people they lead. Without self-care, activists are particularly vulnerable to burnout. One way leaders can express care for fellow activists is by acknowledging that some topics may be **triggering** and/or distressing to participants as a result of their past experiences. By having a shared understanding that allows people to remove themselves from potentially triggering discussions, a precedent for being responsible for one's self-care will be set.

Self-care comes in many forms and should be discussed and demonstrated in a holistic manner. Activists should be encouraged to take time for emotional and spiritual care, rest, eat well, pursue hobbies, and exercise. DeRay Mckesson, mentioned earlier in this chapter, warns activists not to be martyrs and to enjoy joy and beauty to refuel so there is something to pour into the work. Some self-care practices, such as meals, music, and dance, are cultural. Other self-care practices may include quiet time alone, reading, or an earlier bedtime. For some, participating in activism is part of their self-care. Self-care should not be defined as a luxury or as unnecessary. Patrisse Khan-Cullers, a co-founder of the Black Lives Matter movement, practices self-care by cooking, traveling, praying, and spending time with her family. She also makes time for fun by going to the arcade, roller skating, and having park days. Women of color scholars have long argued that practicing self-care, especially for women of color, is a radical act of activism because too often they are expected to care for everyone else while neglecting themselves. Self-care is healing, growth, and, ultimately, survival.

Acts of self-care can be particularly difficult to practice for activist leaders because they may fear admitting to themselves or their colleagues that they need some time to recharge. However, it is imperative that they do. Social justice leaders, by their nature, feel deeply about the human condition and are susceptible to feeling every hurt and defeat in their environments. Many will try to take on all the burdens of the people around them, but of course, that is not healthy. Leaders need people with whom they can confidentially discuss their leadership challenges and triumphs, whether that person is another activist, a counseling professional, or somebody else outside of the work. The pairs of activists mentioned throughout this chapter (Bayard Rustin and Martin Luther King, Bella Abzug and Gloria Steinem, and Wilma Mankiller and Charlie Soap) helped each other in this way. Additionally, writing about activist experiences—whether through private journaling, writing for another outlet, or taking on a book project—can be therapeutic, and the reflection can aid in the leadership process.

Review

In this chapter, five characteristics of effective social justice leaders were explored, including good communication skills, the desire to call out injustices, a willingness to be vulnerable, sharing power, and solution-oriented community involvement. Leaders were specifically encouraged to pay close attention to developing communication skills that are centered on inclusivity and empathy and to manage imposter feelings and practice self-care. Leaders who embrace the advice in this chapter will find that they are not alone in their leadership challenges. Effective, empathetic leaders committed to social justice are always looking for ways to grow and improve.

Discussion Starters

1. Bayard Rustin, Bella Abzug, and Wilma Mankiller are all lesser-known social justice leaders. What are your thoughts on why they are not better known? Are there other leaders you admire who have been written out of history?

2. What do you think of Martin Luther King and Bayard Rustin's relationship? Does the footnote regarding Bayard's sexuality and MLK's reaction to it make you think any differently about MLK?

3. The author shared five characteristics of effective leaders. Do you agree with the list? Would you add other characteristics?

4. Do you or anyone you know struggle with imposter feelings or lack of attention to self-care? What are your suggestions for managing these challenges? What are some other common leadership challenges for people committed to social justice that you've seen?

Further Reading/Viewing

Alinsky, S. D. (1971). *Rules for radicals: A practical primer for realistic radicals*. New York, NY: Vintage Books.

Bobo, K. A., Kendall, J., & Max, S. (2010). *Organizing for social change: A manual for activists* (4th ed.). Santa Ana, CA: The Forum Press.

Clance, P. R., & Imes, S. A. (1978). The impostor phenomenon in high achieving women: Dynamics and therapeutic intervention. *Psychotherapy: Theory, Research & Practice, 15*(3), 241–247. doi:10.1037/h0086006

Khan-Cullors, P., & bandele, a. (2018). *When they call you a terrorist: A Black Lives Matter memoir*. New York, NY: St. Martin's Press.

Levine, S. B., & Thom, M. (2007). *Bella Abzug: An oral history*. New York, NY: Farrar, Straus, and Giroux.

Mankiller, W., & Wallis, M. (1993). *Mankiller: A chief and her people*. New York, NY: St. Martin's Griffin.

Preskill, S., & Brookfield, S. D. (2009). *Learning as a way of leading: Lessons from the struggle for social justice*. San Francisco, CA: Jossey-Bass.

Rettig, H. (2006). *The lifelong activist: How to change the world without losing your way*. New York, NY: Lantern Books.

Ricketts, A. (2012). *The activists' handbook: A step-by-step guide to participatory democracy*. New York, NY: St. Martin's.

Schultz, H. (2012). *Onward: How Starbucks fought for its life without losing its soul*. New York, NY: Rodale Books.

Singer, B., & Yates, N. (Director). Singer, B., & Yates, N. (Narrator). (2003). *Brother outsider: The life of Bayard Rustin* [Motion picture]. USA: California Newsreel.

Soap, C., & Kelly, T. (Director). Heller, P. M., & Powell, L. (Executive Producers). (2013). *The Cherokee word for water* [Motion picture]. USA: Kamama Films.

Sullenberger, C. (2012). *Making a difference: Stories of vision and courage from America's leaders*. New York, NY: HarperCollins.

Young, V. (2011). *The secret thoughts of successful women: Why capable people suffer from the impostor syndrome and how to thrive in spite of it*. New York, NY: Random House.

Figure Credits

Mothers of the Movement (pictured here at the Democratic National Convention in 2016) advocate for the children they lost as a result of police force and/or other gun violence.

CHAPTER 9

Working in Groups and Building Coalitions

N OW WE TURN our attention from individual leadership discussed in Chapter 8 to the greater collective. Most social justice activists are far more comfortable working with a team than they are going it alone. In fact, people committed to social justice often prefer flexible roles for participants and rotation of leadership with no fixed leaders within their **groups**. When the civil rights legend **John Lewis** (see Chapters 3 and 7) co-founded the **Nashville Student Movement** as a college student in the late 1950s, the group chose a central committee (not a single individual) that could represent and speak for the larger group. The chair position rotated so no one person owned the title. The committee was focused on group effectiveness, not individual power. They believed "leaders" should follow the people and the people could lead themselves.

While activism can be accomplished by an individual or groups, **coalitions** have proven to be far more effective than either when it comes to social change. It is important to note the difference between a group and a coalition. Groups are individuals who come together for one common cause. You read about one such activist group in Chapter 7: Concerned Student 1950 organized against the president at the University of Missouri. Coalitions happen when groups with similar interests partner together in unity. Concerned Student 1950 became even more influential when it worked as a coalition with the football team and other student groups. There have been other great examples of successful groups and coalitions in recent years, including Free Ryan Ferguson (also in Missouri), the #metoo movement, and the unlikely partnership of Lucia "Lucy" McBath and Rev. Rob Schenck, as illustrated in the documentary *Armor of Light*.

Ryan Ferguson was wrongfully convicted of murder at 19 years old and served 10 years of a 40-year sentence before activists, led by his father and other family members, got his conviction overturned. His dad drove a Toyota wrapped with Ryan's photo across the United States while on a speaking tour. He also started a Free Ryan Ferguson Facebook page where people around the world posted photos of themselves holding "Free Ryan" signs. This is an example of a group coming together on social media in solidarity with the goal of seeing Ryan's conviction overturned.

The women of the #metoo movement were *Time* magazine's Person of the Year in 2017. The hashtag originated a decade earlier when Tarana Burke founded a nonprofit to aid survivors of sexual harassment and assault. The hashtag gained popularity in 2017 after Harvey Weinstein, a media mogul, was accused of sexual harassment and assault by many high-profile women in the entertainment business. Alyssa Milano, a Hollywood actress, asked her followers on Twitter to respond with #metoo to give people a sense of the far reach of sexual harassment and assault. There were 12 million posts and reactions to Milano's tweet within 24 hours. This example also illustrates a group effort. However, if Milano had partnered with Burke's nonprofit (like many people wanted her to do), perhaps there would have been an even more inclusive and effective coalition.

In November 2012, 17-year-old Jordan Davis sat in a gas station parking lot in his friend's Dodge Durango while the driver went inside the store. He and the two other passengers passed the time by listening to rap music. Michael David Dunn, 47 years old and in town for a wedding, pumped his gas and demanded that the young men to turn the radio down. One of the passengers complied by turning the music completely off. Jordan turned the music back on and made it clear to Michael that the radio was not going back off. Michael, who was licensed to carry a gun, pulled a gun from his glove box and emptied 10 bullets into the other vehicle—killing Jordan and wounding the driver (who had come back to the vehicle) and two other passengers. Michael fled the scene but was later captured and found guilty of one count of murder and three counts of second-degree murder.

A coalition of civil rights (Jordan and friends were ethnic minorities; Michael was white) and gun control activists protested outside the courthouse nearly every day. After the trial, Jordan's mother, Lucy McBath,[1] partnered with Rev. Rob Schenck, best known for anti-abortion activism, to fight for gun control. Theirs appeared to be an odd coalition. Rob is a leader amongst white Evangelicals, many of whom believe it is their God-given right to pack guns in their glove boxes, just

---

1   Lucy McBath was elected to the U.S. House of Representatives from Georgia's 6th district at the end of 2018 and assumed office in early 2019.

like Michael. Lucy belonged to Mothers of the Movement, a group of women whose Black children had been killed by the police or as a result of gun violence. Rob's career and reputation have certainly suffered amongst his base followers, but he—like Lucy—believes he is following the will of God. Coalitions often bring groups together that appear disparate but have a shared goal.

Tips for Effective Work Groups

The goal of any effective work group is to experience synergy—the feeling that the group accomplished a task in a way that is superior to what an individual could have accomplished alone. Often when a person has a poor group experience, it is likely that the task at hand could have been solved by one person rather than unnecessarily bringing together a group that ends up wasting everybody's time. Of course, wasted time is not the only reason groups fail. Many other characteristics contribute to the potential success of working groups, including the number of group members, establishment of group rules and norms, meeting environment, and preparation. Group success boils down to the four Cs: cohesiveness, commitment, consensus, and collaboration.

Number of Members

A working group is most efficient when it consists of the smallest number of people needed to get the job done. Most of the time, the magic number is about three to seven people. Any fewer than three people, and there will not be enough diversity of opinions and labor to get the job done. Any more than seven members, and the group can get stuck in inertia as a result of the number of people who want to be heard. Granted, most activist work involves more than seven people, but it is important that tasks or problem solving be assigned to smaller groups when work needs to be accomplished, especially if the work needs to be accomplished quickly.

Establishment of Rules and Norms

When a working group initially comes together, it is important to discuss preferences for how the group will function. Rules tend to be written down or stated, whereas norms develop informally over time. Some common questions that will be addressed through rules and norms include: Who will facilitate meetings? Will the meetings be at fixed times or rotated? Can people bring guests, including their children, to the meetings? Will there be formal votes, or will the group operate by consensus? Will the organization have a constitution and bylaws? Will **Robert's Rules of Order** be used? How long will meetings last? How often will the group meet? Will there be an agenda? Will someone need to keep minutes? How many meetings can a person miss and still be in the group? How will the group ensure everyone has an opportunity to weigh in on decisions?

Unfortunately, too many groups do not have discussions about rules and norms until problems arise. Then it is often too late, and the discussion about any problems feels personal to some members of the group. If it is important that people behave with certain expectations from the beginning, then it is best to establish rules about those topics. Otherwise, the evolvement of norms may work for the group, but there may come a time to codify or write down the norms so they are rules.

Meeting Environment

The group of three to seven people needs places to meet that are conducive to getting work accomplished. For some groups, that meeting place may be a coffee shop or restaurant. For other groups or other tasks, those environments may be too noisy or otherwise distracting. In those instances, the group may want to meet in a room at the public library or in a member's living room. Time of day is also important. Some people do not function well early in the morning or late at night. If group members function better at different times of day, it might be a good idea to vary meeting times. Also, keep in mind that some people may have a very hard time concentrating during a meeting that is more than an hour in duration.

When groups meet, it is advised to arrange seats in such a way that everyone is facing each other. It makes it easier to communicate when both verbal and nonverbal messages can be read. Some common distractions in meetings include hunger, light, noise, and temperature. As an individual, it is important to prepare for these common distractions by packing snacks and/or dressing in layers. Light and noise levels are often controlled by the meeting's host, who should be willing to make adjustments for guests' comfort because, ultimately, comfort does affect people's abilities to concentrate on the task at hand.

Preparation

To get the most out of group meetings, the individuals involved need to show up prepared, having completed the assignments they agreed to do. For example, a person may have volunteered to file a city permit for a protest. If that person fails to complete that task, then the group may have to delay an event that was already advertised. It is also important that members fully engage during group meetings. This level of engagement may require research to be conducted between meetings and/or that people attend the meeting with a willingness to be vulnerable, which may require sharing personal stories or fears with group members. A lot of attention is given to assigned or emerging leaders, but a group needs far more prepared and engaged followers than it needs formal leadership.

The Four Cs: Cohesive, Committed, Consensus, and Collaborate

Effective work groups need to be cohesive, committed to the cause, willing to operate by consensus, and able to collaborate. A *cohesive* group shares a collective sense of identity and genuine respect for members of the group. This cohesiveness does not happen quickly. For it to occur, members have to see that their cohorts are trustworthy and equally committed to the greater cause. *Commitment* is demonstrated by showing up to meetings prepared and on time. It means marching at a rally even when it is raining and boycotting a restaurant even when the marriage equality activist will really miss those Chick-Fil-A chicken nuggets and waffle fries. Commitment sends the message that a person is in it for the long haul and that the cause is a top priority in their lives.

Groups can make decisions in many ways, including by majority rule (more than half of the members agree), supermajority rule (usually requires two-thirds or three-fourths of the members agree), working consensus (all members can "live with" the decision), and absolute consensus (everyone absolutely agrees). Activist groups tend not to make decisions by majority or supermajority rule because activists naturally empathize with people outside the majority. After all, at one point, slavery and segregation were accepted by the majority of voting Americans, but it was still wrong. *Consensus* building (sometimes referred to as the Quaker method) is tough. It requires compromise—when a person gives up something they want for the greater good—and *collaboration*—when parties negotiate until they find a solution everybody likes. When the leaders of the Mexican American Youth Organization (MAYO) would meet (see Chapter 3 for more information about MAYO), they would use a combination of *Robert's Rules of Order* and dialogue in an attempt to achieve consensus. Every person in attendance was given the opportunity to comment on each agenda item.

When a person cannot agree to a consensus, they should propose an alternative solution that can be considered and debated by the group. It is frustrating for a group when a person vetoes ideas but gives no alternative solutions. Absolute consensus (when everybody agrees) should be reserved for the most important decisions. Reaching any type of consensus takes considerably more time than ruling by majority vote, but in the end, a decision reached by consensus makes a team more cohesive and committed.

Tips for Effective Coalitions

The use of coalitions in social justice activism dates back centuries. During Prohibition, Protestants and suffragists came together to fight against the distribution of alcohol (see Chapter 2). Their motivations were different (Protestants were motivated by religious beliefs against alcohol consumption; suffragists were concerned that alcoholic husbands were putting their wives and children in physical danger), but they were able to work together because their end goal was the same. Although generational differences made collaboration difficult for the members of the Southern Christian Leadership Conference and the Student Nonviolent Coordinating Committee, they found a way to work together during the U.S. Black civil rights movement (see Chapter 3) to end segregation and give equal access to the ballot box.

Krysten Sinema[2] was a member of the Arizona state legislature for 7 years, beginning in 2005 (when she was only 28 years old), and had a successful history with coalition building. She co-chaired Arizona Together—a coalition fighting against a 2006 state amendment that would have banned same-sex marriage and civil unions in Arizona. The usual liberal suspects joined the coalition, but Krysten

Figure 9.1 Sen. Krysten Sinema (D-Ariz.) during her ceremonial oath of office in 2019.

---

2   Krysten Sinema was elected to the U.S. Senate representing Arizona at the end of 2018 and assumed office in early 2019.

knew they needed more than the **American Civil Liberties Union** (ACLU) and **Planned Parenthood** to defeat the initiative. The amendment did not recognize unmarried families and therefore would have outlawed the ability to extend healthcare benefits to any unmarried romantic partner. With that information in hand, Krysten and her allies recruited 50 more groups to the coalition, including teachers, police officers, firefighters, and retired persons. Together, they defeated the initiative.

Krysten advises activists to form relationships with people who are different from themselves and to find common ground. People in a coalition need a common purpose and goals. Otherwise, there is no sense of accomplishment or hope for a resolution to their concerns, which will cause people to disengage and stop attending meetings. Krysten warns that a common mistake made by social justice leaders is ignoring their coalitions until they trot out the partner organizations for a press release. Meaningful work is never accomplished if the organizations are not consistently working together to set goals and accomplish tasks. In coalition work, it is best to start with easy decisions first and to leave large chunks of time between coalition meetings so people can refresh themselves and have time to focus on the common purpose and goals.

Helpful Documents

Whether engaging in a small work group meeting or a large coalition gathering, there are some documents that can be of benefit, including a constitution and bylaws, meeting agendas, timelines, minutes, and a strategic plan.

Constitution and Bylaws

Some groups are so informal and temporary the members do not believe the creation of formal documents such as a constitution and bylaws are a good use of time, and they may be right. Other groups are tied to national organizations and/or grow so large the members feel the need to codify informal rules and norms. A constitution will be a shorter document that contains the mission and the principles that will guide members. It typically includes the formal name of the organization, the purpose, a statement about the membership, organizational structure, a broad ruling about how often the group must meet annually, what constitutes a **quorum**, and the rules for amending the constitution. The constitution provides the framework of the organization.

The bylaws establish *specific* rules and guidelines by which members are supposed to function; this document should strengthen and not contradict the constitution, which is the organization's primary document. The bylaws could include more specifics about the structure of the organization, including how leaders are chosen and their specific responsibilities; the standing committees and their purposes; information about voting and who gets to vote; an attendance policy; how the budget will be handled; how to remove an officer or committee chair; and how to amend the bylaws. It is best not to put a lot of narrow specifics, such as the time of day a committee needs to meet, in the bylaws because times may change depending upon the schedules of the committee members. Some groups like to include very specific details in a less formal handbook that can be easily amended.

The constitution and bylaws, should your group have them, need to be available to new members and, like the strategic plan mentioned below, should be reviewed often and amended as necessary.

Agendas, Timelines, and Minutes

The meeting facilitator should call for agenda items and make sure the agenda is distributed at least a few days before the meeting. An agenda will include a list of everything that will be discussed at the meeting. Some agendas are quite lengthy, with the addition of treasurer and standing committee reports; others are much shorter, simply sticking to new and old business. Some people like to note time limits for discussion items. The early distribution of an agenda will allow participants to read through it and prepare for discussion.

Agenda Template

Heading should include date, time, and location. A list of invited participants can also be included at the top of the agenda.

   I. Call to Order. The leader should try to start the meeting on time. This time is also good for recognizing any guests.

   II. Discussion and Approval of Minutes from the Previous Meeting.

   III. Treasurer's Report if applicable.

   IV. Standing Committee Reports if applicable. Put the names of the people responsible for reporting. No votes or extended discussion should occur during this time.

   V. Unfinished Business. Items from previous meetings that still need to be resolved. Votes can take place during both Unfinished and New Business.

   VI. New Business. Items that are up for discussion for the first time.

   VII. Next Meeting. List the time and date of the next meeting and summarize what people need to do to prepare for that meeting.

VIII. *Announcements. Allow people to make announcements about upcoming events, things to celebrate, etc.*

IX. *Adjournment. Formal end of the meeting.*

. . . .

During the first couple of meetings of a work group, a timeline of tasks, people responsible, and due dates should be created. This organizational tool helps alleviate confusion and keeps people accountable to the group. The timeline can be revisited often and adjusted as necessary.

Table 9.1 **Example of a Timeline**

Task	Due Date	Person(s) Responsible	Completed	Needs	Notes
Parade Permit	04/14/19	LaKeisha	Form is completed.	Email address of contact at City Hall	Rishi will send name of his contact.

The group will need to decide who will take minutes; it could be one person, or the responsibility can be rotated amongst attendees. Minutes should follow the agenda but include meeting details, especially the details of the decisions that are made. They are the institutional memory for the organization. Like the agenda, minutes should be circulated before the meeting so members can offer edits and vote on the approval during the beginning of the next meeting.

Strategic Plan

While agendas, timelines, and minutes should be referenced in every meeting, a strategic plan is more of an overarching document like the constitution and bylaws. Groups and coalitions centered on activism need goals, both long-term and short-term. Strategic plans allow a group to plan where they are going, be good stewards of time and money, and take ownership of their plans and goals. The plan (which should include goals, activities, due dates, and people responsible) does not have to be far out into the future—about 18 to 24 months is great. It can be organized in a table, much like the timeline example above.

Goals should be tied to the mission of the group or coalition and need to be measurable so milestones can be easily recognized and celebrated. For example, a group may set a goal to increase the number of people at an annual rally by 20 percent. To identify goals, it may be best to survey members (if it is a large organization) or host a retreat (if the group is smaller). Once a few goals are identified, then specific activities necessary to reach the goal must be established. To increase attendance at rallies, an activity may be to boost posts on Facebook twice a week and/or increase the budget for fliers so more canvassing can occur. It is important to continually update the strategic plan so it is always 18 to 24 months out.

Challenges for Groups and Coalitions

Group and coalition work have their challenges just like individual leadership does. The two most prevalent challenges for group and coalition members are **groupthink** and group conflict. The former occurs when the members of the group get along too well and do not think about issues critically enough. While the latter can be healthy, if handled incorrectly, it can cause a group to become fragmented and less effective in their fight for social justice, which, unfortunately, has happened many times in the history of activist movements.

Groupthink

Groupthink occurs when highly cohesive groups have members who do not want to voice dissent, remaining silent even if they do not agree with the direction of the conversation and/or the decision. This lack of dissent or conflict can be detrimental to groups and coalitions. Most famously, it is believed that groupthink is to blame for the Space Shuttle Challenger explosion in the mid-1980s. That poor group decision cost seven lives, including the life of a public-school educator who was chosen to be the first teacher in space. The Challenger was set to launch from the coast of Florida on a January morning in 1986, but the unusually low temperature made it too cold for the O-rings to seal properly, thus causing "blow-by" and resulting in an external tank explosion. The malfunction brought the space shuttle down in flames within 73 seconds from launch as millions of American schoolchildren watched in horror during a live broadcast.

It was later discovered that NASA was warned the night before by its contractor, Morton-Thiokol (M-T), to delay the launch until the temperature warmed. During a 5 ½-hour period, a couple of conference calls took place between 34 engineers and NASA managers. Initially, all 14 of the M-T engineers and managers said they opposed the launch, stating that the O-rings had never been tested for temperatures below 40 degrees Fahrenheit. The NASA managers did not want a delay and pressured M-T to reverse its recommendation. One of the NASA managers employed shame and sarcastically asked M-T personnel if they expected NASA to wait until April to launch. The M-T team asked for a break from the call. Once they were off the phone, the M-T managers dismissed the engineers and decided to tell NASA that their results were inconclusive and to proceed with the launch if the agency wanted to. When asked if there were any objections, none of the 34 people on the call voiced any, although it is now well known that two of the M-T engineers were sure the decision would be fatal. It was obvious to the two dissenting engineers that their opinions were not welcome.

It is important that healthy dissent is encouraged within groups and coalitions and that a culture of groupthink is discouraged. One way to accomplish this task is to appoint a devil's advocate or two at the beginning of any deliberation. This important responsibility can be assigned or rotated, or names can even be drawn out of a hat. It is best if the role is not played by the same person all the time because people may start to tune them out. The person fulfilling the devil's advocate role must provide other points of view whenever they are lacking in the conversation. For example, if the group wants to boycott a distributor's tomatoes because they do not believe the distributor pays its employees fair wages, then the tough topic of how the boycott could negatively affect the employees should be discussed. Disagreements and debate can lead to new, better approaches and is an important precursor to beneficial change.

Conflict

Dissent, while necessary and good, can cause conflict in groups. How that conflict is managed can make or break a group, a coalition, or even a movement. Such a split occurred in the mid-19th century when abolitionist William Lloyd Garrison and freed slave and abolitionist Frederick Douglass could not agree on the role of violence in the abolitionist movement (see Chapter 2 for their stories). These once very good friends began to attack each other publicly in their newspapers. Their partnership, which had produced speaking tours, legislation, and Douglass's autobiography, was finished. Sometimes things get too personal during deliberations, and *ad hominem* (see Chapter 7) attacks may occur. Instead, it is important to remember to be hard on the problem but soft on the person, particularly when that person is an ally.

The Student Nonviolent Coordinating Committee, mentioned above, prided itself on decentralization of leadership and decision-making by consensus. However, the group grew too large, and many of the participants did not know or trust each other. The closeness and cohesiveness disappeared, causing the group to eventually fall apart. People generally have one of three responses to conflict: flight, fight, or unite. *Flight* occurs when a person decides not to engage. In fact, they may disengage during the conflict itself and will not be interested in a resolution. They may be too angry, scared, or apathetic to engage any further. They may also quit showing up to gatherings because of the discomfort unresolved conflict can create. A person who *fights* believes in a win/lose approach to dialogue and puts being right ahead of the interpersonal relationship(s). Anyone who chooses to *unite* values both the deliberation and the relationships. They want a resolution to the conflict.

To create a resolution, everyone involved has to desire an end to the conflict and be willing to support a culture of respect and concern to achieve the goal. It is always best to allow some time to pass after the initial heated exchange. When the appropriate parties come back together, a person who is viewed as neutral should state the issues briefly and without judgment. The folks involved should ask nonaccusatory open questions of each other to seek to understand and satisfy curiosity. Some questions might include: What values are influencing the decision? What are some things you want to know more about? In what areas do we agree? What are some other options that can be considered? Cooperation and active listening are encouraged during this exchange. Healing cannot be rushed. During these exchanges, people often discover they have a lot of common ground and that their area of disagreement is surprisingly minimal.

Review

In this chapter, tips for effective group communication and coalition building were discussed, encouraging groups to pay attention to multiple aspects, including number of people in a group, their work environments, preparation for meetings and events, and organizational documents. Finally, the chapter ended with common challenges faced by groups and coalitions, including groupthink and conflict. Leadership and group work are not always easy, but like-minded activists are much stronger together than they are apart.

Discussion Starters

1. Think about a group in which you are a member. What are some formal rules of that group? What are some informal norms? How did you learn the norms?

2. Think about some groups or a cause you believe would benefit from a coalition. What groups could make up that coalition? What is their shared purpose?

3. What have you seen done when a conflict within a group appears unresolvable?

Further Reading/Viewing

Disney, A., & Hughes, K. (Director). Hughes, K., & Anisko, E. (Producers). (2015). *The armor of light* [Motion picture]. Culver City, CA: Samuel Goldwyn Films.

Janis, I. L. (1989). *Crucial decisions: Leadership in policymaking and crisis management*. New York, NY: Free Press.

Lewis, J. (1998). *Walking with the wind: A memoir of the movement*. New York, NY: Simon & Schuster.

Sinema, K. (2009). *UNITE and conquer: How to build coalitions that win—and last*. San Francisco, CA: Berrett-Koehler Publishers, Inc.

Vaughan, D. (1996). *The Challenger launch decision: Risky technology, culture, and deviance at NASA*. Chicago, IL: University of Chicago Press.

FIGURE CREDITS

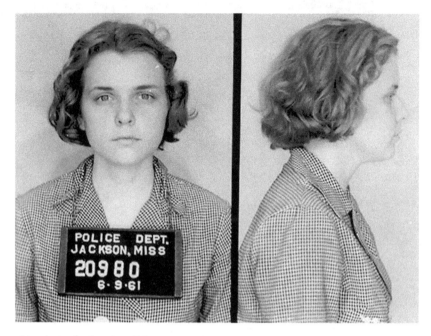

Mugshots of a Freedom Rider.

CHAPTER 10

Risks and Rewards of Social Justice Activism

V ERY FEW THINGS are certain when a person is labeled an activist, but one fact that is guaranteed is that friends, family, and acquaintances will think of you differently once you start taking decisive stands on issues related to social justice. Many times, this adjusted opinion is positive, and as a result, people's respect for you increases as they begin to see you as a social justice crusader who is selflessly educating and advocating. On the other hand, some naysayers will see you as needlessly judgmental, overly sensitive, and involved in issues that should not concern you.

Shortly after your author left Iowa and returned to Oklahoma (see Chapter 1 for the longer narrative), I received a direct message on Facebook from my only non-university friend during my time in the Hawkeye State. We met at church, and I had become close to her extended family, spending many Sunday dinners and holidays with them. My friend (let's call her Hailey) was upset with some recent updates on my Facebook profile, where I had proudly changed my political affiliation to "Feminist" and my religion to "Jesus was a Socialist." I guess that last comment sent her over the edge. In the DM, she told me I had lost my way and the university had corrupted my morals. She then blocked me on Facebook and stopped accepting my calls. We never spoke again. The loss of that friendship did not sting nearly as badly as the loss of Rusty. This time was different, though, because, unlike with Rusty, this time I felt I was finally on the right side of history.

In short, there are both risks and rewards when it comes to social justice work, and it is imperative that budding activists are aware of both, as well as their legal rights and responsibilities, before taking on the work in a serious way.

Risks of Being a Social Justice Activist

This chapter will begin with the bad news first: the risks of activism, which range from personal attacks and loss of privacy (more likely) to personal injury and death (less likely). It is impossible to predict or control how naysayers will react. A simple action—such as posting a petition online—could be the end of an already strained friendship, or more severely, it could cost a person their property and/or safety if they are financially dependent on the person who is offended. Every activist and would-be activist has to figure out their line in the sand—just how far they are willing to go for a cause.

Personal Attacks

Rev. Al Sharpton, a modern civil rights leader, media talk show host, and pastor, has been parodied for years on comedy sketch shows such as *Saturday Night Live*. He has been ridiculed for his hair, his wind suits, his weight, his communication style, and his advocacy. He believes ridicule and distortion are burdens of social justice leadership. It is not uncommon for activists to be called egotistical and humorless (e.g., the "PC police"). Gloria Allred, an attorney who often takes on pro bono cases representing women and children, has been accused of both. In 2002, former NBA star Charles Barkley told Gloria to "shut up" on national television regarding her concern about pop music icon Michael Jackson holding his baby over a fourth-floor balcony. Charles accused Gloria of seeking out high-profile cases and believing she was God. More recently, late-night talk show host Jimmy Kimmel said he doubted the women accusing **Bill Cosby** of sexual assault solely because the women were represented by Gloria and said, "She is in league with the devil."

Lindy West is a well-known blogger and journalist who has written about fat acceptance, feminism, sexual assault, social justice, and humor in publications such as Jezebel.com, *The Guardian,* and *The New York Times*. In 2013, she appeared on the television show *Totally Biased with W. Kamau Bell* to discuss rape jokes told by comics. Lindy had done stand-up, was dating a comic, and wrote jokes for other people who performed comedy. She felt rape jokes further traumatized sexual assault survivors who were in the audiences of the comics. The counterpoint was presented by Jim Norton, a comic and radio talk show host who believed the topic of rape could be funny and should be used in comedy. After the televised debate with Norton, Lindy received thousands of email and social media messages from detractors telling her she was too fat, humorless, and ugly to get raped.

Some social justice activists have been challenged regarding their religious faith. Carlton Pearson was an influential Pentecostal bishop leading a megachurch in Tulsa, Oklahoma, and traveling the world preaching. In the mid-1990s, he had a revelation that hell was not a place where God sent people after death. In particular, he was concerned about people in developing countries who did not have access to a **salvation message**. He did not believe they were condemned to hell—an ideology that contradicted what he had preached for years. As a result of his **paradigm** shift, Carlton was declared a heretic by his peers and, within a year, lost his church due to lack of members and funds. Another person from Oklahoma, Sara Cunningham, was also questioned about her faith. The doubt came after she accepted her gay son and started to attend Pride parades to give free "mom hugs" to members of the LGBTQ+ communities, many of whom were estranged from their parents. For 20 years, Sara had attended a conservative church but had to switch to an LGBT-affirming church after living a life of "radical inclusion." Members of her former church no longer accepted her or her family.

Loss of Privacy

Many of the people included in this book, including civil rights activists Rev. Dr. Martin Luther King, Jr., **Malcolm X**, César Chávez, and José Angel Gutiérrez, were all surveilled by the U.S. government. After MLK became well known during the **Montgomery Bus Boycott** in 1955, he was watched by the FBI for the next 12 years until his assassination. In 1964, shortly after it was announced that he had won the **Nobel Peace Prize**, he received an anonymous package claiming proof of his infidelity and encouraging him to commit suicide. MLK suspected it was from the FBI, and later, a Senate committee confirmed that the document—dubbed the "suicide letter"—did indeed come from inside the FBI.

Rachel McKinnon posted a photo of herself on Twitter after she won a major track cycling race and broke a world record doing it. Additionally, she was the first transgender woman to ever win the championship. She immediately received negative comments from strangers, mostly claiming she cheated and did not belong in the race. As a result of the criticism, she changed her phone number and Twitter name, stopped taking photos anywhere near her home, set items to private that used to be public, created online block lists, and removed personal details (such as her address and phone number) from her résumé.

Cecile Richards, long-time president of **Planned Parenthood**, was a victim of **doxing** and had her personal email address shared without her permission on a right-wing blog. Within hours, her inbox was full of the same message copied and pasted thousands of times by readers of the blog. The messages declared that Cecile was a baby killer, was going to hell, etc. More than anything, the situation was inconvenient: she had to search through all the spam to find legitimate emails.

Compromised Relationships

Strained relationships are a common concern for budding activists who hold views that are different from those of their family members and lifelong friends. James Zwerg, a **Freedom Rider** who was a resident of Wisconsin, was disowned by his middle-class white parents, who believed he was "throwing away" his education with advocacy work. During the Freedom Rides in 1961, James's mom wrote to U.S. Attorney General Robert Kennedy, claiming her son had been "duped into subversive attitudes" and asking his advice regarding counseling opportunities for her son. Eventually, James's dad had a heart attack, and his mom had an emotional breakdown, both of which caused their son to live with tremendous guilt.

Lecia Brooks, the outreach director at the **Southern Poverty Law Center** (SPLC), educates the public about Confederate monuments, forgotten U.S. Black civil rights history, hate groups, etc. She struggled with acceptance from her family at an early age. They did not like her youthful desire to "fight the power," and that lack of acceptance and support has followed her into adulthood as an influential staff member at the SPLC. Carlisha Williams Bradley experienced strain in her childhood friendships. In college, her consciousness about Black history was raised after she made new friends, but as a result of her new ideology, she experienced resistance from her childhood friends. They were surprised to find she no longer idolized the same images of beauty they did. As her consciousness raised, old friendships drifted apart, and she grew closer to people who challenged her to grow and have a greater understanding of herself. Carlisha is a goodwill ambassador to the Republic of Gambia and the founder and executive director of Women Empowering Nations, a nonprofit devoted to the educational and economic empowerment of girls.

Mental Health

Isolation, trauma, burnout, and depression are common mental health challenges faced by those who dedicate their time to advocacy. Many activists put impossible expectations on themselves, their colleagues, and their work. Aidan Ricketts, a social and environmental activist, suggests activists think of themselves as the tortoise rather than the hare, remembering that "slow and steady" wins the race. Experienced feminist activists Jennifer Baumgardner and Amy Richards recommend rewarding oneself often with whatever healthy activity (e.g., a walk, shopping, reading) makes them happy. Sometimes the toll is too much, though, and a person may need some mental health counseling and/or some time off from the work.

Activism certainly took its toll on Elizabeth Eckford and Anne Moody during the U.S. Black civil rights movement. Elizabeth was one of the students who made up the Little Rock Nine. In fact, there is an iconic Pulitzer Prize–winning photograph showing her in sunglasses wearing a white dress trimmed in gingham with a very angry white classmate yelling from behind her. The time of desegregation in Arkansas was traumatic, and for the Little Rock Nine, it included yelling, name calling, spitting, shoving, and death threats—all directed at them and their families. While the other eight students in Elizabeth's cohort eventually settled outside the South, she joined the Army and then returned to Little Rock and lived in anonymity for 20 years. After a local newspaper reporter spoke to her in the mid-1970s, he said she appeared to be on the brink of a breakdown. She would lie in her bed for hours staring at the wall and instructing her family to tell reporters she was dead.

In 1968, Anne Moody published *Coming of Age in Mississippi*, a book that symbolized the Black college student activist experience of the 1960s. Today it is required reading in many high school and college literature and history courses. Like Elizabeth, Anne is the subject of an iconic photo: hers is of a sit-in in Jackson, Mississippi, in which she appears with three other people, all with food dripping from their heads. Not long after publication of her book, Anne disappeared from the public eye and moved to New York City, moving back to Mississippi in the early 1990s. She never felt safe back in her home state and would insist that her son or someone else accompany her wherever she went. She granted only one interview (in 1985) after the publication of her book in 1968 and before her death in 2015.

Loss of Income and Property

Sisters Angelina and Sarah Grimké were born at the turn of the 19th century into a large wealthy family in Charleston, South Carolina. Their father was a member of the state's supreme court, and their mother came from a family of wealthy politicians. The Grimkés were also slave owners, a fact that bothered the sisters, who would secretly and illegally teach their slaves how to read. As adults, Angelina and Sarah left their family plantation and moved north to Philadelphia, where they attended anti-slavery meetings, gave lectures, and penned opinion pieces. They gave up their lives of luxury and leisure to struggle financially and fight for abolition.

In 2016, Colin Kaepernick was a quarterback in the NFL when he started silently protesting by kneeling (an action that is commonly performed to show respect to an injured athlete) during the national anthem. Colin's goal was to call attention to police brutality and racial injustice. Pretty soon, other players and cheerleaders joined him in taking a knee, which garnered media and political attention. Colin also pledged to give $1 million to organizations that worked in historically oppressed communities. During the next season, he found himself a free agent who was never signed by a team. It is estimated that Colin lost nearly $90 million as a result of his activism.

A family home belonging to the deceased father of José Angel Gutiérrez, a leader of the Chicano civil rights movement (see the Foreword and Chapter 3), was burned to the ground. Gutiérrez had recently announced that he planned to move back to his hometown of Crystal City, Texas, to help organize a school walkout. Soon after that information was released, a couple of white youth were spotted by neighbors near the home right before the fire started. Once the firefighters arrived, they claimed the fire was too far advanced, and they watched it burn rather than try to stop it or slow it down. The event was never ruled an arson, though the house had no electricity or tenants at the time of the fire.

Arrest

Over the years, activists have been brought in on a number of legal charges. Suffragist Alice Paul was arrested in 1917 for obstructing traffic when she and her colleagues brought their protest signs to the front gates of the White House. She famously went on a hunger strike while in prison, which resulted in forced feedings that garnered public sympathy. John Lewis's first arrest was in 1960; the charge was disorderly conduct during a restaurant sit-in. The situation put a strain on his relationship with his conservative Southern parents, who were shocked and ashamed by the arrest. The neighbors gossiped about how much trouble John was getting into at college. It took years for him and his parents to repair their relationship.

One of the most famous arrests of a social activist is that of Angela Davis in 1970. Angela had recently lost her job as an assistant professor of philosophy at the University of California, Los Angeles for being a member of the Communist Party. She received threatening mail as a result of the controversy and bought a few guns that she gave to private guards who provided her with security. Some of those guns were used for a very public attempted kidnapping and murder of a local judge. Fearing arrest, Angela went on the run, and the FBI eventually found her in a New York City hotel. She was charged with first-degree murder, kidnapping, and conspiracy. She was not initially offered bail, which resulted in an international "Free Angela" campaign. In 1972, Angela was acquitted of all charges after a 13-week trial.

Ramero "Ramsey" Muñoz's Chican@ activism dates back decades; he was best known for running for governor of Texas twice in the 1970s on the **La Raza Unida** (RUP) ticket (see Chapter 3 for more information about RUP) and received hundreds of thousands of votes. He was a former football player at **Baylor University** and charismatic lawyer, and many of his followers believe his white political opponents became concerned about Ramsey's political power, particularly with the growing Hispanic communities in South Texas. Ramsey drew large crowds and was asked to speak at universities throughout the country, where he was well received. Everything changed in 1976, when he was accused of conspiring to bring marijuana from Mexico to the United States. He admitted he heard about the conspiracy from one of his clients but believed he should keep it quiet because of attorney-client privilege. He was told he would be given leniency in the marijuana case if he would tell law enforcement more about the workings of RUP, but Ramsey refused and pled guilty.

In the end, Ramsey received sentences for conversations about drug sales that happened in two cities, and he served 5 years in prison and permanently lost his law license. After he was released, Ramsey made a living as a paralegal, and while he was in Dallas in 1994 meeting with clients, he was suspiciously pulled over by police, who found 40 kilos (about 88 pounds) of cocaine in the trunk of the car Ramsey was driving, which belonged to another person. Ramsey and his supporters thoroughly believe he was set up and paid the ultimate cost of being an outspoken Chican@ activist. In late 2018, after serving nearly 24 years in prison on a life sentence, Ramsey was granted **compassionate release** from federal prison.

Injury and Death

DeRay Mckesson and other protestors were trained by street medics in **Ferguson,** Missouri, because they believed ambulances rarely came to protest sites. The activists learned how to flush out eyes when sprayed with tear gas and how to help other protestors in distress. DeRay utilized the training the very next day when he was teargassed during a protest. That night, with his eyes burning, he hid from the police (who were enforcing an imposed curfew) in the floorboard of his car. On another day, DeRay said he feared for his life while he was participating in a sit-in at a police station and an officer dragged him out on his back. DeRay wrote in his 2018 book, *On the Other Side of Freedom,* that another officer looked to be contemplating whether to shoot or tase him during the incident.

In August 2017, white supremacists held a Unite the Right rally in Charlottesville, Virginia, to protest the removal of a statue of Robert E. Lee, a Confederate war hero, from a local park. They carried torches and chanted phrases such as "You will not replace us" and "Jews will not replace us." The rally drew counterprotestors, who chanted, "Whose town? Our town!" An angered white supremacist drove a car into a crowd of counterprotestors, killing Heather Heyer and injuring 28 other people. Heather was 32 years old and deeply committed to civil rights. She knew the risks of attending the protest but did it anyway. Heather would often share her favorite quotation: "If you're not outraged, you aren't paying attention." These were the last words she ever posted on Facebook.

Medgar Evers unsuccessfully attempted to register to vote when he came back from serving his county in World War II. In time, he became the **NAACP's** first field secretary in Mississippi and moved to the state's capital city of Jackson, where he had a house custom-built with high windows and no front door—making it tougher to shoot at his family or gain access to the inside of the house. Medgar and his wife taught their three very young children how to crawl to the bathroom (staying under the windows) in case of gunfire. Additionally, the children's beds sat on box springs with no frames to keep them low to the ground. The precautions were not enough to save Medgar, and in June 1963, he was assassinated in his driveway a little after midnight by a sniper shooting from a vacant wooded lot across the street.

Minimizing Legal Risks[1]

There are now nearly 30 amendments to the U.S. Constitution; the first 10, referred to as the Bill of Rights, were authored by James Madison (who would go on to become the fourth president of the United States) and ratified by the states in 1791. The intent of the Bill of Rights was to grant individuals more protections and liberties than what was implied within the U.S. Constitution. Three amendments—the First, Fourth, and Fifth—are of particular importance to people seeking to advance social justice. It is also important to note the passage of the 14th Amendment in 1868, which officially required that the Bill of Rights apply at the state levels.

. . . .

First Amendment

Congress shall make no law respecting an establishment of religion, or prohibiting the free exercise thereof; or abridging the freedom of speech, or of the

---

1   The information provided here is for educational purposes only and is not a substitute for professional legal advice. Always consult an attorney licensed in the state of the demonstration before pursuing actions that may subject you or your allies to civil and/or criminal liability.

press; or the right of the people peaceably to assemble, and to petition the Government for a redress of grievances.

The First Amendment guarantees the right of people to engage in nonviolent speech and assembly, including protests and marches in public places, even if the protestors' views are unpopular. Demonstrators have the least amount of constitutional protection on private property, and if they are asked to leave by the owner, they should do so or risk being charged with trespassing. Keep in mind that acts of violence, **defamation**, obscenity, statements that cause panic (e.g., yelling "Fire!" in a crowd when there is no fire), and **"fighting words"** are *not* protected by the First Amendment. The government can also impose reasonable "time, place and manner" restrictions on the exercise of free speech; however, the restrictions should not be based on the views of the activists. Instead, the restrictions must be limited to what is necessary to achieve a "compelling governmental interest," such as protecting public safety, allowing for flow of traffic, etc. For example, the government cannot require folks advocating against a water treatment plant to hold their protests at 3 a.m. in a faraway small public park while allowing everyone rallying for the plant to demonstrate in the middle of the afternoon in front of City Hall or some other place with heavy foot traffic.

Fourth Amendment

The right of the people to be secure in their persons, houses, papers, and effects, against unreasonable searches and seizures, shall not be violated, and no Warrants shall issue, but upon probable cause, supported by Oath or affirmation, and particularly describing the place to be searched, and the persons or things to be seized.

The Fourth Amendment relates to a person's privacy and guarantees that no search of property[2] should take place unless consent is provided by the owner or a search warrant is produced with date, time, location, and a list of what can be seized.[3] You are under no obligation to provide consent. If you do not consent, it is best to state "I don't consent to the search" rather than to remain silent. If a search

2   A pat-down of a person, often referred to as a "Terry stop," can occur without a warrant if the officer has a reasonable suspicion that the person is armed and/or engaged or about to engage in criminal behavior.

3   There are some exceptions to the requirement of search warrants. For example, during a traffic stop, a car can be searched without a warrant if there is probable cause. Also, law enforcement can seize any evidence in plain view or anything that is seen during a protective sweep.

does take place (even without your consent), never physically touch an officer or attempt to put your body in the way of the search. Save your objections for the courtroom, where it may be possible to have illegally seized evidence thrown out by the presiding judge.

Fifth Amendment

No person shall be held to answer for a capital, or otherwise infamous crime, unless on a presentment or indictment of a Grand Jury, except in cases arising in the land or naval forces, or in the Militia, when in actual service in time of War or public danger; nor shall any person be subject for the same offence to be twice put in jeopardy of life or limb; nor shall be compelled in any criminal case to be a witness against himself, nor be deprived of life, liberty, or property, without due process of law; nor shall private property be taken for public use, without just compensation.

The Fifth Amendment is designed to protect a person when they are taken into custody by law enforcement. A detained individual should be read their Miranda rights by law enforcement before they are interrogated. Mirandizing has been required by the U.S. Supreme Court since 1966 and is intended to ensure that a person in police custody is aware of their rights to remain silent and to not make self-incriminating statements. To evoke these rights, you should explicitly tell the officer that you "wish to remain silent" and that you want an attorney. Those words and that request puts a bubble of protection around you—as long as you stop talking.

Example of Phrasing of Miranda Rights

You have the right to remain silent. Anything you say can and will be used against you in a court of law. You have the right to an attorney. If you cannot afford an attorney, one will be provided for you. Do you understand the rights I have just read to you? With these rights in mind, do you wish to speak to me?

Miranda rights apply to only those people who are in police custody. Anything said to the police before being Mirandized may be admissible in court, as long as the presiding judge believes law enforcement did not ask questions that were interrogating or intended to draw out incriminating responses. Be aware that statements not elicited by law enforcement, such as comments to fellow protestors made in the back of a police car, can still be used against you by the prosecution in some states, even if you had previously invoked your right to remain silent. These are considered voluntary statements, and any statement made voluntarily by you is considered a waiver of your right to remain silent. The same is true of "excited utterances" or other outbursts you make not predicated upon police interrogation.

Interactions With Police

If you choose to demonstrate, participate in a march, picket, or even observe these events, there is the risk that you will experience an interaction with law enforcement. Below are some tips for interacting with police officers during activist events.

- Before a planned demonstration, organizers should familiarize themselves with state and local statutes, ordinances, and regulations, including when and if permits are required and how to file for them.

- Organizers should designate a police liaison who is trained and ready to interact with law enforcement during the demonstration. It is a good idea for the liaison to contact local police before the event to provide the liaison's name and contact information.

- All demonstrators should be told to direct questions from law enforcement to the designated liaison.

- People need to be assigned to watch police interactions at public events and to record those interactions, if state regulations allow for it. When recording, it is a good idea to keep a safe (noninterfering) distance from the interaction and to state out loud "I am recording" near the beginning of the recorded interaction. Have video cloud backup in case the recording device is seized by the police.

- It is best to be polite to police officers during all interactions with them. You will likely be treated better during the interaction, and if there is video released, the general citizenry will view you, your colleagues, and your cause more favorably.

- When questioned by an officer, direct them to the police liaison, if there is one. If the officer insists on talking with you, say as little as possible to the officer without being argumentative. Ask "Am I being detained?" If their answer is no, then you are participating in a **consensual encounter** and likely do not have to provide any information.[4] Alternatively, you could ask "Am I free to go?"

- If you are not being detained and have been told that you are free to go, then slowly walk away from the officer with your hands in plain view. Never run from a law enforcement official.

---

4   Consult the state statutes and/or an attorney licensed in the state of the event regarding when and if ID must be disclosed when requested by law enforcement.

- If you are being detained, ask the officer "Why?" They should be able to give you a reason.

- Everyone has the right to be spoken to by law enforcement in their native language. Police officers have access to translators by phone. Ask for one if needed.

- If being detained, you need to provide the officer with your name, address, and date of birth, if asked. Depending upon the state, you may also have to provide identification.

- If you would like to have an officer of the same biological sex provide the pat-down, then ask for it.

- Ask for the officer's name, agency, and badge number and remember it.

- Obey the instructions of the police and submit to arrest, even if you believe you have done nothing wrong (again, fight it in court). Keep "obstruction" and "resisting arrest" off your record.

- If you are arrested, things of value (such as jewelry) have to be removed from your person when you are booked into jail. It is best to leave those items at home when heading out to a public demonstration.

- If you must have prescribed medications with you at a demonstration, bring them in original containers with the label showing that the medicine is legally prescribed to you. Otherwise, you could end up with an illegal possession charge.

- Organizers should have a plan for securing the release of anyone detained during a demonstration. It is best to communicate with a bondsperson prior to the event to have a good understanding of state requirements regarding bonds and to get an estimated amount of money that may be required to get a person released from jail.

- Write down everything you can remember after interacting with the police. Try to provide names and contact information of witnesses.

- If you are injured, take photos as soon as possible and daily thereafter until the injuries are no longer visible.

Rewards of Being a Social Justice Activist

Risks of activism can certainly be discouraging and maybe even a little scary, particularly for a new activist. Just remember that for every risk that makes the news, there are thousands of rewards silently unnoticed. The Rev. Dr. Martin Luther King said it best while encouraging a group of very tired marchers at the Alabama State Capitol: "The moral arc of the universe is long, but it bends toward justice." He believed that in the end, good would triumph over evil. Below are a few of the benefits of the work experienced by social justice activists.

A Clear Conscience

People become activists because of a raised consciousness related to a social justice issue or issues. In other words, they know there is a problem and want to be part of the solution. There is a desire to learn more about the issue by reading, having conversations, watching documentaries, etc. There is also a desire to do more by talking to others, attending public meetings, posting to social media, signing petitions, etc. As discussed in other parts of this book, ignorance is no longer an option once a social justice consciousness-raising has occurred; it is impossible to unknow what is known. To do nothing only leads to frustration, anger, and hopelessness.

Carlton Pearson knew his awakening regarding hell would likely cost him his church, but he felt it was an epiphany given to him by God that he could not ignore. Today he has found a spiritual home in the Unitarian tradition, is preaching again, and travels the globe spreading the message of "radical inclusion." Recently, a movie about his life appeared on **Netflix**. Like Carlton, Sara Cunningham and her family also left the church because they thought the church's interpretation of the Christian Bible was too narrow. For Sara, she wanted the church to accept and embrace her gay son. When they refused, she left with a clear conscience. In early 2019, actress Jamie Lee Curtis announced plans to make a movie based upon Sara's self-published memoir, *How We Sleep at Night* (2014).

Take No Excuses Attitude

Doing activist work gives a person a sense of purpose and a feeling of independence and power. Activism is the perfect antidote to feelings of victimhood, passivity, meaninglessness, and isolation. Aidan Ricketts believes embracing advocacy completes the process of a person moving from childhood to adulthood, no longer relying on the government or other agencies to do the right thing. Instead, activists use their voices and political power to demand what is right without taking any excuses while feeling empowered to reject paternal, demeaning explanations.

Though the Rev. Al Sharpton endured many years of ridicule related to his advocacy and fashion choices, he came out on top. Since 2011, Al has hosted a successful political talk show, *PoliticsNation with Al Sharpton*, on MSNBC. The show is highly rated, particularly with Black viewers, and it features A-list guests. As a social justice activist, he uses the show to highlight underreported news stories. Al has an assertive style both on and off the air and makes no apologies for his thoughts and beliefs, no matter how much he is critiqued.

Colin Kaepernick has taken a similar attitude toward his critics. At the end of 2018, the shoe company Nike featured Colin in an advertising campaign with the message "Believe in something even if it means sacrificing everything." The television advertisement, with Colin narrating, initially aired during the NFL season opener. While there were some negative reactions and people burned their Nike products on social media, sales actually increased by 10% for Nike. Colin, independent and powerful, filed a case against the NFL, accusing the owners of colluding to keep him out of the league. In early 2019, the lawsuit was settled for an undisclosed amount of money.

Support of Great Allies

In 2018, high school senior Seth Owen was given a choice by his conservative parents: he could continue to attend a church that preached against his sexuality or he could move out of his family home. He chose the latter, spending the last few months of his high school career virtually homeless. To make matters worse, when he received his financial aid package to Georgetown University, the university had included his parents' income as part of the expected family contribution, even though his parents had withdrawn all financial support. Seth needed $20,000 to attend Georgetown. When his teachers found out about the gap, they sprang into action, using **GoFundMe** to raise the money needed. In the end, allies raised more than $100,000. Seth plans to use the extra money to start a scholarship for other students in predicaments similar to his own.

While in junior high school in the late 1960s, Lecia Brooks was inspired by **James Brown's** Black empowerment funk anthem, *Say It Loud, I'm Black & I'm Proud,* but had a hard time gaining acceptance from her family as a result of her newfound consciousness regarding race. Instead, she turned to a discussion group of her teenage peers for support. Her allies played an important role in her identity development, providing her with a **safe space** to talk about race where people would listen and gently challenge her when necessary. She later volunteered with the sponsoring program and was consequently employed by them for 12 years.

Robert Jensen, a race and gender scholar who is anti-pornography, had a similar experience to Lecia's when he was in graduate school, in that he had to go outside his "home" to find the support he needed. Robert felt his journalism professors and fellow students were all defenders of pornography, which left him with no one to discuss his emerging thoughts regarding feminist critiques of the industry and the First Amendment. He had to go outside the academy to an activist group that was fighting the sexual exploitation industries (pornography, prostitution, stripping) to get a countering opinion. He was glad he did. The experience introduced him to community organizing and led him to a mentor who he felt contributed to radical politics in a principled way.

Acting as a Role Model

Three months after Ramsey Muñoz was granted compassionate release from federal prison, he served as grand marshal of the 20th annual César Chávez March in his hometown of Corpus Christi, Texas, where the frail Ramsey was celebrated and serenaded by **mariachis**. Today, the home of Medgar Evers in Jackson, Mississippi, is a museum and designated **National Historic Landmark**. People come from all over the world to visit the site and pay their respects to the U.S. Black civil rights leader. Chances are that you have already developed a few activist crushes of your own—people for whom you would travel great distances to see in a parade or visit a site where they lived or took political action. These activists have inspired you with their wit, their courage, and their charisma.

Both Michelle Obama and Ruth Bader Ginsburg are two modern-day activists with a devoted following. Michelle, the former first lady of the United States, took on childhood obesity as her activist cause during her time in the White House. She was seen on television planting a garden with schoolchildren to promote better food choices and dancing with kids to encourage increased physical activity. In 2018, she published a memoir and went on an international book tour that attracted millions of fans and filled up stadiums typically reserved for concerts and sporting events. Ruth (often referred to as RBG or even the "Notorious RBG"), an associate justice on the Supreme Court of the United States, has developed a bit of a cult following amongst activists, especially feminists. Like Al Sharpton, she has also been parodied on *Saturday Night Live,* but unlike those of Sharpton, depictions of RBG appear much less mean-spirited. Her legal decisions always fall on the side of social justice, even if it means she is in the minority opinion. In fact, she famously wears a special "dissent" collar on days when a decision is rendered in which she is in the minority on the Supreme Court, and merchandise (e.g., lapel pins, cuff links, earrings) depicting the collar are popular. Other products depicting RBG—including t-shirts, dolls, coffee mugs, candles, etc.—are readily available online.

It is true that as an activist you will meet and work with lots of inspiring people, but what you may not notice is that you are becoming an inspiring person yourself. People will watch how you react to both the good and the bad and how you treat others. Sometimes you will receive a note or a kind word, but oftentimes your admirers will say nothing, assuming from your self-confidence that you do not need a reminder of how great you are.

Positive Karma

As discussed above, Cecile Richards was doxed by an angry blogger who gave out her personal email address, but not all of the news was bad. While going through thousands of spam emails, she opened a message from a woman who had received Cecile's email address when her mother-in-law forwarded it to all of her anti-choice friends, encouraging them to spam Cecile. This woman did not spam Cecile but instead wanted her to know that Planned Parenthood helped her in college and that she was grateful. That message of gratitude arrived during a trying time when Cecile needed it the most.

Many of the activists mentioned in this book have won prominent awards, including the Nobel Peace Prize and the Presidential Medal of Freedom. They have also been the subjects of books and movies and had National Historic Landmarks designated as a result of their work. In 2014, novelist Sue Monk Kidd published *The Invention of Wings*, a book of historical fiction about the Grimké sisters. It debuted

Figure 10.1 Fans of Justice Ruth Bader Ginsburg celebrate her birthday.

at the top of *The New York Times* Bestseller List. Most recently, Lindy West's book, *Shrill*, was the inspiration for a **Hulu** series of the same name. Like Medgar Evers's home, MLK's home is designated a National Historic Landmark, and so are many other places where he spent time, including churches, sites of protests, and the motel where he was assassinated. Obviously, these activists went through some hard times as they sacrificed selflessly for the greater good, but ultimately, the good karma was returned to them in private notes of gratitude, public accolades, book deals, television shows, movies, and designated landmarks.

Personal Development

There is no doubt that John Lewis's journey during the U.S. Black civil rights movement prepared him to be the effective U.S. congressman he has been since he was initially elected to represent Georgia in 1987. In 2016, at the age of 76, he led a sit-in of 170 lawmakers on the House floor to protest for better gun control legislation. The moment was reminiscent of the sit-ins he led in restaurants, at lunch counters, and in bus stations nearly 60 years earlier. John also makes regular pilgrimages to Selma, Alabama, to retrace his steps during the 1965 march from Selma to Montgomery—the march John claims ended the U.S. Black civil rights movement.

Another person involved in the U.S. Black civil rights movement who has experienced personal development is Elizabeth Eckford from the Little Rock Nine. While she understandably struggled with seclusion and avoided the limelight for many years after so publicly taking part in school desegregation in Arkansas, she began accepting speaking engagements about 20 years ago. She tells compelling narratives regarding her experiences and relates those experiences to things that are happening today to youth of color. She has a conversational style that is wholly embraced by audiences.

Performing activist work moves a person like John and Elizabeth into the fifth and final stage of the feminist identification model discussed in the Preface. As a reminder, Stage 1 is living every day with no recognition of oppression. It is a state of ignorance. Stage 2 is an initial consciousness-raising regarding marginalized folks and oppression. Stage 3 is a response of anger to the oppression and seeking out relationships with like-minded individuals. Stage 4 requires identifying with a group and being able to comfortably use a label (e.g., gay ally, environmentalist) in one's activist identification. It is not uncommon for people to spend long periods of time in one stage and to perhaps even slip back into a previous stage for a time. Any movement upward on the scale is personal development, but the ultimate goal is to achieve Stage 5.

Table 10.1 Feminist Identification Model

Downing & Roush (1985)	
Stage 1: Passive Acceptance	Acceptance of traditional sex roles
Stage 2: Revelation	Awareness of marginalization and oppression
Stage 3: Embeddedness-Emanation	Seeking relationships with like-minded people
Stage 4: Synthesis	Integration of new social justice identity
Stage 5: Active Commitment	Doing the social justice work

Achieving the Goal

Ultimately, the greatest reward for a social justice activist is ending oppression, making the world a better place, taking care of the environment, promoting equity, etc. Realistically, the end goal is not always achieved in an activist's lifetime. For example, neither Elizabeth Cady Stanton nor Susan B. Anthony were alive when women won the right to vote in the United States (see Chapter 2). Both of them had spent nearly their entire adult lives fighting for something that was never achieved during their lifetimes. They simply passed the torch on to Carrie Chapman Catt, Alice Paul, and their allies.

The same will likely be true for Lilly Ledbetter, who sued Goodyear for pay equity and lost (see Chapter 5). The legislation she helped pass after her retirement will help women in the future, but she will never personally financially benefit from the legislation. Her retirement income from Goodyear, which was based on an unfair salary, has not changed. In fact, today, she has to turn down some speaking engagements because she simply cannot afford the expense of the travel. It is likely that Lilly will not see women receive equal pay for equal work during her lifetime. She will simply pass the torch, just like Susan and Elizabeth.

However, Lilly would have never been in management at Goodyear if it were not for the activists who came before her—the suffragists who desired the gender equality they saw modeled by the people of the **Haudenosaunee Confederacy** (Iroquois); the labor activists who achieved 40-hour workweeks and safety standards; and the people of the women's liberation movement who insisted that women be represented in the corporate world. So goes the story for every movement. Someone starts the work, moves it along as far as possible, and finds successors; those people and their allies move the work along, find successors, etc. until the work is finished. To sit still is to let the oppressor win.

Review

There you have it—the good, the bad, and the ugly of social justice activism. No one ever said it was going to be easy, but the work is necessary. It is best to approach it with full knowledge of the risks and rewards and the stories of the people who have gone before you. Many of them experienced what they considered minor inconveniences, but others paid a heavier price—leaving the work with their lives intact (albeit with an emotional toll) and others who left the work as a result of death.

Myrlie Evers-Williams, the widow of Medgar Evers, tells the story that a few nights before Medgar's assassination, he held her tight, cried, and told her that he did not have much longer. He got up the next day and carried on as usual with his NAACP responsibilities. Much like other activist leaders, he continuously expressed responsibility for the work. He loved his home state of Mississippi, and he would say that if he moved from the state, it would unfairly leave the people who weren't mobile to do a disproportional amount of social justice work. Granted, Medgar did more than his fair share, but the sentiment was as true then as it is now. People should share the burden of halting oppression. It is not a problem for just the oppressed.

Discussion Starters

1. What concerns give you the most pause as a social justice activist? What risks have you encountered or feared that were not mentioned in the chapter?

2. What are your thoughts regarding the tips for interacting with law enforcement that were offered in this chapter?

3. What rewards are most persuasive to you? What would make the risks worth it?

4. Which stage of the feminist identification model do you think is the most difficult for people to get past?

5. Where are you when it comes the feminist identification model mentioned in the Preface of this book? Where were you when you started the book? Has there been progress?

Further Reading/Viewing

Beals, M. P. (2003). *Warriors don't cry: A searing memoir of the battle to integrate Little Rock's Central High*. New York, NY: Spark Publishing.

Cort, R.W. (Producer). Leder, M. (Director). (2018). *On the basis of sex* [Motion picture]. New York, NY: Focus Features.

Cunningham, S. (2014). *How we sleep at night*. Scotts Valley, CA: CreateSpace Publishing.

Downing, N. E., & Roush, K. L. (1985). From passive acceptance to active commitment: A model of feminist identity development for women. *The Counseling Psychologist, 13*(4), 695–709.

Glass, I., Stern, J. D., Forster, M., Goldstein, J., & Shipp, A. (Producers). Marston, J. (Director). (2018). *Come Sunday* [Motion picture]. Los Gatos, CA: Netflix.

Greenstone, J. H. (2010). Learning the meaning of one: Reflections on social justice education. In M. K. Trigg (Ed.), *Leading the way: Young women's activism for social change* (pp. 76–86). New Brunswick, NJ: Rutgers University Press.

Grossman, R., Sartain, S., Kauffman, M., & Tollin, R. R. (Producers). Grossman, R., & Sartain, S. (Directors). (2018). *Seeing Allred* [Motion picture]. Atlanta, GA: Apparatus Productions.

Hollars, B. J. (2018). *The road south: Personal stories of the Freedom Riders*. Tuscaloosa, AL: The University of Alabama Press.

Jensen, R. (2007). *Getting off: Pornography and the end of masculinity*. Boston, MA: South End Press.

Kidd, S.M. (2014). *The invention of wings*. New York, NY: Penguin Books.

Lynch, S., Smith, S., Lambert, C., & Ruszniewski, C. (Producers). Lynch, S. (2012). *Free Angela and all political prisoners*. New York, NY: Realside Productions.

Margolick, D. (2012). *Elizabeth and Hazel: Two women of Little Rock*. New Haven, CT: Yale University Press.

Mckesson, D. (2018). *On the other side of freedom: The case for hope*. New York, NY: Viking.

Moody, A. (1968). *Coming of age in Mississippi*. New York, NY: Random House.

Obama, M. (2018). *Becoming*. New York, NY: Crown Publishing Group.

Ricketts, A. (2012). *The activists' handbook: A step-by-step guide to participatory democracy*. New York, NY: St. Martin's.

Sharpton, A. (2013). *The rejected stone: Al Sharpton and the path to American leadership*. New York, NY: Simon & Schuster.

West, L. (2016). *Shrill: Notes from a loud woman*. New York, NY: Hatchette Book Group.

FIGURE CREDITS

Glossary

A

Able-bodied Privilege benefitting from access to places and opportunities that are available to people who are able-bodied.

Activism acts that require direct action (e.g., strike, street march) by groups or individuals seeking change as a result of their commitments to social justice.

Activists people who actively seek social or political change.

Advocacy the act of lending support to a cause or action that is often less confrontational than activism.

Alice Walker U.S. American novelist, poet, and activist; best known for the novel The *Color Purple*, which was published in 1982 and later made into a movie and Broadway musical.

Allies friends and other supporters of people who are marginalized or otherwise oppressed.

Amazon the largest e-commerce marketplace in the world.

American Civil Liberties Union founded in 1920, the ACLU is a nonprofit organization dedicated to protecting people's constitutional rights.

American Psychological Association founded in 1892, the APA is the largest scientific and professional organization of psychologists in the United States.

Americans with Disabilities Act of 1990 a civil rights law that prohibits discrimination based upon ability status.

Anglos white English-speaking Americans with European origins.

Arlington National Cemetery U.S. military cemetery established during the Civil War in Arlington County, Virginia, near Washington, D.C.

Assimilation adopting the values and norms of the dominant culture.

Asylum protection granted by a nation to a person who flees another country as a political refugee.

B

Baby Boom Generation people born between the mid-1940s and early 1960s who came of age during the Vietnam War era.

Baylor University a private Christian university in Baylor, Texas, with nearly 17,000 students.

Bill Cosby a comic and actor whose height of fame occurred from the 1960s until the 1990s; he was convicted of sex offenses in 2018 and sentenced to prison.

Boarding School Movement the practice of separating American Indian children from their families and sending them to residential programs with the primary objective of assimilating them into the dominant Euro-American culture.

Brown v. Board of Education of Topeka Supreme Court case in which it was unanimously decided that state laws establishing separate public schools for Black and white students were unconstitutional.

C

change.org an electronic platform where people can post petitions and collect signatures.

Cherokee Nation headquartered in Tahlequah, Oklahoma, the nation spans 14 counties in Northeast Oklahoma.

Choice Feminism the belief that any choice is a feminist decision as long as women have all options available to them and are able to make their decisions without intervention.

Cisgender (cisgendered) when a person's gender identity matches the biological sex assigned at birth.

Classism prejudice for or against people belonging to a particular social class.

Co-opting the act of a member of the dominant culture absorbing aspects (e.g., music, fashion, language) of a minority culture as one's own.

Coalitions when groups of similar interests partner together in unity for a common purpose.

Collectivism the cultural value of putting the needs of the group before the needs of any one individual in the group; collectivist countries include Japan, China, Korea, Brazil, India, and many others.

Compassionate Release immediate early release from prison based on medical or humanitarian changes in the prisoner's situation.

Consciousness-Raising a heightened sense of awareness, particularly around oppression and marginalization.

Consensual Encounter a police-initiated conversation in which the other person (or people) does not have to engage; it is treated like a conversation that could happen between two people meeting on the street.

The Cosby Show popular television sitcom depicting an affluent Black family that aired from 1984 until 1992.

Critical Pedagogy a teaching philosophy that encourages students to take control of their learning and discourages classroom models in which teachers provide all of the content knowledge.

Cultural Appropriation the act of a member of the dominant culture absorbing aspects (e.g., music, fashion, language) of a minority culture as one's own.

Cultural Erasure gradual suppression or removal of history, tradition, language, artifacts, etc. that belong to a group of people.

D

Defamation making statements that are known to be untrue with the intent to damage the reputation of a person or entity.

Desegregation process of ending segregation based upon race and/or ethnicity.

Dialogue the practice of engaging in focused conversations with the goals of increased understanding, addressing problems, and questioning thoughts and actions.

Doxing publishing private or identifying information about a person on the Internet, typically with malicious intent.

E

Entitlement an arrogant belief that one is deserving of special treatment and privileges.

Epictetus a Greek philosopher who was born in 55 A.D.

Equal Employment Opportunity Commission a federal agency founded in 1965 that enforces civil rights laws within workplaces.

Equal Justice Initiative a nonprofit organization founded in 1989 that provides legal representation for people who may not have received fair trials.

Equality treating everyone the same.

Equity giving people what they need to be successful.

Ethnocentric a belief that one's cultural values and ways of being are superior to other cultures.

F

Feminism a belief in equality of the sexes.

Feminist a person who believes in the equality of the sexes.

Ferguson a suburb of St. Louis, Missouri, in which 18-year-old Michael Brown, Jr., a Black man who was unarmed, was shot by a white police officer in the middle of the street in 2014, setting off community protests that received national attention.

Fighting Words personal insults directed at a person or a group that are likely to create a violent reaction.

Fort Laramie Treaty of 1868 A 17-article agreement between the U.S. federal government and several American Indian nations. Many promises were made, including guaranteed exclusive tribal occupation of reservation lands and the barring of settlers from land used for hunting.

Freedom Riders civil rights activists who took part in the Freedom Rides.

Freedom Rides bus rides throughout the U.S. South in 1961 made by U.S. Black civil rights activists to bring attention to illegally segregated spaces inside bus terminals.

G

GLAAD a nonprofit organization founded in 1985 whose primary focus is monitoring representations of LGBTQ+ communities in the media.

GoFundMe an electronic crowdsourcing platform where people can bring attention to and raise money for an activity, product, or cause.

Grassroots Leadership a nonprofit organization founded in 1980 that focuses on civil and human rights and seeks to end mass incarceration.

Great Compromise of 1850 a set of laws passed by Congress as a result of fierce debate between lawmakers who favored slavery and those who opposed it. The compromise admitted California as a state with no slavery and stopped the sale of slaves in Washington, D.C., but forced people to return captured slaves to their masters and allowed for the people in the new territories of Utah and New Mexico to decide on slavery for themselves.

Groups individuals who come together for one common cause.

Groupthink thinking or making decisions as a group that discourages healthy dissent or disagreement from individuals within the group.

H

Haudenosaunee Confederacy meaning "They made the house," symbolizing all the nations of the Confederacy coming together as one. Founded in 1142, from east to west, the original nations of the confederacy are the Mohawk, Oneida, Onondaga, Cayuga, and Seneca.

Hegemony dominance and control by a person or group of people.

Henry "Skip" Louis Gates, Jr. a public intellectual who specializes in literary criticism centered on race and ethnicity.

Heteronormativity a worldview that most values a romantic partnership between a cisgender female and a cisgender male.

Hillary Rodham Clinton the Democratic Party's nominee for U.S. president in 2016; her former positions included First Lady of the United States, U.S. Senator, and U.S. Secretary of State.

Historical Trauma the cumulative unresolved emotional harm endured by historically oppressed groups (e.g., American Indians, Latinx, Asian Americans) and carried by their descendants.

The Holocaust a genocide during World War II by Nazi Germany and its collaborators that resulted in the deaths of 6 million European Jews.

Homogenous (homogeny) a grouping that is the same or very similar.

Hulu an entertainment subscription service that provides streaming of movies and television shows.

Hyperbolic exaggerating to evoke strong feelings and make an impression.

I

Ideology a system of beliefs and values held by a person or a group of people.

If These Walls Could Talk a film released in 1996 that portrays women from different decades coping with unplanned pregnancies.

Implicit Biases attitudes and stereotypes based upon a person's appearance that reside in our subconscious.

Imposter Phenomenon fear that a person will be exposed as a fraud or someone unworthy of their success.

Indigenous Peoples original settlers of a given region.

Institutional Discrimination discrimination of marginalized people by society and organizations, either intentionally or unintentionally.

Intersectionality an approach that values multiple identity categories—including sex, race, class, religion, ability status, sexuality, etc.—and how those categories are interwoven to create a person's worldview.

Iron Lung a cased fitted over a person's body to mechanically aid in breathing that was most utilized during the polio epidemic of the 1940s and 1950s.

J

James Brown an American singer and songwriter; commonly referred to as the "Godfather of Soul."

Japanese American Internment Camps places in the United States where more than 100,000 people of Japanese ancestry were forced to relocate during World War II as a result of a U.S. presidential executive order.

Jim Bakker hosted a popular Christian talk show with his then-wife Tammy Faye from 1974 to 1987, when he resigned as the result of an alleged rape and subsequent cover-up.

Jim Crow a derogatory term used for people who are Black. The name is derived from a slave character played by a white actor in blackface during the 1830s.

John F. Kennedy Profile in Courage Award an award created in 1989 by the Kennedy family to honor public officials who display political courage.

John Lewis co-founded the Nashville Student Movement as a college student in the late 1950s and has served as the U.S. representative from Georgia's 5th district since 1987.

John Wayne an American actor and filmmaker best known for starring in Westerns in the mid-20th century.

K

Ku Klux Klan a white supremacist hate group founded in 1865 in Tennessee.

Kyriarchy a set of norms that extend patriarchy beyond sex and gender to include race, class, ability status, sexuality, and other identifiers.

L

La Raza Unida a political party that was active in the 1960s and 1970s with the goal of getting Mexican Americans elected to local, state, and national offices.

Labor Union an organization of workers who come together collectively to bargain for better working conditions, attain better wages and benefits, and support the integrity of the shared trade.

LGBTQ+ the "LGBTQ" part is formed based on the following terms: lesbian, gay, bisexual, transgender, and queer. The plus symbol allows for a clearer representation of people who are lesbian, gay, bisexual, transgender, queer, questioning, intersex, gender nonconforming, pansexual, asexual, straight allies, etc.

Lilly Ledbetter Fair Pay Act of 2009 an act that amended the Civil Rights Act of 1964 allowing for the 180-day statute of limitations for unfair pay to reset with each paycheck and not just with the initial paycheck under the discriminatory action.

Lobotomy a surgical procedure, mostly performed in the 1940s and 1950s, in which nerve pathways within the brain were severed to treat mental illness.

M

Malcolm X a U.S. Black civil rights leader who spent most of his activist career as a proponent of the Nation of Islam and the supremacy of Black Americans.

March on Washington for Jobs and Freedom held in August 1963 and attended by 200,000 to 300,000 people, the primary objective of the march was to advocate for the civil and economic rights of the Black population in the United States.

Marginalizing (marginalization) treating a person or group as if they are insignificant and outside the norm.

Mariachis a group of musicians who perform a style of music that evolved in various regions in Mexico, beginning in the 18th century.

Matilda Joslyn Gage a U.S. suffragist and abolitionist who lived from 1826 to 1898 and was active in the New York movement.

Mecca a city located in Saudi Arabia that is considered Islam's holiest city because it is the birthplace of the Prophet Mohammed and the Islamic faith.

Medgar Evers first field secretary of the Mississippi NAACP; in June 1963, he was assassinated in front of his house by a sniper.

Meritocracy a belief that a person should be given opportunities based upon talents or abilities and that no consideration should be given to a person's sex, race, socioeconomic status, or other factors that result in marginalization.

Microaggressions verbal or nonverbal communication, both intentional and unintentional, used to convey negative, unwelcoming messages to marginalized people.

Millennial a person who became an adult during the new millennium; they were born between 1980 and 2000.

Misogyny a dislike for and prejudice against women.

Mister Rogers' Neighborhood a popular half-hour children's program on public television hosted by Fred Rogers that debuted in 1968 and ran for 31 seasons.

Montgomery Bus Boycott a year-long boycott of buses led by Rev. Dr. Martin Luther King, Jr. in Montgomery, Alabama, during the mid-1950s that ultimately resulted in desegregation of the buses.

N

NAACP a civil rights organization founded in 1909 to advance justice for people of color, particularly people with Black ancestry.

Nashville Student Movement co-founded in the late 1950s by John Lewis and Diane Nash at Fisk University, the members initiated the Nashville sit-ins in the early 1960s and were later part of the leadership of the Freedom Riders.

Nation of Islam a Black religious and political movement founded in Detroit, Michigan, in 1930.

National Historic Landmark historic places, as deemed by the U.S. Secretary of Interior, that hold national significance as a result of their ability to illustrate U.S. heritage.

National Organization for Women founded in 1966, NOW fought for women's full, equal inclusion in society.

National Prize for Arts and Sciences in Mexico one of the Mexico's most prestigious awards; it is awarded annually in six categories.

National Women's Conference of 1977 held in November 1977 in Houston, Texas, the 3-day gathering involved 2,000 female delegates from every U.S. state and territory who set an agenda for American women.

Netflix an entertainment subscription service that provides streaming of movies and television shows.

New York Fashion Week a semiannual series of events in New York City when international fashion collections are made available.

Nobel Peace Prize a prestigious international peace award given by the Norwegian Nobel Committee annually (with some exceptions) since 1901.

O

Objectifying viewing a person, particularly a part of their body, as a mere object to be enjoyed by the onlooker.

Old Testament the first of the two parts of the Christian Bible; takes place before the birth of Jesus Christ and written by Israelites who Christians believe were inspired by God.

Oklahoma Education Association founded in 1889, the organization advocates for education professionals in Oklahoma.

Oppressive causing unnecessary constraint, particularly on people who have been historically marginalized.

Other(s) (Othering) causing a person to feel like an outsider.

P

Paradigm(s) (paradigmatic) a belief that a person holds about a cause, concept, culture, project, etc.

Patriarch a person who subscribes to the patriarchy.

Patriarchy (patriarchal) a set of norms that values a traditionally masculine perspective and encourages traditional gender roles.

Person-First Language putting a person before their descriptor ("man who is gay" instead of "gay man") to show value for the person before the adjectives.

Pine Ridge Reservation Oglala Lakota reservation of nearly 30,000 residents located in the southwest corner of present-day South Dakota.

Pistol-Whip the act of using the handle of a handgun like a club or baton to strike a person, usually on the head.

Planned Parenthood a nonprofit founded in 1916 that provides health services, including birth control, emergency contraception, pregnancy testing, Pap tests, STD testing and treatment, abortion referral and services, HIV services, patient education, and other general health services for both men and women.

Plutonium a radioactive silver medal initially produced and isolated in 1940.

Plymouth Rock the traditional site of disembarkation of the *Mayflower* Pilgrims who colonized Plymouth Colony in 1620.

Political Correctness the use of language and policies to better include members of marginalized groups.

Postfeminism the belief that feminism is no longer necessary because sexism no longer exists.

Postracial (Postracist) the belief that racism no longer exists and, therefore, efforts to eradicate it are unnecessary.

Postsexist a belief that sexism no longer exists.

Predominately White Institution colleges and universities where more than 50% of the student population identifies as white.

Presidential Executive Order a directive from the U.S. president that has much of the same power as a federal law.

Presidential Medal of Freedom bestowed by the president of the United States, it is one of the two highest civilian awards in the country.

Privilege Guilt culpability felt by people of privilege for the historic and modern-day oppression of marginalized groups who do not share their same privileges, whether it be class, ethnicity, race, sex, sexuality, religion, ability status, etc.

Profiling the act of targeting a person based upon sex, race, socioeconomic status, age, etc.

Protestants members of a branch of Christianity that separated from the Catholic Church during the 17th century for what they perceived to be excesses of the Catholic faith.

Q

Quakers members of the Society of Friends movement (with roots in 17th-century England) who valued all people equally.

Quorum the minimum number of people required at a meeting to take valid votes on action items; for most groups, it is a simple majority.

R

Reparations the idea that some form of compensation needs to be made to descendants of Africans for the labor provided and pain endured during the Atlantic slave trade.

Rosie the Riveter depicted with a denim shirt and red bandana with her arm bent to flex her muscles, she was the star of a campaign aimed at recruiting female workers for defense industries during World War II.

Rhetor a person engaged in rhetoric.

Rhetoric the art of persuasion.

Robert's Rules of Order a manual of parliamentary procedure used to govern meetings.

S

Safe Space a place free of judgment or harm.

Salvation Message the belief that people will have eternal life as the result of Jesus Christ's crucifixion, as long as they accept that Jesus Christ is their savior.

Savior Complex a condition of a privileged person who believes it is their responsibility to save a marginalized person from oppression.

Separate but Equal Doctrine the belief that racial segregation was constitutional as long as the facilities provided for people who are Black and people who are white were somewhat equal.

Seventh Generation an indigenous ideology that urges the current generation to make decisions, especially about the environment, for the benefit of descendants seven generations in the future.

Shabbat the Jewish Sabbath and day of rest.

***Silent Spring* (1962)** a popular book documenting the harms caused to the environment by chemical pesticides.

Social Justice a commitment of people who work to promote a society in which diversity and difference are celebrated and not ignored or belittled.

Social Justice Consciousness heightened sense of awareness regarding the need for the promotion of a society in which diversity and difference are celebrated and not ignored or belittled.

Social Justice Orientation a person's beliefs or attitudes about the importance of diversity and difference.

Social Movement a series of activist events that are coordinated to focus on one issue over a long period of time.

Socratic Pedagogical Method a classroom method, named for the Greek philosopher Socrates, in which probing questions are used in a dialoguing fashion to challenge assumptions and aid the student in developing a deeper understanding of the topic.

South African Apartheid racial segregation that promoted white supremacy in South Africa from 1948 until the early 1990s.

Southern Poverty Law Center a nonprofit founded in 1971 that is dedicated to civil rights legal advocacy and education.

Sovereignty authority of a state or nation to govern itself.

Spectacle an event in which a person of privilege treats marginalized people as if they are entertainment, a hobby, or a community service project.

Standing Rock Sioux Tribe citizens of the Lakota and Dakota Nations; more than 8,000 people live on reservation land situated in North and South Dakota.

Status Quo the existing social or political state of affairs.

Stokely Carmichael developed the Black Power movement, first as a leader of the Student Nonviolent Coordinating Committee and then as a leader of the more controversial Black Panther Party.

Stormfront Website an Internet site launched in 1996 to promote white nationalism.

Student Nonviolent Coordinating Committee a U.S. Black civil rights organization founded in 1960 and led mostly by college students.

Suffrage right to vote in political elections.

Sundance Film Festival the largest independent film festival in the United States.

Systemic relating to an organization, group, set of laws, etc. and not an individual.

T

Tammy Faye Bakker Messner hosted a popular Christian talk show with her then-husband Jim from 1974 to 1987; after her divorce from Jim in 1992, she became an ally for LGBTQ+ communities.

Title IX a federal law that bans sex discrimination in schools that receive federal funds.

Tokenism symbolically involving a few people from marginalized groups to give the appearance of equity and equality within the organization.

Tony Awards awards recognizing excellence in live Broadway theatre annually since 1947.

Transformational Leadership leadership that causes change in individuals and social systems.

Trayvon Martin a 17-year-old Black male who was shot by a member of the community watch in a Florida neighborhood in 2012; it appeared to be a shooting inspired by racial profiling.

Treaty of Guadalupe Hidalgo signed in 1848, it ended the Mexican-American War and gave the United States the Rio Grande as a boundary for Texas and ownership of California and a large area comprising roughly half of New Mexico, most of Arizona, Nevada, and Utah, and parts of Wyoming and Colorado.

The Trevor Project a nonprofit organization founded in 1998 dedicated to suicide prevention efforts among youth (ages 13–24) who identify as LGBTQ+.

Triggering arousing feelings or memories associated with a particular traumatic experience.

Truth personal belief that derives from a set of rules or a guide (e.g., religious texts, family rituals, the law) that are not considered debatable by the person who subscribes to them.

truths personal beliefs that are considered flexible, evolving, and debatable.

Turning Point a moment of clarity when a person sees the oppression and privilege that surrounds them and believes they must do everything possible to achieve social justice.

Twerk a type of dance that involves the person performing it to get into a squat and thrust their hips.

U

Underground Railroad a network of safe houses and other places used to help slaves escape to free states or Canada before the Civil War.

United Nations the largest international organization (with nearly 200 member states) formed to promote peace and increase political and economic cooperation among its members.

U.S. Immigration Reform Protests of 2006 large-scale mobilization efforts in response to national legislation that would raise penalties for illegal immigration.

V

Vernacular everyday language of a particular culture or group of people.

Vietnam War a conflict between North Vietnam and South Vietnam from 1955 to 1975, with U.S. soldiers fighting for South Vietnam and the end of communist rule. The war was controversial in the United States, and the country's involvement ended in 1973.

Viva Kennedy Clubs organizations made up of Mexican American voters—primarily in Texas, Arizona, and Southern California—who supported the election of John F. Kennedy for U.S. president in 1960.

Voting Rights Act of 1965 Signed into law by President Lyndon B. Johnson, it aimed to overcome legal barriers (e.g., Jim Crow laws) at the state and local levels that prevented Black voters from participating in elections.

W

Watergate Scandal a U.S. political controversy in the early 1970s in which Republican U.S. President Richard Nixon was accused of involvement with a break-in at Democratic National Committee headquarters (which was located in the Watergate office complex in Washington, D.C.) and then covering it up; as a result, Nixon resigned from office in August 1974.

Whistleblowers people who expose corruption within an organization with which they are affiliated, typically as an employee.

White Centric catering to Anglo experiences as the norm.

White Fragility a defensive response by white people when they are confronted about personal actions or language that is considered oppressive.

White Guilt culpability felt by people who are white for the historic and modern-day oppression of people of color.

White League a paramilitary organization founded in Louisiana in 1874 and active for 2 years with the dedicated purpose of voting Republicans (the party of Abraham Lincoln) out of office by intimidation of Black voters and their allies.

White Nationalism the belief that white people are from the superior race and should have their own separatist nation.

White Nationalist(s) a person who subscribes to white nationalism.

White Privilege benefitting from the positive assumptions that are made about people who are white and their levels of education, criminal history, and upward mobility.

Women's Liberation Movement during the 1960s and 1970s, groups of women organized to fight for women's rights, including equal pay for equal work, representation in media, access to health care, expression of sexuality, etc.

Woke a state of awareness regarding injustices in society.

Wounded Knee Incident of 1973 an occupation of Wounded Knee, South Dakota, in the Pine Ridge Reservation by approximately 200 Oglala Lakota Sioux and followers of the American Indian Movement. The occupation lasted for 71 days.

Index

CPSIA information can be obtained
at www.ICGtesting.com
Printed in the USA
LVHW040721100820
662719LV00005B/291